D0445023

# All the Things We Never Knew

# All the Things We Never Knew

SHEILA HAMILTON

SEAL

Copyright 2015 Sheila Hamilton

Seal Press
A Member of the Perseus Books Group
1700 Fourth Street
Berkeley, California
sealpress.com

All rights reserved. No part of this book may be reproduced or transmitted in any form without written permission from the publisher, except by reviewers who may quote brief excerpts in connection with a review. Some names and indentifying details have changed to protect the privacy of individuals.

Library of Congress Cataloging-in-Publication Data is available.
ISBN: 978-1-58005-584-0

10 9 8 7 6 5 4 3 2

Cover design by Faceout Studio, Derek Thornton
Interior design by Tabitha Lahr
Printed in the United States of America
Distributed by Publishers Group West

To Sophie—your willingness to lovingly embrace things just as they are allowed us all to move forward

# Introduction

I missed much of the unfolding of my husband's mental illness. By the time I'd pieced together the puzzle of who David actually was, he was falling apart. My once brilliant, intense, and passionate partner was dead within six weeks of a formal diagnosis of bipolar disorder, leaving my nine-year-old daughter and me without so much as a note to understand his decision. He'd left us hundreds of thousands of dollars in debt and with no plan for helping us recover from the profound grief of his suicide.

David's employees never called to tell me he wasn't showing up at the job sites where his company was remodeling high-end residences and commercial businesses. By the time David experienced his first full-blown manic episode, we'd already been keeping separate bank accounts and separate lives. He isolated himself from me with lies and infidelity. I returned the salvo, alienating myself from him by pretending I didn't hurt.

David's parents may have known about his struggle with mental illness, but they never let on.

Mental illness, unlike breast cancer, isn't celebrated with big marches or pink ribbons. The stigma is stifling, and it prevents most people from seeking help. David refused to accept the label of bipolar disorder. He could not imagine a life of medications and therapy, which had helped him so little. David's path is not unique. Suicide is now the tenth most common cause of death for men and women. Every thirteen minutes, another American dies from suicide. What could we have done differently? What should we have known? According to a 2008 report by the National Institute of Mental Health, research shows that risk factors for suicide include depression and other mental disorders and substance abuse disorders (often in combination with other mental disorders). More than 90 percent of the people who die by suicide have those risk factors.

It is my belief that many people could benefit from hearing more about how psychiatric conditions unfold. In the years, months, and days leading up to David's death, I didn't classify him as mentally ill. I missed many signs. I ignored others, believing it could get better. And I scrambled, as the world came crashing down around us, just to maintain my own sanity and the health of my daughter.

Our daughter celebrates her birthday each June. I can't help but measure her birthdays with an equal sense of apprehension and elation. She's a teenager now, and still no signs of the brooding, the polarity, the darkness that descended on David like Portland's thick gray clouds in January, refusing to budge. Yes, she has his intellect, but she also has my relatively sunny nature. She is physically stunning with long, muscular legs and a waist that defies her voracious appetite. She has David's European cheekbones. The color of her skin is his. Her ears have the same shape. There are times I find myself staring at one of her features for too long. She bats me away: "Mom, enough."

But David's genetics also carry a downside. "There's a 50 percent chance your daughter will present with the same disorder," a well-meaning psychologist once advised. "It is most common between the ages of sixteen and twenty-one."

I knew the statistical odds by heart. After David's death, I'd read every book I could get my hands on about bipolar disorder. I'd measured the likelihood of a gene mutation against the things I could influence—what she ate, how much sleep and exercise she got, the unconditional love that I gave her.

But the genetic risk of mental illness is such that my daughter is keenly aware of what she can't do. She understands heavy drinking would kill brain cells that she may need to rely on for higher functioning. She'll never be able to safely experiment with drugs. It's a burden a teenager shouldn't have to take on, but more than half of people with bipolar disorder commit suicide. The numbers are intractable, unchangeable. Read fifteen studies and the numbers come up consistently grim.

And yet, there is much to celebrate.

There have been tremendous breakthroughs in brain science from 2005 to 2015. The ability of scientists to study aberrations in MRI imaging has led to new thinking about the treatment for brain disorders. The work of Dr. Bruce Perry at the Child Trauma Academy in Houston, Texas, is focused on brain disorders in children, but the applications may also be relevant to adult populations.

When children are subjected to abuse, neglect, absent parenting, or drug and alcohol exposure, brain development can be severely stunted. Perry's ability to define treatment based on the child's current brain functioning is of particular interest to me, since I watched my husband's behavior regress to that of a child during his hospitalization. I had no context at the time for understanding exactly what was happening to him, or to me.

If I were faced with the same predicament today, I would forcefully advocate for the type of care Perry has successfully practiced: the neurosequential model of therapeutics (NMT), which is a sensitive, neurobiologically informed approach to clinical work. NMT helps match the nature and timing of specific therapeutic techniques to the development of the patient. This research was not available ten years ago and is only now starting to be practiced in some mental health facilities.

NMT's reliance on somatosensory activities like music, movement, yoga, and therapeutic massage allows healing at the most elementary level. A traumatized brain is incapable of processing the subtleties of group therapy. It is impossible to ask people who have just suffered a manic episode to start sorting out their bills. It is crucial that we understand the limitations of the people we are attempting to help.

I strongly believe that the litany of medications David was prescribed did very little to help. In fact, his first suicidal thought came just days after being prescribed an antidepressant by a well-meaning physician-friend. Medication has helped millions of people, but it fails tens of thousands of families every year. We have relied for too long on an approach to mental illness that relies on pharmaceuticals and fails to take into consideration the whole person—mind, body, spirit.

The collaborative problem-solving method developed by Dr. Ross Greene, of Harvard, is an important milestone in communicating with people suffering from brain disorders. Though the technique was developed for children, it offers an important template for caregivers. David's early behavior of withdrawal and isolation in our marriage made it impossible for us to solve disagreements or disputes in a collaborative and mutually satisfactory manner. The collaborative problem-solving model employs empathy, consideration of real-life consequences, and collaborative brainstorming to arrive at a place of solution that is both realistic and mutually satisfactory. It may have offered a creative form of communication that I simply did not have at my disposal.

If we knew then all the things we understand now, I might have been more equipped to do more than watch my beloved husband's decline in a state of denial, grief, and fear. I would have had more resources and wouldn't have felt so woefully unprepared for marriage to a person with a mental illness. Instead, I compartmentalized our problems in order to deal with the needs of my child and a demanding job. And in my ignorance and fear, I too allowed our lives to spiral out of control.

In the aftermath of David's death, it took years to stabilize my family's financial future and the emotional current of our lives. Once I came to terms with what killed David, I did an enormous amount of research to learn more about mental illness and what we can all do to be more compassionate to the people in our lives who are touched with brain disorders.

I have learned so much from my involvement in the Flawless Foundation, a nonprofit advocating for people with brain disorders. My interest is in preventing another loss of life as exquisite as David's. If we begin modification at the earliest ages, we might improve the chances of mitigating the onset of mental illness.

Dr. Elisabeth Kübler-Ross has described the five stages of grief as denial, anger, bargaining, depression, and acceptance. When a loved one commits suicide, that list is incomplete. We are haunted by the questions "Why would he?" or "What could I have done differently?"

Suicide is an unnatural choice and leaves carnage for the living. I'd propose one more stage of grief to Kübler-Ross's list in the case of suicide: forgiveness. It was not until I reached this stage of forgiveness that I was able to sort out my own failings from those of my husband. In accepting responsibility for my part in David's death, I was able to understand his sense of futility and his unwillingness to face his illness. I forgave him. And in doing so, I've been better able to understand his decision.

My hope is that our story—told from the other side of this sixth stage—will be a catalyst for positive change in the ways we approach, regard, and respond to the social fallout of mental illness.

# Chapter One

The doorman scanned two pages of names before he found ours—Colin MacLean "plus one." That was me: the plus one. It was strange to be known that way and even stranger to be wearing a dress. For the last three months, I'd worn nothing in the evening but sweat-pants, the uniform of crisis. I tugged at the hem of my black silk dress to pull it down farther.

The young doorman nodded and opened the door, "Enjoy your evening."

The knot in my stomach tightened along with my smile. The tension was highest just below my rib cage.

The restaurant was one of Portland's trendiest, with a long marble bar and two stories of dining. The art was modern, and the place thumped with electronic dance music. Dozens of young men and women were moving on the dance floor. The bass bounced off the acoustic ceilings and the glass windows, amplifying the beat. The party took up both floors of the restaurant. Upstairs, dining tables had been pushed aside so guests could hang over the banister to watch the dance floor.

One of them, a young man with sticky, gelled hair, yelled down at my date, "Hey, MacLean, you're late!"

Colin waved and then gently folded his long fingers around mine. *A true gentleman,* I smiled to myself. He opened car doors for me. He was the first to stand whenever a woman left or rejoined a group at the dinner table. He thanked waiters and waitresses for their service and did it all sincerely. It was a type of chivalry I hadn't seen in a long, long time, certainly not from my soon-to-be ex. The marriage was over, except for the formalities, except for David's signature on the papers. I caught myself nervously biting the inside of my lip and forced myself to stop and be in the moment.

The focus of this party, the birthday boy, was a local real estate agent, a hugely successful, balding, middle-aged guy who liked his newly single life and women under thirty. He was jammed between several women in the middle of the dance floor, oblivious to his newly arriving guests.

I'd been dating Colin for only about a month, but he already seemed like the guy I'd been searching for back in my twenties, when my list of must-haves seemed important. He called when he said he was going to call. He was, as a mutual friend described him, "one of the last remaining good guys." But I was like a detective trying to uncover Colin's dark side. I'd even paid a background check company to make sure he didn't have a record, a history of violence, or a history of pretending he was someone he wasn't. Men aren't always as they appear, but they are what they hide.

I watched his profile as he summed up the party: a wonderful nose, perfect in its lines except for a slight bump at the top. It would have been too perfect in its geometry without the break. I liked a man with a few scars, stories to tell about his various broken bones. He was the most stylish man there, taller than the rest, in a black jacket, white tuxedo shirt, and jeans. He smiled easily and shook hands with nearly everyone he passed. The owner of the restaurant made it a point to wind his way through the crowd. "Well, now the party begins," he said, shaking Colin's hand and then kissing me expertly on the side of the cheek. I wanted to relax into Colin's breeze. Instead, I felt like a hurricane was looming.

An oversized mirrored ball hung from the ceiling, spinning slowly, throwing bursts of light onto people's faces. Like so much in my life, it seemed precarious. Would it drop and smash into pieces? The exits were guarded to keep the party private. I felt my underarms begin to sweat. Part of me felt trapped. Before, I loved parties, the thrill of too much everything: music, people, alcohol. Now in my early forties, my world had been reduced to worrying about my estranged husband, a man I no longer loved. He was in trouble, I knew, suffering from a sudden and acute mental breakdown; tonight he was safe, though. Tonight he was at our home with his mother to watch him. I reminded myself of this and tried to ease the knot below my breastbone, but it had become a part of my physical landscape, like worry lines. A young woman with blonde hair extensions teetered toward us. Colin squeezed my hand and started weaving us through the couples.

I wriggled loose of his grip. "That's okay; I'll get a drink first," I said, smiling, finally breaking free. It was all too much, too fast. I shouldn't have come. I had convinced myself I was ready to rejoin the social scene. But I was wrong.

The bar was pure chaos. The bartender held two bottles in his hands, pouring, shaking, then pushing drinks toward a line of loud customers. I waved in the bartender's direction. Nothing.

"I'll have a vodka martini, double," I said. Still nothing.

"*Vodka martini!*" I yelled, and he finally looked my way, nodding.

The light from my phone distracted me from the bartender. "Unknown number," the phone read.

I took in a breath. Sophie. It must be my nine-year-old calling from her sleepover. I pressed the talk button and held the phone against my ear.

"Ms. Hamilton? Sheila Hamilton?" I could barely make out the man's voice. The music thumped louder than ever.

"Hold on, hold on. I can't hear you." I walked through the middle of the crowd with the phone to my head. Colin saw me striding toward the bathroom and mouthed, *Everything okay?* I nodded, trying to keep the panic from my face. I pushed past sweaty bodies to the small unisex bathroom.

Inside, I yelled loudly into the tiny speaker of my cell phone. "Sorry. I'm at a birthday party. Who is this?"

"It's Officer Todd Rodale from the Clackamas County Sheriff's Office."

My body suddenly felt heavy, too heavy to stand. *Bang, bang, bang!* The door shook like someone was kicking it from the outside.

"Hey!" a drunk yelled. "I've got to piss."

*Unisex bathrooms,* I thought. *What a stupid invention.* The guy would have to wait. "Sorry, Officer, go on," I said into the telephone. I plugged my other ear to drown out the drunk, and the music, and the absurdity of the place.

"Ms. Hamilton, we got a report that your husband broke into a woman's home in the Columbia Gorge and stole her gun."

I pushed the phone closer to my head. "What? I'm sorry, did I hear you correctly—he has a what?" My soon-to-be ex was supposed to be at the home we'd shared. His mother was supposed to be watching him. This must be a mistake. The dim light of the bathroom made the scene feel like a bad dream.

The cop repeated the words *gun* and *husband* and *woman.* He said they were looking for David, that my husband knew the "victim," and that they considered this man I was not yet divorced from "armed and dangerous."

My husband was on Larch Mountain, the officer said. I repeated the information, scrambling to make sense of the bizarre story. I stopped cold at "shots fired."

"We didn't know how to reach you," said the cop, "so I called the radio station. I'm a big fan of yours."

I drew in a breath. I'd tried so hard to keep the drama of my personal life from most of my coworkers at KINK-FM—and I'd never mentioned on air how serious the problems were.

"I hope you don't mind that they gave me your cell phone number," said this cop, this fan.

Shame, humiliation, nausea—the storm moved through my body. I stood up to interrupt the bile rising in my stomach and caught a reflection of my face in the mirror. Red blotches covered my neck and ears. My foundation had disappeared from the sweat. My eyes, which Colin described as a deep emerald color, were bloodshot and pinched. I was pressing the cell phone so hard against my head that my blonde hair was mushed against one ear. The face in the mirror was a mug shot.

The jerk banged on the door again. Now there were several people yelling. One voice came through loudest. "Get the FUCK out!"

I unlocked the door and poked my head out. The crowd outside was larger, the comments louder. "Please," I said. "It's an emergency." I closed the door, locked it, and put the phone to my chest for a brief moment while attempting to slow my breathing. "Where should I meet you?" My voice sounded like that of a person in shock. The sheriff's office was forty miles east of the city. "Do you have a pen?" he asked.

I heard myself try to answer, watched myself from above, like a moviegoer, conscious of what was happening but no longer mouthing words or reacting to pain. It was someone else down there, some mixed-up woman in a black dress and "no-run" mascara running down her face. She looked pathetic, trapped in an overly expensive bathroom. Gleaming Kohler faucets and no way out. "No, I don't have anything with me but my phone."

"Meet us at the Clackamas County Sheriff's Office in Troutdale." He said it twice to remind me. I was numb, trying to calculate how I would navigate a forty-mile drive. He must have known I was in shock. He added, "Sorry I had to call you under these circumstances."

I opened the door slowly. A young man in a tuxedo looked at my face and fell silent. Another guy booed as I walked past. His date elbowed him in the stomach.

*Don't cry, don't cry, don't cry.* My body felt hollow. I nearly tripped on the step down to the dance floor. A blonde in a tight tube dress stopped dancing to stare at me.

Colin saw me from a distance and pushed through the crowd until he could grab my hand. "Let's get out of here," he said, squeezing my fingers.

The young doorman was surprised. "Leaving so early?" he chirped, and then he stopped when he saw my face. "Well, okay, you two have a good night." He shoved his hands in his pockets and watched us walk away.

Inside the car, my words spilled out. I felt as if I'd been injected with a super shot of amphetamines. I was unraveling, almost babbling. "He's stolen a gun, Colin. He could do something really dangerous."

"Whoa, slow down," Colin said, taking a deep breath. "Start from the beginning."

## STIGMA

According to the Substance Abuse and Mental Health Services Administration, nearly one in five American adults (18.5 percent), or 43.8 million adults, had a mental illness in 2013. Yet, despite the prevalence of mental illness, the stigma surrounding it persists. Some people still believe that mental illness is a weakness of self, or a choice that can be managed by "pulling oneself together."

Dr. Graham Thornicroft, senior study author at the Institute of Psychiatry of King's College, London, says, "The profound reluctance to be a mental health patient means people will put off seeing a doctor for months, years, or even at all, which in turn delays their recovery." Thornicroft's team collected information from 144 studies involving 90,000 people around the world. Stigma ranked as the fourth highest of ten barriers to care.

Self-stigmatization can be even more potent and destructive. David's worsening mental health resulted in a sense of shame so great that his doctors say it complicated the most extreme of his symptoms. He was "unreachable," as one caseworker told me. Secrecy acted as an obstacle to early intervention in his illness.

If David had been diagnosed with diabetes at a young age, members of his family, school, and church would have undoubtedly mobilized support. His caregivers would have communicated his need for dietary changes, exercise, and/or insulin. This was not the case when David exhibited the earliest signs of depression.

The myth persists that mental illness is a character flaw. It is my hope that one day disorders of the brain will be treated with as much care, compassion, and tenacity as diseases of any other organs in our bodies.

# Chapter Two

He drinks too much coffee. That's what I thought when I first laid eyes on David eleven years earlier. He was juggling construction plans and a pager while he ordered a double-shot cappuccino. He checked his watch, ran his fingers through his hair, and then fumbled through his wallet for a few crumpled bills.

I would later interpret this first impression of David in a much different light. Disorganization and anxiety are two of the early warning signs of bipolar disorder, but on this day, I was immediately drawn to his erratic, discombobulated energy. I thought his lack of bravado was refreshingly different.

I'd slipped away from my job as a reporter for the Portland ABC affiliate, KATU, to refuel for the long night ahead. David was dressed in 501s, a white, organic cotton shirt, and black European dress shoes. His hair was thick and brown, and he was deeply tanned from what I later learned was a month cycling in the California desert. Whatever he said to the barista made her crack up with laughter. His teeth weren't perfect, and his grin was a little lopsided, maybe a tad shy—infectious.

"Are you a builder?" I asked, nodding at the construction plans he held. We spoke as he was picking up his coffee order.

"Are you CIA?" he replied, the wrinkles at the corners of his eyes turning up.

People shuffled around us to get to the cream and packets of fake sugar. "I need a contractor to finish a deck," I said. "My neighbors are beginning to ask when I'll be getting the piles of two-by-fours off my lawn."

"Let me guess: A, your builder went bankrupt; B, your builder walked out on the job; or C, your builder broke up with you." He smiled and then handed me his card. "It's always A, B, or C."

"B," I said, looking at the card. *Mica Construction*. "Pleased to meet you, Mica."

"No, I'm not Mica. That's my company name," he said. "David. David Krol."

I looked at the card again. "Polish?" I could tell by the spelling and by his strong cheekbones and jaw. He was handsome in a way none of my girlfriends would approve of, too manly for them, with a beard that wasn't trimmed down to the nub and thick brown hair that looked like it could use a good cut. But he was tall and strong, with intense blue eyes. I was tired of dating metrosexuals who had more hair product on the counter than I did. This guy probably got his hair cut at his girlfriend's house. I checked his ring finger and suppressed a strange bubble of excitement inside me.

He grinned. "You are CIA. Okay, read me my rights."

I laughed and shook my head, no, no. "Oh, never mind."

We walked out the door together and stood in the parking lot. The day was good by Portland standards. Sun peeked through budding magnolias. The rain was giving us a break for now. He smelled like Tom's toothpaste and a kind of soap I couldn't identify. He drew a breath in, as if he was going to say something important. "Well, I better get going. I've got a bid meeting, uh, ten minutes ago." He laughed, juggling the plans and his coffee while checking his watch.

"Oh, yes, me too. I've got a story that needs a really good editor. Know any?"

His eyebrows lifted, his first overt sign of interest. "So you're a reporter?" he asked. "Who do you write for?"

I moved my shoulder closer to his. "TV," I said. "I'm a television reporter."

He looked confused. His phone rang. He lifted his finger apologetically as he turned to answer. My heart sank.

"Okay, so sorry," he said after hanging up. He held onto the cappuccino cup with his teeth while he placed the phone back in his pocket. "TV, huh?" he said. "I wish I had one so that I could say something relevant."

I laughed. This man was different. Interesting. Gorgeous. Completely unaffected by my career. It was the first time in years I'd felt this kind of powerful attraction to a man, an immediate and deep connection, uncanny, unexplainable, except to blame it all on a biological burst of pheromones. "Call me," he said as he got into his car. "I'll forget unless you do."

He drove away in a yellow Mercedes that we would later call Old Yella. It would be the car we made out in, argued over politics in, and eventually strapped a baby seat in. We patched and replaced and limped along in that car, treating it as if it were a beloved but aging, and sometimes neglected, member of the family. It was perpetually in need of repair.

I called him the night of our first meeting, leaving the basic information about my deck on his voicemail. He didn't rush to bid the job. I buried myself in breaking news, but every time I came up for air, the builder was the first thing on my mind. I called him again and left my number at work and home, trying to sound casual. "Uh, hi, David, the deck job is still there if you're interested."

Nothing. Why wasn't he calling? I'd been dating a string of lawyers and doctors who came after me like the flu in February. In hindsight, I might have been less interested if David had been like the others: doting, responsible, nice. It is almost embarrassing to admit that his ambivalence toward me propelled me further. It made me want him all the more.

A week later, he finally called, offering a lame excuse. "I'm busier than I'd like," he apologized. Still, he showed up the next day to look at the deck. As he stood on the front deck, I smiled at the items he'd brought with him: a tape measure, a bottle of French pinot, a baguette, a section of soft French Brie, and four radishes.

"That's an interesting bid package," I said.

"It can make work a lot more tolerable," he smiled. "Unless you don't like French wine."

He showed me the label and then read the name in a perfect accent. I nodded my appreciation.

"I like French wine. But stinky cheese doesn't really go well with tape measures." I pretended to block the door.

"This tape measure is surprisingly robust," he said. "Goes with everything. Can I come in?"

I stepped aside and gestured him in. He had a builder's build, the kind you get without having to go to the gym. He had to duck through the entryway, which meant he was at least six foot four. He wore the same kind of jeans he'd had on at the coffee shop and a black dress shirt.

I felt like a schoolgirl, standing nervously in the dining room, trying to decide what to do next. I looked down at the floor. The shoes. Yes, the shoes. "Those look well-loved," I said of his Italian shoes. A.Testoni, I could tell from the natural seams and hand-woven twine.

"Bologna, fifteen years ago. I thought I would die when he told me how much it would be to have them made." He gazed at the shoes as if he was remembering the smell of Italy.

"But worth it?"

"They weather like hiking boots. Worth every last lira."

His dialect, I found out, was from Quebec, where he grew up, along with the half-dozen countries he'd adopted as his own. His lips were full and soft. There was a tiny scar that barely showed beneath his moustache. I'd reported on a doctor who fixed cleft palates in children, and the scar was exactly like the ones I'd seen on dozens of pictures of orphans. "It was brutal," he said, when he saw me looking at the scar. "Seven surgeries later, I still can't breathe."

I turned, embarrassed that I'd been studying his face so intimately.

Embarrassed that he seemed to be able to read my thoughts. Within hours of knowing David, I sensed an enormous vulnerability, a part of him that was wounded and in need of care. His strong exterior was so unlike his interior, and his ability to remain coolly aloof, even while talking about his own disability, was already confusing to me. Over the years, David's feelings of being different would only increase, a sort of self-fulfilling prophecy. His favorite saying was "We're born alone; we live alone; we die alone." I found it odd that he left out the most important part: "Only through our love and friendship can we create the illusion for the moment that we're not alone."

Over wine, he told of his life and travels: Morocco, Spain, and Mexico, warm countries where a single man and his backpack could blend in with ease. He'd log or pull construction jobs in his home base, Canada, and then travel until his money ran out. He'd been married once, a marriage of convenience, he said, so that he could get a green card in the United States. "We were young, twenty-something, both of us. We met in a traveling circus."

My eyes widened. "No way."

"No, really. I'd joined to take care of the Clydesdales, the only horse in the world that doesn't make me feel gigantic. Jen was doing something more legitimate." He paused, studying a painting on my wall. "I cheated on her, and she ended up gay," he said. "We're really good friends now, though."

My reporter instinct kicked in. "Cheated" is a big word for anyone to use in casual chat. I suppressed whatever thread I should have followed for an innocuous question.

"And the uh, woman, you cheated on her with?"

"We spent ten years together. The craziest, spookiest, most

fucked-up years of my life." He said it affectionately and poured the last of the red into his glass. "We're lucky we both got out alive."

I let the line sink in, unsure of what to make of it. Two long-term relationships, both described in ominous terms. Was he trying to make himself sound like an unlikely partner? Did he care? Years later, a therapist would describe how we, like everyone, followed our unconscious patterns in our seeking out of partners.

That day, however, it simply felt like we clicked. The wine bottle was empty and the sky had darkened before we got around to looking at the unfinished deck. I turned on the lights so he could measure. He hopped from one two-by-four to the next with the agility of a tightrope walker.

"Yeah, we could do this," he said. "But it would be a couple of weeks before we could get started." He snapped back the tape measure and gathered his things from the table. "Let me know what you decide." He looked at me intently, as if he might reach out and brush my hair to the side.

Instead, he walked to the front door and held out his hand. "It was really nice meeting you."

A wave of electricity went up my spine. My head was light from the wine. I was airy, ethereal. He lifted his eyebrows as if to say, "Are you okay?"

I straightened my blouse. My chest was warm. He scribbled a quote for the work on a piece of yellow paper and drew two exaggerated lines under the number. "Voila!" he said. "Painless."

I shifted from one foot to the other, hoping he'd ask to stay. He didn't. When I closed the door behind him, I wondered what was happening to me.

The yellow sheet he'd left wasn't an estimate at all; it read "sweet dreams" in scribbled letters. I could barely make out the handwriting.

One Sunday afternoon, shortly after I started seeing David, I got a call from Jim, a mutual fund manager I'd been halfheartedly dating for several months. He described a tenderloin he'd lovingly basted for several hours. He went on about the roasted potatoes, garlic-infused leeks, how he'd found the perfect bottle in his wine cellar, just calling to be opened after twenty years. All in all, he said, it was the perfect summer's evening on his deck overlooking the city. Was I available?

All during the phone call, David was standing on the porch, in a pair of bike shorts and a jersey, waiting for me to set off on a ride. David was not a traditional date who planned and plotted romantic opportunity. Instead, he'd call or pop by unexpectedly, and we'd end up taking long walks around my neighborhood. Today's bike ride was one of the first attempts David had made to plan something in advance. I had no idea how strongly David felt about me at this point in our relationship. Oddly, his aloofness made him even more mysterious, more desirable. As he waited for me to finish the call, he tenderly checked the health of my hanging basket, squirting water over the magnolias and then deadheading some of the dormant flowers.

"I'm so sorry, Jim. I'm tied up tonight," I said, lowering my voice.

Jim's disappointment was palpable. He didn't speak for a moment. Then he cleared his throat. "Well, how about brunch tomorrow?"

David peeked his head into the door, smiling broadly, his hair pushed back and his eyebrows lifted. "You ready?" he asked.

I lifted my finger—*just one moment, I'll be right there*—expecting to feel conflicted and confused. David smiled, miming for me to hang up the phone. He was so charming when he was like this, playful even in a head-butting competition with another man. I felt a weakness, a stirring that was so biologically driven, so unexpected. *Imagine children coming from this man*, I thought to myself.

But Jim didn't give up easily. He repeated himself, and I was jarred back to the phone. "You there, Sheila? Are you there?"

David walked toward me, mischievously thrilled to interrupt my phone call.

"Uh-huh." I nodded as David slid behind me, his arms around

my waist, kissing the back of my neck. I didn't believe in fate. The biological clock was baloney. I'd rationalized a life without children because kids would prevent me from getting to the top of my career. How do you pick up and move to the next big television market with an infant? How do you go to Europe on a moment's notice with a toddler? I was in my early thirties and hadn't seriously considered children until now. I made a mental note to myself to remember the details of that day, the heat in the kitchen, David's purple jersey with "Trek" emblazoned on the back, the way the hair on the back of my neck stood up when he breathed on me.

Jim's voice became irritable. "Sounds like you're busy."

David kissed my earlobe. My palms throbbed. My heartbeat interrupted my own thoughts, *whoosh-whoosh.*

Jim cleared his throat.

"Hey, Jim," I said, "I'm really sorry. But yes, I'm uh, um, I'll call you later, okay?"

Our bike ride ended at David's house, a bungalow he'd remodeled on the east side of the river. He told me how he'd found it while out one day walking, a home that was in such dilapidated shape that the aluminum gutters had holes the size of golf balls and the deck was rotten. Now, the home gleamed with copper gutters, fresh paint, and carefully sealed hardwoods on the deck. The small yard was framed with healthy azaleas, maples, and rhododendrons. We'd left our bikes on the front porch as he took me on what he described as the "quick tour."

The living room was lovingly cared for, looking as if a woman might have placed the rugs, hung paintings, and lined the bookshelves with dozens of worn hardbacks. The reading chair in the corner looked like an antique, with long, dark cherry arms and a tattered cushion. *I could hang out here*, I thought to myself.

In the dining room, a long table was the sole piece of furniture, one of the most stunning tables I'd ever seen, with room for ten. "I made this table from Brazilian hardwood," David said. The seams of the hardwood table fit together perfectly. It was shined and sealed, with a vase of large lilies placed in the center. We moved through the dining room into a bright kitchen with white tile and floor-to-ceiling deck doors that looked out on a hardwood deck and garden. David slipped through the door. "Come on out here, meet Sunny-Side Up and Tex-Mex."

David raised chickens! The red coop looked like it had been created precisely for the corner of his garden. This little fact about my new boyfriend thrilled me no end. "The city actually gives out permits for a certain number of coops in the city," he said.

Through the chicken coop wire I saw two chickens, one with orange feathers, the other with brown and white markings.

David opened one of the pens and held up a beautiful brown egg. "Now, *that's* organic."

He talked to the chickens through the wire as if they were his children, speaking sweetly to them. "Don't get nervous, girls. Bad for the eggs." I couldn't help loving the contrast; this big, six-foot-four man gently stroking his chickens' egos. "You ready for the best eggs in Portland?" he said after gathering several more eggs in his T-shirt.

I was famished from the bike ride. "Absolutely!"

I sat on the back deck sunning myself while David puttered in the kitchen. Beyond the chicken coop, David had planted a huge garden, with raised beds sprouting starter plants for tomatoes, cucumbers, onions, and herbs. The back of his garden was lined with sunflowers. It was so peaceful here. I let the sun sink into my bones. Portland's long rainy season could leave me feeling so sun deprived; it felt good to let the weekend heat sink deep. David's cherry trees and rose bushes were thriving. The sound of Leonard Cohen played softly through the windows. I felt punch-drunk, cared for, and connected. I closed my eyes and dozed.

When I woke up, David was coming through the door holding a tray filled with food.

"Your eggs are ready, Madame." David presented the tray of fresh eggs, toast, and a strong cup of coffee, just the way I like it, made in a French press.

He served the meal with small Italian salt and pepper shakers and a white linen napkin. "I love eggs for dinner," I said. "It's beautiful."

"So are you," he replied, setting the tray down beside me. It was the first overtly affectionate thing David had ever said to me. He was not loose with his words. He touched my arm, and a current moved through me. He watched me without flinching. I wished I hadn't just finished a sweaty bike ride.

"I've never heard you say anything like that before."

"Yeah," David said, poking his eggs with a piece of the toast. "I'm not much of a romantic."

I started to disagree but then thought better of it. He wasn't a romantic in the way that other men were, offering trips or jewelry as a showing of their affection. But he was completely authentic. David was his own person, and he appreciated me and my ambition. He wasn't the richest man in the world, or the CEO of a major corporation. He told me he hadn't bothered to finish his college education in Montreal, a fact that would later make much more sense. But despite the lack of a degree, he was by far the most intelligent and sensitive man I'd ever met, and the most mysterious. I had the uncanny sense that I already knew him, though, and that his serious, contemplative side could be very good for me.

I leaned over to kiss him. He did not rush me, or hurry me. His lips were full, a sweetheart shape that met my own naturally. I was ready to put down roots with someone. This tender gardener had won me over.

We spent most of our weekends together after that: hiking, skiing, mountain biking. Finally, I was with someone who loved the outdoors as much as I did. We traveled whenever we could both get away. We spent many of our summer weekends in the gulches, arches, and peaks of Canyonlands, hiking and bouldering, then cooling off in the local rivers and lakes. The red rock was millions of years old, as grand as any setting I'd ever known. I wanted David to love it as much as I did, and from the smile that settled on his face in the desert, I could tell he was enthralled.

One night in Capitol Reef National Park—three hours from my childhood home near Salt Lake City—we stayed up to watch a particularly active lightning storm. The strikes could have been miles away, but every time one hit the ground, it electrified the room with bright light and an energy that spooked me. The house where we stayed was owned by a college friend, a geologist who had bought land in the Torrey area before it became unaffordable.

Just as the sky thickened with dark, brooding storm clouds, David threw a jacket over me and said, "Come on, we can't miss this!"

We both ran barefoot into the storm, a wild, chaotic wind and rain that drenched us in minutes. He drew me in close, held out his left arm, and snapped a photograph of us while the dawn broke and a bolt streaked the sky behind us. Our eyes still held the excitement of those strikes, living so close to something so beautiful. And so dangerous.

## EARLY TREATMENT

The National Institute of Mental Health reports that "unlike most disabling physical diseases, mental illness begins very early in life. Half of all lifetime cases begin by age fourteen; three-quarters have begun by age twenty-four. Thus, mental disorders are really the chronic diseases of the young. For example, anxiety disorders often begin in late childhood, mood disorders in late adolescence, and substance abuse in the early twenties. Unlike heart disease or most cancers, young people with mental disorders suffer disability when they are in the prime of life, when they would normally be the most productive."

The study quoted above found that in the United States, mental disorders are quite common: 26 percent of the general population reported that they had had symptoms sufficient for diagnosing a mental disorder during the past twelve months. However, many of these cases are mild or will resolve without formal intervention.

According to David's doctors, his presentation of bipolar disorder was unusual because he had compensated for his illness for most of his adult life without psychiatric medication, counseling, and/or hospitalization.

David's sister, a psychologist, said David had informally reported periods of depression in his teens, twenties, and thirties. He experienced significant impairment in his forties, affecting his mood, anxiety level, and ability to sleep. Untreated psychiatric disorders can lead to more frequent and more severe episodes and are more likely to become resistant to treatment.

The Early Assessment and Support Alliance (EASA) project has shown unequivocally that early intervention in mental illness works. EASA supports youth ages twelve to twenty-five years old and offers a holistic approach to psychosis. The two-year intervention includes community education and outreach; intensive multilevel treatment that includes medical care, mental health care, occupational therapy, and vocational support; and strong support to keep young people independent, in school, and tied to employment.

Tamara Sale is Oregon's EASA program development director. "The current system of mental health care in most places in the United States is broken," she says, "forcing people into long-term crises and government disability by not providing access to services or evidence-based practices. . . . The approach we have taken has been a fundamental cultural shift. Now, there is greater awareness in the community about being proactive and persistent with psychosis intervention."

A case study by the Robert Wood Johnson Foundation says that the EASA program "has reduced hospitalizations for psychosis, helped young people maintain critical family and social support, and helped keep them in school." "If a young person starts to develop psychosis in Oregon," says Sale, "there is someplace to turn." According to the case study, a person who is hospitalized for an acute psychotic episode is at heightened risk for another episode and typically faces a longer recovery process. Sale adds, "If you can identify people before they've lost contact with reality, it is much easier to keep them on track."

# Chapter Three

David's upbringing against the backdrop of the Canadian Rockies fascinated me. His father had been a fighter pilot for the Royal Air Force, a forester in the Canadian Rockies, and a Harvard business school grad and business executive. So when David asked me if I'd like to travel with him to meet his parents, I didn't hesitate. We'd known one another just three months, but this was crucial intelligence; I wanted to see what he was like with his parents.

"What should I wear?" I asked, thinking I already knew the answer. "Something nice, a dress, or a skirt?"

David laughed. "No, please, no. Let's drive up. Bring a swimsuit and some shorts. There's such good swimming along the way."

Just as David had promised, we'd driven in Old Yella, talking and listening to a dozen new CDs I'd brought for the trip. We stopped for a dip in the Columbia River and again just south of the Canadian border. David loved the water, and he seemed to have internal GPS for finding the best swimming and fishing holes. He looked more at home in a canoe than in a car. I watched him drive as he hummed along to Fleetwood Mac, and I thought, *I could do this forever.*

We arrived in Victoria, British Columbia, just after dinner. My hair was tangled from the ferry ride, and the long, hot drive had left a kind of humid stickiness on the backs of my legs. The ranch home they'd bought was modest, on a half acre of manicured lawn, lined with dozens of magnolia trees and rose bushes. This was a part of the world that literally oozed the benefits of good soil, ample rain, and just the right amount of sunshine.

David's mother met us on the front steps and shook my hand warmly. "Well, your legs go on forever, don't they?" she said, smiling.

"It's really nice to meet you," I said. Seeing Alice in her proper white slacks, silk tank top, and sensible flats, I wished I'd trusted my own instincts about what to wear when you meet someone's parents for the first time. A printed red-and-white scarf was tied Jackie O–style on her head, and she wore no makeup. She was stunningly beautiful, even in her mid-sixties.

David's father came to the door and smiled a grin so contagious I couldn't help but chuckle—*So that's where David's charm comes from*, I thought. "Shee-laa," he cooed. "I've heard so much about you." Lew's blue eyes twinkled in the summer light; his skin was moist and thick, with few lines, even though he was deeply tanned. He had a full head of thick silver hair, the color many older people try to replicate in the salon after they've given up on blonde or black or auburn. His short-sleeved shirt looked casual enough, but a fiery red ascot peeked out at the top of his neckline, throwing the whole look off. Wow, what a character.

"Come in, come in," Lew said. "You must be parched. What can I get you?"

We settled in the living room, designed with the most basic of pieces: a couch, two chairs, a nice Persian rug, a couple of lamps, a coffee table, and a bookcase. No nonsense. Alice stirred iced tea in the kitchen while we chatted. They'd moved all over the world, Lew said. This last move was from Italy to Victoria, B.C., the midway point between Portland and Montreal. I tried to calculate mileage as a reason for settling down somewhere; it seemed as good as the next.

"David says you are a journalist. What newspaper do you write for?" Lew asked.

"Oh, I don't write for newspapers anymore," I said. "I'm in television."

"Mm." Lew's look turned. "There is nothing as valuable as the printed word, as far as I'm concerned."

"Agreed," I said, trying to cheer him back to the jovial point where we'd begun upon our arrival. "But television is about writing, too." I started to explain my belief that the best stories married strong writing with powerful imagery. He stopped me midway through my sentence.

"Television is a scourge on our society," he said bluntly.

I recoiled. David looked amused by the exchange; he'd warned me his dad was moody, charming, and complicated. I'd seen all of it in the course of twenty minutes.

"I think I'll freshen up," I said. "David, would you show me where we'll be staying?"

Alice interrupted, standing and blocking my route to the hallway. "David will stay in here," she said politely, pointing to a small den with a foldout bed. "And you can take the guest room."

"Yes, yes, of course." I blushed.

I surveyed the guest room Alice showed me. A Bible lay on the bookstand with a proper reading light and a bookmark midway through the pages. The single bed was covered with a lace bedspread, something my grandmother would have approved of. A portrait of Jesus hung above a chest of drawers, his face flooded with light and grace, his long hair cresting at the top of a white gown. He looked beautiful, I thought—and like Jim Morrison.

David had never mentioned that his parents were so religious. He called himself "a screwed-up Catholic schoolboy" when we talked of his private education and the mind-numbingly long Sunday services. I had followed the lead of my parents who, while deeply spiritual, had never really attached to the religion that dominated our state, Mormonism. I unfolded my clothes and placed them carefully in a chest of drawers. The top drawer had been cleared for my things.

The isolation and strict order in the house made me feel unsteady. My own family, however flawed, would have broken out a round of beer or a bottle of wine by now. Someone would be telling an inappropriate joke. And there would be laughter, lots of it.

I came back into the living room to find Alice darning a pair of socks—*who does that?*—and Lew reading the newspaper, a pair of reading glasses balanced on the crook of his nose. Alice was built similarly to David's sisters, whom I would meet later. They were all tall and lithe with beautiful bone structure. Her nimble fingers worked quickly, and only once did she reach for her reading glasses, when she was re-threading the needle. I watched this scene and found myself drawn to her deliberately attentive pace, the old-fashioned rituals of caring for house and home. Every move Alice made was purposeful; on her way to return Lew's socks to his drawer, she stooped to pick up the ads that had fallen from the newspaper, straightened a table lamp, and ran her finger across the piano. *I could learn a thing or two about how to run a household from this woman,* I thought to myself.

I'd never really learned how to nurture a household and longed for a proper role model; my mother's own domesticity alternated between manic bursts of activity and sheer neglect. I relied on my closest friends for instructions on how to cook a roast, scrub properly underneath a toilet seat, or bring order to a file cabinet. I tried desperately, often failing, to keep a few plants alive.

I followed Alice into the kitchen when she announced she was going to make dinner. When she opened the fridge, it appeared almost bare, the white light shining brightly on just a few items. But she methodically pulled together the ingredients for a lemon rosemary chicken roast, orange vinaigrette-glazed beets, and a delicious rice salad.

"You look like you've worked as a chef," I said, admiring the rapid chop-chop of the knife and the exact size of the tiny red and orange pepper slices.

She softened, whispering, confiding in me. "I was a horrible cook when I married Lew. I couldn't boil water. We both agreed lessons were in order." She laughed at the memory.

"When I first moved to Portland, my best friend would come over and prepare the dinners I would serve," I admitted. "She'd leave it all in a pan for me, with cooking instructions. David has benefited greatly from the skills of my talented girlfriend." I chuckled, more relaxed now. "Now, David is really appreciative of anything I make. Never criticize the cook, right?"

A look of amusement crossed her face, but then just as quickly her eyes changed, as if she was realizing the impact of another woman cooking for her only son. She reached for a bunch of parsley in the fridge. "Ahh, David," she mused. "How he loves to eat."

I helped her slice and dice as she told me stories of David, stories that made me fall even deeper in love with her son—the heartache of his cleft palate, the multiple surgeries he endured until it was barely noticeable. She told me of his tender nature, "by far, the most sensitive," and how, as a boy, David had been eager to win a paper route, rising at dawn to make his deliveries.

"When it came to collecting," she said, amused by the memory, "he was paralyzed. For the life of me, I couldn't understand why that boy couldn't ask people for money."

Denial and mental illness are easy bedfellows, and in that first meeting and many others, David's family gave no indication of a family history of mental illness. I would eventually learn David's family history through his sister, a psychologist, and his medical documents, crucial pieces to a puzzle I'd tried to fit together for more than a decade. But that night, I helped Alice move the food methodically from the kitchen into the dining room, accepting it all as normal—*We all have our quirks,* I thought. Lew and David had been reading the entire time, an oddity given that in my upbringing, the men pitched in with household work.

I caught Lew studying me intently, sizing me up as a potential mate for his only son. His eyes were gazing past his newspaper, and I felt myself being examined, in an almost clinical way, the thickness of my skin, the health of the cuticles on my fingernails, the strength and straightness of my teeth. He smiled when he realized he'd been caught doing a once-over. The charming smile was back. "So, Sheeee-lah," the Cheshire Cat said, "tell me about yourself."

I grew up about as far away from the reaches of the Catholic Church as possible: Utah, land of the Mormons, big mountains, small towns, and the knowing feeling that I didn't quite fit into such a conservative community. We were not religious people and spent our Sundays at rodeos and horse shows rather than church. We lived on a quiet street with huge cottonwood trees and several acres of rolling grass and farmland behind our house. We owned five horses, two dogs, a goat, and a cat—not exactly a working ranch, but a kid's paradise.

Everyone in town loved my father. "Bones," as he was called, was a lanky, gregarious man who had built a thriving general contracting business on the strength of his personal relationships. He won nearly every city and county contract for huge pipeline jobs or sewer systems. As the population grew, so did the number of Caterpillars, graders, loaders, and gargantuan pieces of yellow equipment at his work sites. On the rare days that Dad would call me up onto one of his pieces of machinery, I felt dwarfed and tiny compared to the masculine power around me.

He'd met my mother in high school. "The Tempest in the Teapot," he called her, a feather of a woman compared to his six-foot-four frame. (I would later seek out men of nearly the same height as my father, never doing it consciously.) Donna was fiery and smart and passionate, and she first caught his eye wearing a tight pink sweater and bobby socks that showed off her slim ankles, or so he said.

My father's nicknames defined him. Bones, for his length, and "Glue Tips," for his good reach and sure hands as a tight end on the football team. He won a football scholarship at BYU. It wasn't until

Dad returned home from the Korean War that he set about wooing my mother. She wasn't easily convinced, and in hindsight, she said if it weren't for his good genes and long legs, he might never have had a chance with her.

My mother was in her early twenties when she married, and she started having children faster and easier than either of them wished. We were all beloved, and my mother recounts those early years, with five children under the age of seven, as her favorites. I was the middle child, squeezed between two standout older siblings and two mischievous younger ones.

Black-and-white Polaroids of my mother give distinct clues as to where the family started to break. In nearly every frame, you see the stress of a woman trying to do it all too well: standing or kneeling behind five adorable children all in a row with starched rompers and hair that had been twisted or curled into place. Five pairs of polished white shoes, never a scuff, never a detail wrong. The house is orderly in every shot. My mother is dressed as if she were having a professional photograph taken every day: trim and groomed, her hair in an updo even as she battled the reality of motherhood—diapers, puke, and colic. But there is sadness in her eyes, and I would later learn my father's approval was as rare as a full night's sleep.

In kindergarten, I saw, for the first time, a huge pile of dirty laundry on the laundry room floor. Mom was rarely up when I returned home from school. She started excusing herself from making dinner to stay in her room, and eventually she was absent from every family meal.

I remembered watching my father stir a marinara sauce after working all day long, his work shirtsleeves rolled up as he tested the sauce again and again. The steam from the spaghetti noodles whistled into his face, making him sweat above the stove. "Who's hungry?" he'd asked, forcing a cheeriness to his voice.

I was five when she slipped into a full-blown depression. Nobody called it that. All I knew was that I rarely saw my mother. One morning I stood outside the door of her room and offered a knock. "Mama," I asked, "are you sick?"

No answer.

I slid my back down the door and waited. My brothers and sisters played rambunctiously in the hallways, and I shushed them.

The next morning I left toast at her door. By that afternoon, the edges of the bread had curled upward.

More days followed, with no improvement. I fished a dirty shirt out of the hamper to wear to school, not understanding the gravity of what that meant until a teacher pulled me aside and asked me if everything was all right at home. I lied. "My mom's on vacation."

I missed her laugh—a shush of air that came out uninhibited, her white teeth flashing as she threw back her head, slapping her hand on her thigh. I missed her lying down beside me at night to tell me what a special girl I was, that I was loved beyond the moon and the stars.

I tried new ways to move Mom from her bedroom. One day, I brought her a Coke, with five ice cubes, the way she liked it, and put it by the door. It spilled, and I cursed myself for being so stupid. "She's not even in there," I told my youngest brother as I scrubbed the carpet with a white bathroom towel.

Several more days went by, as my father hushed any discussion of why Mom wasn't feeling well, offering instead to make us pasta or pizza for dinner and instructing my older brother on the ways of the household.

By the time my father insisted on professional help a few weeks later, we'd all learned how to pack our lunches, wash the laundry, vacuum the floor, and finish our homework without supervision. We coped.

I started spending most of the time away from my house, in the garden or in the tree house. Nobody really seemed to notice my absence anyway. Time passed more slowly without the frequent visits from my mother's friends, without her remodeling the living room (again), and without the magical conversations we had about what I was reading or writing.

My older sister soon learned to saddle our horses, and we would ride in the fields behind our home. I avoided the house, my mother's lingering sadness, and the heartache of losing touch with the one person who reveled in my stories, my theatrics, and my funny dances on the fireplace stage. Dad took her to a hospital and brought back bottles of pills that were supposed to make her better. One day she was up, folding the laundry, going through the motions of being a good mother. She attended our horse shows and clapped whenever we won a ribbon or trophy. But there was a hollow beneath her eyes that frightened me.

I would be an adult before I learned the true cause of my mother's pain, a family secret that unfairly left the burden of dysfunction on my mother.

One day, after we had been dating about nine months, David and I hiked up Hamilton Mountain on the Washington side of the Columbia River. The hike was the kind I liked, a tough climb with an amazing view at the end—in this case, a stunning vista of the Bridge of the Gods and, on the Oregon side of the river, Multnomah Falls, with a peek at Portland to the west.

Hiking always seemed like a good time to talk, and as we made our way up the mountain, I finally said out loud what I'd been thinking about for months. I wanted to have a child. I wanted a life beyond my own. I found myself breathlessly telling David how I'd come full circle on the question of children, largely because of his presence in my life. He'd brought a dimension to loving that felt sustainable, a connection as viable and strongly rooted as the old growth around us. He was the only man in my life that I'd ever considered having children with. I loved him for bringing out a side of me that I'd either ignored or marginalized for far too long. I knew I was risking our relationship when I told him I was planning to have a baby, either with him or without him.

He stopped walking, turned, and looked at me, breathing hard. His face was flushed, his eyes were lifted, an expression I hadn't yet seen from David—one of pure joy. I didn't really know what he'd say. In fact, I'd surprised myself by laying my feelings out so bluntly. But what he did next changed my life: he proposed to me, on the spot, in a way that was completely his own. "Well, we should get married then, right?" he asked.

It was not the most romantic gesture, but it was David's way, completely authentic and unplanned, and I didn't hesitate. "Yes, yes, of course!" I dropped my backpack on the trail and kissed him squarely on the lips. "What are we waiting for?"

I was as sure as I could be that I loved David—loved him very deeply. A decade later, I would relive that moment, asking myself whether that was the hour that David began to feel trapped or suffocated by my version of happiness. He had never been one to fall in line or make decisions to please others. I expected he wanted a life together as much as I did.

We were married on December 7, 1996. The tearoom, where we would be married, was decorated with a fifty-foot Christmas tree. There were huge silver snowflakes hanging from the ceiling. The grand staircase I would walk down was carpeted in red, the banister wrapped in fresh laurels of pine and flowering poinsettias.

My sister Diane wasn't seeing any of the charm. She paced back and forth in the upstairs dressing room like an anxious bride.

"You are a miserable Matron of Honor, Diane." I was joking, but there was a little truth in it.

Diane shook her head, her eyebrows pinched together in an expression I'd come to associate with her blunt and honest approach to the world. "What's going on with David? It's like he's drunk or stoned or something."

I stiffened, looking away from her for fear I'd say something I'd regret. My ring finger was bare for now. My fingers weren't trembling. Why would she say something so profoundly troubling today, of all days?

"Are you serious?" I asked.

"Sheila," she said, "something is *wrong* with him."

I suppressed a bubble of anger long enough to consider my sister's worrying statement. She was not trying to be mean—she was seeing something I wasn't.

David had called from his home that morning to tell me he hadn't slept well, that he'd caught a bad cold and would be taking cough medicine just so he could get through the ceremony. I shifted in my makeup chair.

"He's sick, Di," I said, defensively. "Give the guy a break."

She rolled her eyes and shook her head. "He's not relating to other people. He's more than sick. He's checked out."

I stood up, straightening my dress as if it would also smooth the impact of Diane's observations. I trusted her judgment. But what was I to do? Call David at the last minute and accuse him of "not relating"?

Neither of us had touched our champagne. I heard singing below, a woman known as Portland's Queen of Soul. The acoustics were so clear; why couldn't I feel the same? My sister was asking me to view my wedding day through a lens I didn't own—the lens of skepticism and doubt. Diane hadn't mentioned her concerns previously. Why now?

One hundred of our closest friends were downstairs waiting, seated in front of a huge fireplace. I stood up, hugged my sister awkwardly, and rounded the corner to the grand staircase.

"It will be all right," I assured her.

She kissed my cheek. "I hope so, She," she said.

It was time.

My tall, handsome father, waiting for me in his stately tuxedo, took my elbow and guided me carefully down the stairs. I was the centerpiece of a wonderland, like something out of *Bride* magazine. I was about to marry a wonderful, exciting, adventurous man, and I felt like I was outside my body. Diane's words haunted me. Was David ready for this? Would he pass out and collapse during the ceremony? Every step heightened my anxiety; my legs went stiff, and I felt as if I would fall off my heels, tumble down the stairs.

I spotted my mother in the front row, beautiful, smiling broadly. She was better now—her marriage had survived the early turmoil, and she loved my father, despite their checkered history. David's parents looked over their shoulders to see me coming and nodded approvingly. It was going to be okay. As I reached the grand tearoom, David stepped forward, calm and stunning in a traditional black-and-white tux with long tails. His eyes were clear, bright blue, and he smiled straight at me. I remember my father smiling as he passed me off to my husband-to-be.

We were going to be okay. Everyone was happy.

That's how it felt at the time. But weeks later, when I opened the wedding photographer's book, I was stunned. My father wasn't smiling at all—his face was ashen, drawn, plagued with conflict. The photo in which David greets me at the bottom of the stairs was as I imagined, David smiling, his head tipped to one side as he takes my hand to greet the crowd. But in dozens of other, more candid shots, David was just as Diane described—his eyes unfocused, his fingers pinched nervously.

Something wasn't right, and Diane had seen it. Yet I refused to believe I'd made a mistake. I had married the man I loved.

## SIGNS AND SYMPTOMS

One in five Americans will develop a mental illness at some point in their lives. Caregivers are often quick to rationalize the behavior of our loved ones—especially if we are unaware of the symptoms of mental illness.

In the early years, I chalked up much of David's behavior to his eccentric upbringing and fierce independence. There are universal symptoms of mental illness that should not be ignored, especially if they become persistent and interfere with daily life. Among the early symptoms I noticed in David but ignored or minimized: a perpetual sense of sadness and negativity, confusion and a reduced ability to concentrate, extreme mood changes, sleep problems, and withdrawal from friends and activities.

David also began to exhibit major changes in his eating habits and developed an inability to control his emotions, resulting in explosive rage or laughing and hysteria. In the latest stages of his illness, David detached from reality, suffering from delusions, paranoia, hallucinations, and olfactory disturbances.

People who have had a biological relative with a mental illness are at greater risk of mental illness, as are those who are enduring stressful life situations, like financial problems, death, or divorce. Other people who may be at risk include those who were exposed to drugs and alcohol in utero, anyone who has suffered from brain damage as a result of serious injury or trauma, and people who have endured military combat or a physical assault.

# Chapter Four

After our wedding, we briefly honeymooned in Hawaii. I got pregnant quickly thanks to a sinus infection and a powerful dose of antibiotics that rendered my birth control useless. Less than a year after our wedding, Sophie was born.

I took four months off to be with Sophie, the maximum amount of pregnancy leave the company offered. For the first time in my life, I was completely, wholly blessed, and I believed David felt that way, too. Mothering Sophie was the most natural, exciting job I'd ever had. As long as I paid attention, Sophie let me know what to do next. I soon came to recognize her hungry cry versus her sleepy cry. I marveled at the miracle of every new kick, yawn, and gurgle. Even with the crazy hours of new motherhood, I hummed with happiness.

Meanwhile, David took on a new seriousness in his role as provider. He worked longer hours, but he also seemed to relish parenting, taking Sophie on long walks, bathing her, and even pitching in with diaper changes. His eyes lit up when he first saw her after a long day of work. I thought he was as happy as I was.

We'd been married a year and a half when I learned that David had never stopped sleeping with the girlfriend he'd had before me.

I'd gone back to work at my job as a television reporter when

Sophie turned four months old. I worked nights so I could be with her during the day, and then switched off child care duties with David at 4:00 p.m. The work, which once captivated me, had become a crude reminder of the world I'd brought my child into. I stepped over a crack baby in an abandoned house; I interviewed an adolescent girl who'd started doing heroin because it numbed her to the pain of sexual abuse. I carried the residue of my reporting home with me to my sweet, untroubled baby girl and found I had to force my job from my mind completely before I could enfold her in my arms. I did not want to taint her with any of the outside world. She would know it all too soon as she grew into womanhood.

One evening I was at the TV station putting together a story on Cesar Barone, a Portland-area psychopath who had finally been convicted of a series of brutal murders in the early 1990s. One of his crimes had stuck with me for years, the random, senseless killing of a Tuality Valley midwife who was driving home late at night after helping deliver a baby. Barone had peppered her car with gunfire, tried to rape the wounded woman, and then dragged her onto the road, where he shot her in the head.

The file footage detailed his early criminal history, starting at the age of nineteen, when he raped his seventy-one-year-old neighbor and then strangled her in her bed. The courtroom video of him showed no remorse, no inkling of feeling or compassion for the families of the people he'd brutalized. Chantee Woodman was another of his victims, a twenty-three-year-old whom he abducted, assaulted so brutally she was unrecognizable, and then shot in the head. Another victim, Margaret Schmidt, was sexually assaulted and strangled in her Hillsboro home. There was also Betty Williams, fifty-one, who died of a heart attack as Barone began sexually assaulting her at her Portland-area apartment in January 1993.

The women he victimized were so unassuming—just driving home from work, reading a book, puttering in the kitchen. He was a monster who had remained at large for years before he was finally arrested. How many others like him were out there? I recorded a voice track, finished the editing, and then delivered the story an hour early. "I can't take this anymore," I said to the eleven o'clock producer. "I'm going home now." He looked at my face and must have known I'd hit the wall.

"Thanks for your good work, Sheil," he said. "Get some rest."

I drove home from work cold and depressed. The house was empty. I opened the door to Sophie's nursery and found it pitch-black inside. Holding her would give me the sense that everything was okay again, but she wasn't in her crib.

"David, where are you? Where's Sophie?" I dropped my purse and my briefcase on the nursery floor and ran through the house flipping on lights. "David? David, honey. Where are you?" Halfway down the hall, I stopped running. Suddenly, I knew where he was.

He was with Jane.

I knew about Jane from the phone bill. I'd seen a number on that month's bill come up over and over again—fifteen- to forty-five-minute phone calls, always at night, always while I was at work. Frantic, I had called the number, heard her voice, and placed her immediately. I'd met her once, while David and I were dating. Although I'd hung up without confronting her, I cornered David the evening I found the bill, during my dinner break.

"Are you having an affair?" I asked him, holding the phone bill in my hand.

He rolled his eyes. "What are you talking about?"

"Jane's number. It's all over the phone bill."

"She's just a friend," he said. "Do I need to ask permission to have friends?"

I was embarrassed to be "that wife," the controlling kind of partner who doesn't allow her husband any breathing room. I accepted his explanation and apologized.

Now, three weeks later, I felt my cheeks go red and heat rise up underneath my sweater. I would not let him turn me into a stereotype I loathed—the jealous woman. I would not suffer the indignity of sobbing, of the puffy face and the stuffy nose, the pinched look of defeat. I stiffened against the shock and the crushing blow. As I sat down, the velvet couch I'd bought for the family room felt like an ice block on my legs.

*Sophie.* Where's Sophie? I let several minutes go by before I picked up the kitchen phone and called his number. "You've reached Mica Construction," the recorded message intoned. I slammed the phone down. Maybe I should go to her house. Maybe I should interrupt them during sex. I walked in circles in my kitchen, then the living room, still too stunned to cry.

I turned on the TV. I called his phone again. I turned off the TV. I opened the packed fridge and stared past all the food into the bright light. Outside, normal families slept, cuddled with their loved ones. I was not normal, not now, not after this. I'd ignored my earlier inclination that something was wrong, and now every instinct in my body told me he was cheating. And he had our baby daughter with him. I felt like vomiting.

Nothing would ever be the same again. I called again and again and again. After several hours of pacing downstairs, my body shivered from cold and shock. I dragged myself upstairs to my bed and undressed. I couldn't cry, couldn't get up to put on pajamas; I couldn't even stand to walk to the bathroom and brush my teeth. I crawled underneath the comforter like a wounded animal.

David finally tiptoed into the house two hours later. He stood in the doorway of the bedroom, holding Sophie in his arm like a football. I hadn't slept, couldn't stop the images of him at Jane's house from firing through my brain. Sophie was wrapped in a pink embroidered blanket David's mother had given her. The look on his face said everything he would never admit to. I turned on the light, surprising him.

"Jesus," I said, holding the sheet to my breasts. "Zip up your pants." I could see his red boxer shorts.

"This is not my fault," he yelled, startling me, holding Sophie with one arm while he fumbled with his zipper. His words sounded hollow and unconvincing, probably even to him. "It's your fault. You're never home."

Sophie cried anxious, high-pitched wails. She needed to be changed and fed. I rose from the bed, awkwardly aware of my nakedness. I took her in my arms, walked into the nursery, and locked the door behind me. I leaned against the door, my neck and shoulders so tight I could not move.

Sophie. I took off her wet diaper, anger rising again when I saw the rash on her bottom. She stared at me, hiccupping and sniffing, before she finally calmed down. I changed her and snapped the buttons on her sleeper, my heart still pounding.

She gulped as she breastfed, hungry and still upset by the yelling. She cupped my breasts with both hands, eyes shut tight, need rising until finally she burped and fell asleep on my chest.

I sat with Sophie for what felt like hours, rocking her in the dark. My thoughts replayed every instance David had been tardy or elusive or refused eye contact when we spoke about his whereabouts. It was painfully familiar. My freshman year of college, I'd popped into a local pizzeria for a slice and saw my father sitting at the bar, holding hands with an unfamiliar blonde woman. By then, I'd heard rumors of his cheating, but it had never occurred to me that he would cheat outside my home town, so close to my school, or with someone who appeared to be half his age.

I hated the way my father blushed, how he stammered and avoided my eyes as he offered up a flimsy excuse about why he was there. I hated how his hands shook as he attempted to introduce me to the blonde woman, who was blinking like a doe about to be shot. I left before she could open her mouth.

I knew I wouldn't be able to tell my mother what I'd seen. It would only wound her further. I now carried the extra burden of my mother's suffering, a lifetime of confusion and misplaced blame over the real problem in our home, a serial cheater. Depression is often referred to as anger turned inward; my father's first affair happened just before her mysterious breakdown. I would not, I vowed, become my mother.

Sophie's weight on my chest was the only thing that kept me from spinning into the ether. The two of us were in the same position when the sun finally rose—trapped. I half expected the bright, cheery star might not choose to rise on such a dark day. My body felt dull and heavy, as if it had endured its own death, still breathing, not yet crying.

Two days later, David and I still hadn't spoken, other than terse cell phone calls about the business of Sophie's day care, her naps, the number of times he'd changed her diaper while I was at work.

I was going through the motions of a life interrupted: at home in the kitchen, preparing for another night shift away from Sophie, zipping breast milk into little bags, the humiliating ritual of mothering from a distance. I knew Sophie had refused the bottle again and again. David had insisted we keep trying. Now, I believed it was because he didn't want me coming home on my dinner break at all, ruining his plans. David interrupted my ruminating, walking through the side door in time to take over his afternoon shift with Sophie. His hair was mussed by the wind, and his eyes were as blue as I could remember seeing them. He dropped the architectural plans he was holding and took three large steps to pull Sophie from her bouncy chair. He held her high in the sky with his big hands, her eyes widening with delight, legs kicking through her romper. David tucked her in close to him like a quarterback, preparing to run the ball, one long arm holding her head and her body. He'd held her that way first in the hospital, endearing himself to me.

I was dressed for work, but the red suit and high heels I'd put on didn't feel like a power suit at all. In fact, it complicated the vulnerability I felt at that moment, watching the man I loved, and now also hated so much, with our child. I sat on the kitchen chair and wept in front of him, the barrier I'd carried for days breaking into a thousand tiny pieces.

"David," I said, "I can't bear this."

He came to me, putting his hand on my shoulder while he balanced Sophie with his other arm.

"It won't happen again," he said softly. "I didn't even sleep with her."

I bristled. "How can you do this, David? How can you stand here, after what I saw, and lie to me? It's worse than the affair. Really, it's despicable."

His eyes softened. "I promise you, I did not sleep with her. I couldn't do it; I couldn't go through with it." He opened the tray to Sophie's infant seat and snapped her in her safety belt. "You must believe me."

I looked for something to trust, some telltale sign that he was changed by the affair. I tried to lock on his eyes, to make him say it again while I stared straight into his soul. Sophie whimpered. His eyes darted away from mine to hers. "There, there, sugar," he said, unhooking the safety belt and lifting her from the chair. He bounced her in his arms as he soothed her. "It will be all right. It's going to be all right."

Several weeks later, my sister Diane came to Portland, visiting for a weekend retreat with a Buddhist teacher. She sat in the passenger seat of my car while we drove through darkening skies, and I told her of the affair.

"Why don't you leave him?" she asked.

I loved her for her straightforwardness. "It's not so simple, Di," I said defensively.

We were headed to the grocery store to buy supplies for dinner. On the way out the door that morning, David had agreed to shop for the chicken and vegetables, but I knew he'd forget, that it would slip his mind and we'd be left without anything to eat.

I found a parking spot and turned off the ignition. "I've played this scenario a thousand times, Diane. I've imagined myself alone, as a single mom, with Sophie, no relatives nearby. My closest friends are childless. The station needs me to work late, or worse, to leave on a breaking news story. Who do I call? What do I do?"

"You make a decent living," Diane said. "More than most single women. You hire help." Grocery carts clanked behind us, the hum of a Safeway parking lot at 6:00 p.m. Large gray clouds hung over the red neon sign. There would be rain again tonight. I wanted to get in and out before it started to pour.

"He's trying, Di. I think I see him trying. And he loves Sophie so much." My voice trailed off, unconvinced of my own reasoning.

"Does he love you?" she asked bluntly. "Does he work to make a true partnership? Is he responsible, honest? Does he elevate you?"

I took the keys from the ignition and gathered my purse. "I can't say. Jesus, I really don't know anything except it's starting to pour."

David showed up at home an hour later, stomping the rain from his shoes, carrying nothing but his drenched briefcase. As soon as he spotted Sophie, he dropped his briefcase on the hardwood floor, scooping her up from her blanket and smothering her with kisses. Diane kept her eyes trained on him, looking for some acknowledgment or an apology for his failure to do what he promised.

David avoided making eye contact. "Hey," he said.

"Hey." My sister exchanged a knowing glance with me about David forgetting the groceries, his unpredictability, and his aloofness. Sophie cooed with delight. Diane shook her head. My emotions were caught between the disdain Diane felt for David and the gushy love Sophie displayed. Every time I thought of Sophie without David, a loss so profound moved through my body that I thought it must be intuition trying to tell me something. I tried to channel some of the gutsiness I used at work, but failed. In this house, with Sophie, I was soft, vulnerable, and not at all ready for an abrupt transition away from David.

David beamed at Sophie, touching her head so tenderly I had to turn away. This was the type of love I'd hoped he might show me one day. I knew now it wouldn't be possible. Sophie returned his affection with the telltale grimace all parents recognize. David laughed. "I'll change her," he offered.

I pulled the salad from the refrigerator. The chicken smelled done. David slapped his forehead on the way to the nursery. "Oh, the groceries. I'm so sorry, honey; I totally forgot."

Diane rolled her eyes, turned, and left the room.

Somehow, we made it through the fall, a blur of work and diapers and me concentrating on the small, magical accomplishments Sophie made every day. I found my purpose in the simple acts of mothering, strapping on the baby pack in the morning and only taking it off for her naps.

We took long, lovely walks together through the park, with Sophie cooing in a tone so delightful it made me smile just to hear her voice. I loved to change her diapers, to bathe and talk and sing to her. The two of us shared as much communication as I needed at the time. Mothering taught me just how much capacity my heart carried. Even though I was sleeping only six hours a night, I woke easily and enthusiastically, eager to see what new accomplishment Sophie might take on during our days together. She was bright eyes and beautiful sounds by now, babbling early and often and pushing herself up off chubby arms to rock back and forth on her haunches, preparing to crawl. I talked or sang with her throughout the day until my dialogue was drowned out by her happy noises, "ba, ba, ba," and "da, da, da." At six months, she had an enormous appetite, with two early teeth to help her chew everything from squash to small bits of chicken and steak. At Thanksgiving, her eyes lit up when she tasted mashed potatoes and gravy for the first time. I kept reading ahead in the baby book to try to keep up with her not-so-minor miracles. The more I loved Sophie, the less I needed of David. The more I concentrated on Sophie, the less I needed to address the pain of my marriage. It was the only defense I had, or so I reasoned. Did I know I was compartmentalizing? Probably. Did I ever imagine it would turn out so disastrously? No, never.

We spent Christmas vacation at my parents' new home in Utah, a sprawling, beautiful house with dozens of windows framing a view of the Great Salt Lake. A series of snowstorms kept the snowplows humming throughout the day. More than two feet of snow was already piled on the front lawn, making perfect conditions for cross-country skiing. My mother assured us Sophie would be fine. "Go, go, have fun, you two. I've done this a few times, you know." David and I exchanged a glance, his more hopeful than my own. We were still being cautious with one another, tentative and polite. But David had never owned up to his affair. And I still mistrusted him.

David and I loaded up our skis and drove in silence to the mountain. Settlement Canyon was such a special place for me. Growing up, I'd spent hundreds of days riding through the passes there. The canyon was the place where I was first kissed. It was where our high school cheerleading squad hiked to light the "T" before the homecoming festivities. It was a place teeming with memories of a more innocent time.

The city had installed a new, heavy gate made of steel, with a small opening for bikes and pedestrians at the entrance to the canyon. Most of the locals were irked by it; people in my hometown were hunters and outdoorsmen who would have preferred to drive their trucks through the canyon, shooting at game. The gate kept out motorized vehicles, and the wildlife had flourished. The snow was untracked in front of us. David headed out in front of me, making long, strong strides with his skis. I followed behind in his tracks.

Because he was raised in Canada, the cold temperatures suited him perfectly. When the temperatures dropped below twenty, David's cheeks grew rosy and his ears got bright, but his hands or feet never got cold. An hour into our ski, I started to feel the sting of frostnip on my fingers and toes. "We should probably turn around," I said. "I'm starting to get really cold."

David's bright expression drooped, his hat slightly lopsided on his head. "Really?" he asked. "Can't we just go a bit farther up the road?"

I didn't want to disappoint him. We'd had such a hard time the past few weeks, and seeing him happy again, looking so relaxed and healthy, made me happy as well. I wanted to bottle that look, that feel, and take it back home with us. I wiggled my fingers inside my mittens. "Okay," I said, "another half hour or so?"

He nodded appreciatively and then skied toward me to offer a huge hug. "Thank you, honey."

We started off up the road together, but David soon pulled out in front. I followed behind in his fresh tracks. His long arms reached out gracefully, his legs moving powerfully between each stride. The snow crunched against our skis, but other than that there was virtually no sound. The mountains were quieted by the snow, blanketed by a cover of powdery white layers. The sun dropped slowly behind the western mountains; I started to shiver, even as I skied faster to try to create more heat.

Suddenly, David stopped in his tracks ahead of me. "Shhh," he said.

I tried to look for what he'd seen that made him stop so abruptly. The trees were empty. A trail of rabbit tracks took off from the left of us. The setting sun cast long, spooky shadows on the deep ravines and gullies; there was nothing moving as far as I could tell.

David pointed to the grove of aspen trees to our right. "There. Do you see it?"

I strained my eyes, my toes numb from cold, my nose stinging from exposure. "See what?" I asked, wishing more than anything that I could turn around and ski as fast as I could home to the safety and warmth of my parents' home.

"See?" he said. "Right there." His glove pointed to three o'clock. I squinted harder.

There it was, camouflaged perfectly in its perch, a great horned owl staring out at us, with the biggest golden eyes I'd ever seen on a bird. Its eyebrows were slanted narrowly at us, its head cocked, mottled brown wings tucked to its side.

"Shhh," David said. He clicked himself out of his skis and slowly, tenderly, took baby steps toward the owl. The owl fluttered its wings, turning its head abruptly to keep its eyes on David, preparing for its escape. Its prominent ear tufts seemed calculating and alert.

David took another step, then another, his weight placed so tenderly he barely made a sound in the snow. He was within a couple of feet of the bird. I'd never seen anything like it. The bird startled me with a deep hooting sound: *Hoo-h-hoo-hoo-hoo*. The sound echoed through the canyon. I caught myself gasping out loud.

From somewhere deep in the tree grove, a loud raspy screech returned the call, the owl's young crying for its mother. The owl looked again at David and then lifted off, its beautiful wings spanning nearly sixty inches. It soared so fast, so precisely, I lost sight of it almost immediately. It was one of the many times David took me to the extremes of his world: places of profound beauty and magic, with little miracles that came along only when I gave up any sense of control. David caught the look of ecstatic gratitude on my face and smiled.

There would be other adventures we shared that would not end so magically. David's insistence at hiking "off-trail" in the Columbia Gorge left him covered in poison oak boils, big red oozing sores that took weeks to heal. Somehow, Sophie and I escaped the allergic reaction to the same poisonous plants.

In Hawaii, again "off-map" at David's insistence, we circled a weedy, scrappy patch of the island for three hours, until I was so tired and pissed off we didn't speak for two days.

On another day, after a long mountain bike ride, we bolted from the hot confines of his truck to take a dip in the Columbia River. We came back to find his truck, our bikes, and my luggage stolen. He'd left the keys in the ignition.

At the time, I reasoned that David had more than his share of bad luck because he lived larger than most people. No risk, no reward. David's nature was that he would go to the end of the road and inevitably want to go further, like an Alice in his own wonderland. Truthfully, I too was curious about what was on the other side. I craved the intensity David yearned for during those wild explorations, and his moods, when high, were contagious. Holding onto the high of euphoria was impossible, and it made our inevitable fall that much harder.

Two weeks later, back home from Salt Lake, I was driving home from the television station to have my dinner break with David and Sophie. A heavy rain turned to slush on the windshield, and then, just as quickly, into fat, sloppy snowflakes. Rushing home for dinner was my way of trying to hold things together—not because I feared losing David so much, but because I didn't want Sophie to lose David. Would he stay in her life if we divorced? I could not say yes for certain. I couldn't accurately plot the course of David's day, let alone what might happen if we divorced. There was still so much about him I didn't understand.

I sat with the engine running in the driveway, watching the wipers wash over the flakes one, two, three times. We were doing better since the affair—weren't we? The wipers thumped a steady beat to Fleetwood Mac, something from the *Mirage* album, the one with the album cover of Stevie Nicks and Christine McVie sandwiching Lindsey Buckingham, both women attempting to capture something that was already gone. The music sounded tired, as if the band was going through the motions. I clicked the radio off and went in through the side door.

David was standing at the front door looking out on the falling snow. I set my briefcase on the kitchen counter and came from behind to hug his big back. I truly wanted to make it work.

"Hi, sweetheart," I said. "Where's Sophie?"

"She's asleep," he mumbled, staring straight ahead into the darkness. "I put her to bed early."

I checked my watch. "But it's only six thirty. I really wanted to see her."

He stared out the window, not acknowledging me. "She was cranky."

I weighed my options. If I told him how important it was to keep Sophie up so that I could see her before bedtime, I'd have another fight on my hands. He was defensive about everything these days, especially Sophie's care. "Isn't it gorgeous?" I said instead, looking out at the snow.

"What?" he turned abruptly, revealing a pen and paper in his hand. "What's gorgeous? I can't see anything gorgeous because I can't hear myself THINK in this house. I can't sit down in this house and read a book. I can't even bear to look out the window because all I see and all I hear are those GODDAMN CARS!" His voice rose to a pitch that scared me. The blood vessels in his neck bulged, and his eyes darted to the window. There were no cars outside.

I was stunned. I began to speak and then stopped myself, not knowing how to gauge this level of anger. I'd seen David upset before, but never like this, never about something so bizarre. We were a block away from a busy street. This was a side street, not a busy boulevard! It was a total overreaction, reminding me of something else that had changed recently. He had a heightened hypersensitivity to sound, to bright lights, to smells, to clothing that wasn't organic cotton.

"What do you mean, the cars?" I pointed toward the street. "I don't know what you mean—David, are you okay?"

He pointed his pen to his yellow pad. "This, these cars! I've counted every car that has come along in the last two hours. Twenty-seven cars! Twenty-seven fucking cars, with their bright lights and fucking loud engines racing to their fucking homes going forty miles per hour. I can't THINK!"

His face was red and splotchy, and he smelled of sweat. Two hours. For two hours, he'd worked himself into a frenzy over traffic.

"If it bothers you, we can move," I said softly. "Again." Even as I said it, I didn't totally mean it. But it seemed crucial to calm him down. Three moves, two years of marriage. When we first married, we'd both sold our homes, mine a quaint Victorian, and his beautiful bungalow, to buy a larger home together in Laurelhurst, one of the most coveted neighborhoods in Portland. But it was too loud, he said, too disruptive to his sleep. Now this one was wrong, too, the house I loved most, with its plantation-style roof and a sweeping deck that opened onto a beautiful garden, with an apartment below for friends and family who visited. The house was wrong? No. A surge of defiance rose up through me.

"This is not about the cars, David. It is not about the neighborhood. This is about you. You need help."

He dropped his pen and paper on the hardwood floor. "Fuck you," he said, coldly. "What I need is a beer." I watched him stomp out the door and through the slush.

*You need a coat*, I thought instinctively, and then I caught my own reaction, protecting him even as he abandoned me, again. I stood at the doorway, frozen, unable to speak or move.

The next morning, David rolled over lazily and cradled me in his arms, as if nothing had happened. I felt my back stiffen against him. I'd brought Sophie into bed with me that night, so exhausted I'd hoped lying with her, rather than rising every time she cried, might make us both happier. My body lived in two worlds: the harmony I felt with Sophie, and the growing disconnect I felt with David.

As I cradled her, I felt a longing for David, the other half of us.

"Look, I've been a jerk lately," he whispered. "I'm really sorry." He curled his arm around both Sophie and me. "I am so grateful to you for bringing me Sophie. I have never loved anyone or anything as much in my life. I will try harder for us." He moved into me breathing, our two bodies connected by this third life, this amazing force between us. His lips touched my spine, soft kisses down the arch of my back, my arms.

My throat tightened as I turned to kiss him back.

In the months that passed, David moved in and out of our marriage as if it were a pair of jeans he could wear or put at the back of his closet. Weeks would go by when David was fine, joyful even at the prospect of spending time at home, gardening, or remodeling a bathroom or kitchen. We made love, ate our meals together, and called one another several times during the day. "I'm just thinking of how lucky I am," he said one day. "And how lost I'd be without my family."

Each time it got better, I thought, *Okay, we've made it. We're past the tough part.* I hung onto those moments of connection, building a case for staying the way Sophie built a pyramid of colored wooden blocks. She was patient, positioning each block so carefully her eyes never left the structure, even as she reached for her next block. It was only when she was smugly satisfied with her work that she swung her arm through the pyramid, crashing it to the ground.

David's sense of self-destruction seemed just as impulsive. A phone call or conversation could set him off, his anxiety building to a point that it twisted his face into a new position. A dark, foreboding sense surrounded him, physically and emotionally. He walked around with a hunch, burdened by this mysterious weight, a weight I could neither tap nor explore.

*My life could be so much worse,* I rationalized. *I love my job. I love this house. Our daughter is healthy. I should be grateful.* I look back on those years, wondering along with everyone else how I stayed for so long. The only answers I can come up with involve my own stubborn sense of optimism and my cowardice. I believed David during the good times, when he told me his family was the most important thing he'd ever had. And given what I now know about how difficult it is to cope with the destructive and alienating thoughts of bipolar illness, I'm in awe of David's capacity for holding his life together as long as he did. I was coping, too, during those difficult years, so that Sophie might grow up in a household with the one man who would always love her unconditionally.

## FOR CAREGIVERS

The symptoms of unipolar and bipolar depression are such that caregivers can feel enormous frustration in attempting to support a person who seems uninvested in recovery. Many family members report loved ones sleeping as much as twenty hours a day, refusing to participate in household chores, and canceling social engagements. People with mental illness may stop attending to their own grooming, causing frustration and embarrassment for other family members.

More than forty million women are the primary caregivers for a sick person, very often the man they married. In *The Caregiving Wife's Handbook,* Dr. Diane Denholm advises caregivers to avoid assuming roles and jobs because someone else thinks we should and to realize that sacrificing yourself completely will not make the sick person well. Also, Denholm advises that the caregiver should never accept abusive or dangerous behavior.

During the acute phase of David's mental health breakdown, loved ones and friends would often call to ask how he was doing. Very few people recognized the emotional and physical toll I was under as I cared for our daughter, kept a household afloat on one income, and managed the emotional heartbreak of witnessing David's deteriorating physical and mental health. I am most grateful for the friends who did not judge, but who listened.

The mental health of the caregiver is also at risk during the time of acute care. Denholm advises taking care of yourself first, by eating well, exercising, and arranging assistance in order to get needed sleep. Denholm says if you become depressed, feel excessively guilty or angry, or fear becoming abusive, it is time to step away from your role, if only temporarily.

# Chapter Five

May 21, 1998. Sophie's cry didn't sound right. It was too distressed, too high-pitched. She woke me from a superficial sleep. The clock said two o'clock; that meant I'd been dozing for roughly two hours after finishing my shift at the TV station. I grabbed my robe from the foot of the bed and ran to the nursery.

Sophie's skin was hot to my touch; she was running a high fever, burning up through her pajamas. Her skin was flushed, her face swollen and lips dry from dehydration. *Damn it*, I thought to myself. This had happened before with Sophie, and I knew what it meant: another trip to the emergency room.

I went back to the bedroom and dressed in the dark, quickly pulling on a pair of jeans and a zip-up hoodie. David stirred in the bed. "She's sick, D. I'm taking her in."

He wiped his eyes, groaning. "Ugh, not again. Want me to come with you?"

"That's okay." I gathered my purse and cell phone. "One of us should sleep." I swaddled Sophie in a blanket, trying to remember how many ear infections she'd had this year. Three times her fever had spiked up above 102, the point at which her doctor said she needed to be seen. These days I could tell how serious it was just by feeling her skin.

Sophie was just short of her second birthday, and the ear specialist had warned us that her Eustachian tubes were still horizontal—the liquid in her ears didn't drain properly. If the infections persisted, he wanted to perform surgery to put in artificial tubes.

I tucked her in her car seat and drove through the night to the Legacy Emmanuel Emergency Room in North Portland. The pediatric waiting room was full of mothers just like me who looked worried, pensive, and haggard.

Three hours later, I drove home with Sophie's fever under control and a bag of pink bubblegum antibiotics by my side. The neighborhood stirred with the beginning of a new day. I made it home, exhausted, daunted. I let the car idle in the driveway, trying to gather the strength to carry Sophie inside.

The infections had started once we put Sophie in day care. David said he needed more uninterrupted time to see clients and architects, so for two hours a day, Sophie went to a neighborhood day care near our home. I wasn't worried at the time—I knew day care could be good for children. But now, with her susceptibility to infections, it felt dangerous every time we dropped her off. Maybe I should be the one to quit. I'd asked David about it once, telling him I'd be willing to take a break from my career to raise Sophie. He argued that I would miss my work, and we needed the money. Now, as I climbed the stairs to the house carrying Sophie in her car seat, my muscles ached.

David was getting out of the shower. He looked radiant, as if the sleep and the water had washed away anything troublesome in his life. His hair was wet, but tousled, as if he'd shaken it partly dry. A white towel was wrapped at his waist; his long legs looked strong and steady. Something inside me stirred for him, but the weight of the car seat, and Sophie's illness, stood between us. "Is she going to be okay?" he asked.

"She'll be fine." I answered. "We're back to the bubblegum routine."

He sighed and dropped his towel to find his clothes. His back was muscled from going to the gym at night after work; his skin was smooth and tanned from swimming at the lake. Even though my ears were beginning to ring and my eyes felt dry and bloodshot, something shifted inside me—I wanted desperately to pull him to the bed with me right then, to make our lives better again, for the three of us.

"I'm late," he said. "Let me put her to bed so you can rest." He took Sophie from me, tenderly kissing her on the forehead. "My poor, sweet baby," he whispered. I could hear the safety lock going up on her crib, the lights going off. I waited in bed, hoping he might return.

"See you this afternoon," he yelled from downstairs. "I won't be late."

The phone startled me. I'd drifted off, dreaming of waiting rooms filled with dozens of screaming sick babies. My assignment editor was on the other end. "We need you to pack a bag," he said. "There's been a massacre at Thurston High in Springfield."

I struggled to make sense of where I was, what was happening, why my assignment editor was calling me in the morning when I wasn't due at work for several more hours. The clock said 9:00 a.m. He rattled off more information, businesslike, uninterested in whether I was prepared to take notes.

"Nels," I interrupted, "Sophie is really, really sick. I need to stay close to home." I heard shouting in the background, the sound of television feeds, and computers rat-a-tap-tapping out the breaking news. On any other day, I would have loved the adrenalin rush. This morning, with my head banging and my body operating on so little sleep, I dreaded the idea that there was more chaos in the world to report on.

"I'm sorry to hear that, Sheila," Nels said, "but we need our senior reporters there now. An hour ago. Really. Get here as soon as you can."

I started to interrupt.

"And bring an overnight bag," he said. "The networks want live shots for the eastern feed."

Five minutes later, I was punching in David's number on the phone. "David," I said on the voicemail, "I've got to go to Springfield. Call me immediately; it's an emergency."

Sophie woke up, crying again, as I tried to track David down. I phoned him several times over as I hurriedly threw things in an overnight bag—my makeup, my hair curlers, the obscene amenities of television news that struck me as strangely out of place, given I was headed to a murder scene. When David phoned back, I breathlessly relayed the information to him.

"I've got to go to work now, David. I'm already late. Can you help?"

"Bring her to my job on Forty-second," he said. "And don't worry. I've got it handled."

"But she shouldn't be out of the house," I argued. "You need to be home with her."

David's voice stiffened. "Look—she's my responsibility now, right?"

I hung up, my heart beating wildly, my mind racing with horrible what-ifs. What if her fever worsened; what if she starts vomiting? Would he know what to do? I showered quickly, loaded a diaper bag with Tylenol and diapers and anything I could think of that might comfort her, and held her tight before loading her into her car seat.

David's job site was just a few blocks away. I checked my watch. Twenty-five minutes had already passed since my assignment editor called.

I pulled up outside a beautiful old Tudor that David was doubling in size for his clients. His pickup, along with his workers' trucks, were all parked in front of the home. I double-parked so I wouldn't have to walk several blocks with Sophie's things. She whimpered as soon as I took her from the calm of her car seat. The sound of saws and hammers, a radio blasting in the background as the men worked, and the dust of remodel greeted me at the door. I normally loved seeing David in his natural surroundings, but now, holding Sophie—who clutched her favorite stuffed animal, Bear—I felt miserable.

"Hi, Sheila," one of David's longtime contractors said, nodding my way as he balanced himself on the two-by-fours that made up the addition.

I offered a fake smile back. "Is David here?"

David appeared from the back of the house, holding his cell phone to his ear. He motioned for me to hand Sophie to him. I wanted him to hang up, to give him all the instructions, everything he'd need to know to care for her, really care for her. He shrugged his shoulders as if he couldn't get off the phone.

I waited stubbornly until he finally hung up, exasperated.

"Here's the Tylenol, here's Bear, there's a few things in the bag you'll need . . ." I started down the list of what I thought were important instructions.

"I've got it handled," he yelled above the noise, holding his arms out for Sophie. Her face was still splotchy, and her eyes darted around with nervousness from the loud sounds.

"Mama, Mama," she cried when I handed her off. Bear dropped to the dusty floor. I reached for it, but David stopped me.

"Go, go, will you? I've got it handled." His phone rang again.

I couldn't move. The noise, and the conflict inside me, made me dizzy, discombobulated. David looked distracted, annoyed by the interference. I squinted to keep the tears back. All I wanted to do was take her back from him and drive far, far away, to a place we could both rest. My cell phone rang. David widened his eyes and turned his chin, as if to say, "GO." I picked up Bear, wiped him off on my suit, and tried to hand him back to Sophie, who arched her back and tried to push away from David.

The car I'd blocked by double-parking blew its horn loudly, *HONK, HONK, HONK!* I looked for a sign from David, any sign that he would say, *Don't go, don't go. Stay and take care of Sophie, of yourself.* Nothing. I forced myself to turn away, ignoring every instinct, including a loud ringing in my ears. I stumbled to the street, reached through David's open window, and put Bear behind the wheel of his seat.

The driver I'd blocked in the road held his hands in the air, as if to say, *What the hell?*

I shook my head. *I'm sorry, so sorry. You'll never believe how sorry I am.*

My cameraman and I loaded our gear into the back of the van. Normally, we'd be talking about the story we were headed to, what we knew, and what we needed to learn before reporting the story. I looked out the window instead, tears streaming down my face. Mike was a bearded teddy bear, a guy who left the priesthood to follow his dream of being a television photographer. He was the best in the business. We'd worked together since I'd come back from maternity leave, and we were deeply respectful of one another.

After about an hour, he said softly, "Everything okay at home?"

"You know, Mike," I said, "I didn't expect it to be this hard."

"You mean reporting?" he asked.

"Everything," I answered. "Nothing comes easy anymore."

We pulled up outside Thurston High School, a red brick school that reminded me of the type of school where I grew up, where nothing much important ever happened. The Thurston High Colt kicked its heels on the sign outside. The lawn was beginning to show signs of greening. There was just a month left until summer break.

Yellow police tape was strung around the school. There were blood spatters on the sidewalk. Our assignment editor said the crime took place just after eight o'clock. They'd found the shooter's car a block away. The boy, Kip, had worn a tan trench coat to conceal his weapons. That was about all we knew, along with the sobering statistics: two dead, area hospitals filled to capacity with teenagers suffering from gunshot wounds.

It was now just before noon, and a few groups of kids were still loitering around outside, talking about the event. Two television stations were already there with their huge satellite trucks. I knew by the end of the day there would be dozens more.

I avoided the teenagers who flocked to the cameramen, who wanted to be on TV just for the bragging rights. A couple of girls in big sweatshirts stood by a tree, ashen-faced, mascara stains around their eyes. I approached them respectfully. "Could you tell me what happened?" I asked.

They looked at me suspiciously, glancing also at the photographer who stayed several steps behind me, honoring their privacy.

"I'd rather not talk to the camera hogs," I said, motioning to the boys crowded around the other television stations.

"Yeah," said one of the girls, "they weren't even there."

I convinced them it was important to tell the story accurately. Mike rolled tape while the girls carefully recounted the moment Kip Kinkel walked into the school cafeteria where kids gathered before class. They said they first thought it was a joke, or they would have ducked for cover sooner. While the surviving students scrambled for safety, Kinkel, who'd also murdered his parents the night before, loaded and unloaded the three weapons he'd brought with him, a .22 caliber rifle, a .22 caliber handgun, and a 9mm Glock automatic pistol. "He just kept shooting," one of the girls said. "The sound is still ringing in my ears."

By the time Kinkel was finished, two were dead, and twenty-five students were seriously wounded. "Jake finally stopped him," one of the girls told me. "After Kip shot Jake, Jake must have thought, what the hell, we're all going to die anyway." She pushed her shoe into the mud.

I thanked the girls and told them how sorry I was for their loss. "Do you know when our moms will be here?" they asked me. My throat seized up and my chest heaved.

"You mean you're still waiting for a ride home?" I asked.

The girl with the longest brown hair answered. "Our moms are at work."

I rushed the tape to the live truck, where Mike and I fed it back to our station and then to the networks. I gathered myself for the live shot and looked into the camera, "Kip Kinkel didn't have many friends at Springfield's Thurston High. His parents were both teachers, and Kip was known as a loner. He entered the school lunchroom and without saying a word, he started firing."

My assignment editor called back. "That was fantastic! Brilliant," he said. "We'll need you to turn around pieces for the five, the six, the eleven, and of course, the network feeds."

"Nels," I said, "can you get someone to relieve me tomorrow morning? I really need to get back to Sophie."

"Sheila," he told me. "This may be the biggest story this year. You should be planning your next move right now."

"Right, Nels. Thanks. I am." My throat was dry, and I realized I hadn't had anything to drink for hours. My shoulders slumped as my body seemed to squeeze out the final ounce of energy. It was the inevitable crash that follows the surge of adrenalin that comes from reporting on big stories. But this time, the fatigue combined with deep sadness and the stark realization that a life of reporting on tragedy was not for me. Since Sophie's birth, I'd lost the ability to be objective, to keep the subject and the people at arm's distance. It was all so personal now. Everything about this day had reinforced the sense of isolation I felt in David's presence and the larger sense of alienation that existed in the world, in schools as small as Thurston. If it could happen here . . .

My cell phone rang—it was David, with news of Sophie. The fever had finally broken.

## HYPERSEXUALITY

Hypersexuality is one of the most troubling and challenging symptoms of bipolar disorder. Doctors Frederick K. Goodwin and Kay Redfield Jamison reviewed the literature on hypersexuality and concluded that 57 percent of people with bipolar disorder report difficulty controlling the urge to have sex with someone other than their partners.

Research by Barbara Geller, M.D., and colleagues in an NIMH-financed study at Washington University in St. Louis found that 43 percent of children diagnosed with mania exhibited hypersexual behavior. The subjects of the study were ninety-three children with mania whose average age was about eleven years.

Hypersexuality can be a component of hypomania, an elevated condition in which the bipolar patient feels energetic and charismatic, and inhibitions drop. Hypomania can be an enjoyable mood state that is like a recreational drug.

But hypomanic individuals can destroy their finances, their careers, and their relationships. David's diagnosis of bipolar II suggests he was in an elevated mood state that manifests itself as irritability rather than euphoria. David was more concerned by his alternating bouts of depression because he felt paralyzed, unable to complete even mundane tasks such as getting dressed or brushing his teeth.

The symptoms of hypomania include rapid, "pressured," or loud speech; increased energy with a decreased need for sleep; lack of impulse control; and hypersexuality. Jamison reported that women with bipolar disorder tend to be much more sexually provocative and seductive than men with the disorder. She found that twice as many women reported increased sexual intensity during hypomania. These women in her study also rated sexual power as the part of mania they liked best.

# Chapter Six

David started working weekends when Sophie turned three. His business was booming, and he felt he needed more time with his clients. I didn't complain. Sophie and I were two peas in a pod, delighted to move through our weekends with a mix of reading, walking and snacking, eating whenever we pleased, or lolling around at farmers' markets or Oaks Park, an antiquated and charming amusement park on the outskirts of Portland. We took in funny movies; we spent hours in the children's sections at Powell's, the iconic bookstore of Portland. We swam at the neighborhood pool and afterward treated ourselves to shaved ice. On weekdays, we spent the morning and part of the afternoon together, before I headed to the station.

I was surprised I didn't miss David more. Truthfully, the less we saw of one another, the better we all got along. Our relationship worked best when it was on David's terms, when I didn't push him or make him attend my numerous benefits or parties. We'd moved past the Jane episode without ever really processing how or why we'd survived it. There was so much left unsaid about why I'd decided to stay. If David had asked, I would have told him, "I won't quit this family." The truth was, I would learn to live without his love. Our sex life was so irregular that when we did move into one another's bodies at night, it was fueled more by hunger than a need for intimacy.

Instead of talking about our difficult relationship, David had channeled his energy into a new direction—work. He said he wanted to be successful, a contrast to the laid-back business style he'd had when we first met.

One night, I invited David to join us after work at a Cuban place Sophie and I loved in northeast Portland. The colors of the restaurant, bold reds, oranges, and gold, suited us. I was thrilled when David said he could join us, and even happier when I spotted a small table for the three of us in our favorite corner.

"You look beautiful tonight," he said.

"Thanks, D," I said, relaxing into a rare moment of appreciation from him. I wore an aqua-blue tank top that set off my tan. I'd become strong and muscled again, swimming daily with Sophie and taking long walks with her to the park.

Families and hip young couples crowded into the restaurant. Sophie munched on tamales, much to the delight of the waitress, who was doting on her. We were both relaxed from a day at the pool.

David took a huge bite of rice and beans, then said, "Do you ever wish you could stop your head, you know, the voices that tell you you're nothing, there is nothing, you live alone, you die alone?"

I put down my mojito. "What do you mean, voices? You mean like the constant chatter, the negativity we feed ourselves?"

He took another huge bite of rice and beans, not bothering to chew before he swallowed. He was simultaneously distracted and wrapped in his own thoughts.

"David," I said, my voice heavy with worry. "Talk to me."

He nodded his head, taking another huge bite and washing it down with a gulp of beer. He seemed ravenous, hurried, talking too quickly. "You mean you can escape your head? You can stop your chatter?"

He seemed to be filling in my half of the conversation, but I wanted to engage him, so I said, "Yes, whenever I can. I walk and try to concentrate only on the feeling inside my body. Sometimes at work, when things get hectic, I lock myself in a sound room and just breathe to interrupt the spinning. It helps, really." I reached my hand across the table for his. He pulled away.

"Sometimes I just feel like such an imposter," he said.

I put my napkin next to my plate, swallowing carefully. "Maybe you should talk to a psychiatrist."

"Daddy, can I have an airplane ride?" Sophie interrupted.

David clipped her nose with his thumb. "In a minute, sugar," he said. "Mommy and I are talking."

"You aren't yourself, David. I think you need help."

He shot me a look of disdain. The clanking sound from the kitchen that had cheered me a half an hour ago now annoyed me. I wished I could wink the crowd away, silence the noise, like a director who edits her film. Instead, here I was, awkwardly, loudly tugging around the edges of my husband's erratic emotions. "David, I am so worried about you. Do you want to go somewhere we can talk?"

"I don't—no, I don't want to talk about it." Then he made his voice stronger, more decisive. "No. Because I'm going to give Sophs a plane ride!" He lifted our daughter from her chair, holding her high in the sky, his biceps flexing each time he lifted her up and down above the table.

"More, more!" Sophie said, smiling broadly, her arms out to the sides.

The waitress came by and cleared our table. "What a beautiful family," she said, smiling at the three of us.

These days, when I drive by that restaurant and see its colorful tables, I remember the intense frustration I felt in never, ever being able to reach David, or to persuade him to get help.

As my sister says, "Well, he was a stubborn son of a bitch, Sheil." The psychiatrists who would eventually treat David framed his behavior in the context of his mental illness, using terms like "recurrent hypomanic episodes," "mild depressions," and "anxiety disorder" to describe his reclusiveness, his isolation, and his fits of anger. They told me his explosive cursing, his infidelity, and his lies were "the illness talking." David, the person, was exempt from his behavior.

But how much of David's behavior was the illness and how much was the stubborn son of a bitch doing exactly what he pleased? Where did the illness begin and the self disappear?

David's parents drove from Victoria to visit us in the fall of 2000. They had seen Sophie only twice, once at her christening, and then again as an infant at David's sister's home in Quadra. I was glad they'd be able to spend more time with their three-year-old granddaughter but worried about the stress David seemed to carry about everything.

He flew into a frenzy before their visit, resurfacing the hardwood floors, scrubbing kitchen windows, clearing out the silverware from the drawers and polishing it with silver cleaner, and then reorganizing it all in perfect rows. I'd never seen him like this before; in fact, we'd had several dinner parties to which David showed up half an hour before our guests arrived. This was definitely different behavior than I'd come to expect. I wasn't sure if the frenzy was a good sign or a bad one. Maybe he was excited to see his parents again. Maybe he was dreading it. I knew it would only annoy him if I asked. David was never big on sharing.

On the evening of their arrival, Alice and Lew were later than expected. The dinner got cold. I'd prepared roasted vegetables, a tenderloin, and a northwest salad with cranberries, blue cheese, and walnuts. I imagined the tenderloin drying, the vegetables hardening, the salad losing its crunch.

Finally, Alice walked through the door carrying a grocery bag full of gifts, all in colorful wrapping with bows and ribbons flowing over the sides.

Sophie stood behind my leg, cautious. When she caught a glimpse of the presents, she wandered to Alice's side. "Can I see?" she asked, clapping her hands and jumping up and down. Alice smiled and tipped the bag down toward her. "Presents—for you, my sweet. But not now—after dinner."

Sophie's smile dissolved. *Oh no,* I thought. *Dinner will be a wreck now.* And sure enough, it was. Alice and Lew took their time with the tenderloin, and Sophie couldn't sit still, couldn't keep her eyes off the presents Alice had tucked away at the top of the fridge.

Another half an hour passed as David and Lew drank wine and I tried to stay engaged with Alice. By 9:45 p.m., Sophie was fried. Her face was splotchy, she twisted her body in uncomfortable positions, and then she crawled out of her chair and onto the floor, wailing.

"I want to open my presents!" she screamed. A full-blown tantrum was about to go down. I rushed from my chair to pick her up from the floor.

Suddenly, Lew bellowed, "DAVID! Control that child. Discipline her—now!" His face was as flushed as Sophie's, and his eyebrows were pointed in a grim display of consternation.

Something went off in David, a bomb buried so deep he probably didn't realize it was in him. He answered in an equally loud voice, unfamiliar to me, filled with more anger and anxiety than I'd ever heard before. "I will not have you tell me how to raise my child in my own home!"

I scooped Sophie up from the floor and ran to her bedroom, holding her in my arms. She was wailing, frightened by the fight unfolding in the living room. I heard a door slam. I didn't know who had left. I tried to calm myself by changing Sophie into her pajamas. Her eyes were still wet with tears as I finished snapping her up.

I wrapped Sophie in a blanket and returned to the living room. Lew and Alice were putting their coats on and gathering their suitcases, still packed, at the living room door. Lew turned to me, his face still flushed with anger. "I'm sorry if I offended you," he said. "But whatever you do, don't spoil your children."

I started to speak, to explain to him that it was past her bedtime and the presents had made it more difficult. He interrupted. "It's clear David does not want us here. We're going back to Victoria."

I stammered the next words. "Where did David go?"

"Off," Alice said. "David being David." She put on her red coat and tied her scarf around her head.

The door closed. I sat in David's chair as Sophie's eyelashes batted slowly, heavily. She was fast asleep, the colorful presents still peeking out from the bag. Sophie would get to open them in the morning.

A week later I received a letter from Lew. It was written in careful handwriting.

> *Dear Sheila,*
> *I am increasingly concerned about David's fits of aggression and erratic behavior. I believe he should seek professional care. You may be aware that David abused drugs as a teenager, and I believe it drastically changed his mental acuity and stability. I am telling you this so that you can make the right decisions regarding his future care. It is unfortunate our visit was cut so short. All my love to you and Sophie,*
> *Lew.*

I folded the letter several times over, considering its contents. I'd known plenty of people in high school and college who took the same drugs David used, garden-variety pot, acid, some cocaine. They were fine today. I couldn't make sense of Lew's ominous warning, and when I later asked David about it, he groaned and pointed out that there was nothing to suggest Lew had ever considered his parenting to be part of David's problems. "He wasn't exactly father of the year," he said.

David refused to apologize; Lew did the same. Alice and I talked on the phone shortly after the disastrous visit, attempting to find some way of reconnecting these two stubborn, like-minded men. They refused to speak to each other, and I finally accepted their decision. But it worried me.

If David replicated this bizarre family behavior, he might one day convince himself he didn't need his daughter either.

## MENTAL ILLNESS AND DRUG USE

The National Alliance on Mental Illness says that nearly one-third of people with mental illness and approximately one-half of people with severe mental illness (including bipolar disorder and schizophrenia) engage in substance abuse. Drugs and alcohol can be a form of self-medication. People may feel that their anxiety or depression is less severe when they use drugs or alcohol. Unfortunately, drugs and alcohol don't treat the underlying disorder and worsen mental illness.

The onset of psychosis during college years is particularly common, given the lack of sleep, an increase in stress, and experimentation with drugs and alcohol. David reported being unable to concentrate in college and having extreme difficulty sleeping. He also used drugs and alcohol during his teen years. David inevitably dropped out of college and showed worrisome signs that indicated his mental health was declining. He lost interest in the care of his apartment and his personal hygiene, he reported increased sensitivity to sights and sounds, and he withdrew from family and friends.

NAMI reports: "Abuse of drugs and alcohol always results in a worse prognosis for a person with mental illness. People who are actively using are less likely to follow through with the treatment plans . . . and more likely to miss appointments, which leads to more psychiatric hospitalizations and other adverse outcomes."

# Chapter Seven

Months later, I was on deadline at work, puzzling over the perfect combination of words and video for my story. We'd been pulled from a longer-format story about cuts in school funding to cover another gang shooting in north Portland. It was the third time I had been called to a particular intersection of Sumner Street in a month. I wished I had time to extrapolate the bigger picture: what the violence meant in relation to recent gentrification in the area, the job numbers, the divisions set up by the so-called Bloods and Crips, offshoots of gangs that had relocated from California.

I'd interviewed a couple of the mothers on the street before; harried and overworked, these women barely had time to get a decent meal on the table, let alone worry about a nearby crack house. One of the women had said it best: "I'm a damn rat on a wheel, that's all. No time to get off. I've got to keep running and running so I don't trip and die."

I was from a far more privileged socioeconomic background, yet I wanted to grab her hand and say, "I know, I know how it feels." As I tried to put the story together, my thoughts drifted away to my own chaotic life: running, always running, a rat on a wheel, scrambling to keep up with ten- to twelve-hour workdays, raising Sophie, trying to find time for paying the bills, buying groceries, cleaning the house.

I'd weighed the option of leaving enough times to understand why I stayed. I believed Sophie would be better off with David in her life, and I was too distant from my family to handle single motherhood. We seemed to leapfrog from crisis to crisis: David's hospitalization for poison oak, my weeklong flu that turned into pneumonia, Sophie's recurring ear infections. As much as David seemed distant and erratic, at least he was helpful in a crisis.

And getting a divorce would be a full-time job. I didn't even have the time to pick up my dry cleaning. We'd have to set up separate households, and David would not make it easy. I had gambled his moods wouldn't get worse, his investment in his business would pay off, and we'd make it. The truth was, we were living further and further apart.

"Sheila," my producer shouted from across the room, "get your story to editing!" I grumbled to myself about sensationalizing crime, feeling that I was part of the problem.

The whiteboard had a scribbled outline of the day's stories and the reporters assigned to them. These days, there were more news shows and less time for research, more rating grabs and less substance. We had two helicopters, not one, because research showed people liked pictures from the air. The investigative unit I had been hired to spearhead had been shelved in favor of more live shots and stories that were less than ninety seconds in length. I loved hosting the longer public affairs program we ran on Sunday afternoons, but the day to day had become grueling, sensationalized. I tried to remember the stories I worked on yesterday—and couldn't bring any of them to mind.

My phone rang, the newsroom bustled with other reporters and editors, and producers rushed around with copies of edited scripts in their hands. We called it the bunker, the place where we spent long hours with nothing more than vending machines to sustain us. There were no windows, so I couldn't tell what the sunset was like.

I let the phone go to voicemail—one more distraction wasn't what I needed. It rang again a few minutes later, and I picked up. "Hello, this is Sheila."

A warm, deep voice spoke up. "Hey, Sheila, I know you're probably on deadline, so I'll keep it short. This is Bill Gehring." He was one of the most respected radio talk show hosts in Portland. I'd heard through the grapevine that Bill was putting together a team of top talent for a new radio station in town, and I'd let other professionals know I was restless. "Let's grab some lunch sometime this week. What do you say?"

Was anyone listening? I lowered my voice and tried to mask the thrill that was moving through my body.

"Hi, Bill, thanks," I managed to reply. "Here's my cell phone so we can talk later."

Later that night, I sat at my desk. The picture I had of Sophie on my desk needed to be wiped down with Windex. She was three and a half now, outgrowing her toddler's tummy in a pink ballerina outfit and tutu.

Three weeks later, the photo of Sophie in her tutu sat on my new desk overlooking Fifth Avenue in downtown Portland. I now sat behind my own microphone at my own radio show.

When the station general manager at KATU had asked me if I wouldn't miss being on television, I answered honestly. "I'll miss the work. I'll miss the thrill of chasing down great stories. I just can't miss any more of my daughter's ballet recitals."

The offices had been custom built for the launch of the new talk radio station. The staff had been pulled from prime stations all across the city. Two producers sat across from me, next to a computer screen, ready to take calls. Sunlight beamed through floor-to-ceiling glass windows. I'd negotiated better pay, and even better, hours that would allow me to tuck Sophie in and be there in the afternoon to pick her up. Plus I had my own talk radio show, discussing politics and issues that I considered important. It was a startup station, a place where I could redefine myself.

"Good morning," I said into the microphone. "This is Sheila Hamilton."

I was driving to work when the first plane hit the World Trade Center. The CBS news cut-in interrupted the song I'd been listening to on the radio, something from the Barenaked Ladies. "How odd that a plane could be that off course," I thought at first. I'd worked in New York several weeks in my twenties, helping ABC with a documentary on a Utah outdoor wilderness camp that was under investigation for child abuse. I'd stood at the top of the World Trade Center. I knew the flight pattern. Planes were not supposed to get that close.

By the time the second plane hit the second tower, I was watching it live on television, disbelieving the surreal screams and the terror the news anchors themselves were attempting to mask.

Nothing in my journalism career had prepared me for this day. I'd been witness to what I thought was the worst disaster I would ever see, the explosion of the space shuttle *Challenger*, when the engineers at Utah's Morton Thiokol had gathered to see the first teacher off to space. It was one of the first national assignments I'd been given; it was supposed to be a fluff story, engineers attending another routine shuttle launch. It was, instead, the first story that would sear a memory into my brain so clearly that I can recall the temperature, the smells, the way the plumes parted as the rocket boosters headed off in different directions in the sky.

I opened the microphone, my hands shaking. The music bed faded. My earphones pressed tightly against my ears. My producer eyed me warily from the glass room where he would be taking people's frantic phone calls.

I spoke very slowly. "I'm Sheila Hamilton. And it is not a good morning. It is a morning you will remember for the rest of your life."

Thirteen hours later, I drove home to Sophie and David. As I drove, the images of people throwing themselves from the upper floors of the towers replayed in my mind, immediate, terrifying. I made it home and walked through the door to find Sophie, now four, sitting in David's lap as he read a book out loud. I rushed to both of them for comfort.

"What's wrong, Mommy?" Sophie sensed my grief. She had her pink pajamas on and carried Bear tucked into her chest as she balanced her book in her lap.

I couldn't speak. I knelt by David's chair and listened to his voice finishing the book they must have read together a dozen times that week, the one about the greedy monster who wanted so many cookies for himself he turned a beautiful tree into a cookie factory. Sophie giggled at all the familiar parts, filling in the lines David skipped.

I couldn't tell her how guilty I felt. I couldn't share with her, or David, that in the minutes before the first plane flew into the towers, killing thousands of innocent people, I'd been contemplating my own escape, from this—this doomed marriage. Somehow, the tragedy of 9/11 made that seem selfish. Myopic. And wrong.

In the weeks that followed the attacks, I followed closely the stories of couples reconnecting, of rushed marriages and canceled divorces. Strangers reached out to one another for comfort. Wayward sons and daughters called home. I understood—just having a family to come home to suddenly made me feel that I'd won the lottery.

I spent the Christmas after 9/11 in a rush of breaking world news and strong opinions on both sides of the political spectrum. Christmas was a blur without the traditional trip back home.

So when the next Christmas came around, a year later, I was determined to let Sophie spend the holiday with her grandparents and cousins, where Christmas was always a huge, happy celebration and David's disdain for the holiday would be less noticeable. We had made it through the year okay; despite the beginning of the war in Afghanistan and the lingering fear of terror attacks, David's business was actually busier than ever. More people were remodeling their dream homes rather than buying or building. He bought two cell phones so he could be on two conversations at the same time, but he and I were as distant as ever.

By early December, I was wrapping the last of Sophie's Christmas presents to send ahead to Grandma's house. I'd tried to select things she would love, chapter books and a toy cash register, a stuffed giraffe that defied gift wrap, and a new snowsuit for snowboarding. At five, she was tearing through books just like her dad and walking around the house spelling anything that seemed relevant. "C-h-r-i-s-t-m-a-s," she'd say happily. "R-u-d-o-l-f." My brother and sister were planning on bringing their kids to Utah as well. Sophie would have playmates, the adoration of Grandma and Grandpa, and a guaranteed white Christmas.

David sat in his favorite chair, reading the paper. "You know how I feel about Christmas."

"I'd really like you to be there with us," I said. "You've missed the last two trips."

He looked up from the paper. "You know how I feel about Christmas," he repeated.

"Yes, but you've got a child, David. You can learn to fake it."

He shrugged his shoulders. "My dad hated it, I hate it, it's gross commercialization and . . ."

"And it's Christmas, David. Find something about it you can celebrate." I pushed the gifts into a huge Ikea shopping bag and headed out the door to the post office.

David walked toward me with his head down, avoiding eye contact. He stopped me before I reached my car. "I'm sorry." He offered to help me load our things. "It just brings back such bad memories. I can't recall a single happy Christmas. Dad hated it and spent most of the day in his room."

I touched his arm. It was cold enough to see my breath, but there was no snow forecast this year in Portland. "David, you can make new memories. For her."

"Okay," he said, finally, "for Sophs."

Two weeks later, David called from work, frantic. "My briefcase is gone. It was stolen."

"Calm down, David. Tell me what happened." I turned down the flame on the stir-fry I was making. "When? When did you last see it?"

His voice rattled. "I was working at the Henson's house, and I left it inside the truck, with all my files, and all the billings, and the change orders, and the . . ." His voice trailed off and he moaned, a strange sound that worried me.

"David, it will be okay." I washed my hands under the sink faucet. "You've got copies of all that stuff, right?"

The line went silent. I knew the answer. We had gone through this before.

Twice, our lives were disrupted by the theft of his briefcase. I spent weeks helping him make phone calls, reconstructing the bids, the work changes, the payments, the bills. After so much misery, he'd assured me he was backing up all his data, making hard copies of everything.

"I'm so sorry, but you need help, David." I leaned up against the wall, trying to breathe. "You have to see someone about why you can't get your work organized. Let me hire an organizational expert for you, a secretary, something. You can't keep doing this."

"I knew it," he said, his voice rising. "I knew that you'd blame me. I get my fucking briefcase stolen, and you're going to blame me. As if I did it!"

I refused to take the heat, to allow him to shift the focus on to me. "At some point, David, you'll have to take responsibility for your continued crises." I had reached a point of fatigue with him, a deep irritation over cleaning up his messes. I no longer made excuses for him when he was late or picked up the pieces of his unfinished projects. I was done propping him up.

"Forget Christmas," he said. "Forget it. I'll have to work."

On Christmas morning, I sat in my father's easy chair, videotaping Sophie as she opened her Christmas presents. She hugged the giraffe tight around the neck, her blonde hair tangled from sleep. Her Christmas PJs said "Ho, ho, ho" in big white letters.

She ran into my mother's lap and curled the giraffe under her arm. "Look, Grandma, he remembered! I told him at Meier & Frank, and Santa even remembered to bring it to Utah!"

My brother's two boys were there, too, tearing into loads of presents under the tree with shrieks of joy and surprise. The smell of bacon and eggs came from the kitchen. We'd tracked Santa's path the night before on NORAD, the website that brings even the most skeptical child around. I honored this precious, fleeting time, when Sophie believed it possible that one man, driven by reindeer, could span the globe delivering every child's wishes.

Sophie opened and closed her new toy cash register, talking to her tow-headed cousin about the "exact amount of change." I kept the camera running, but my heart hurt at the thought of David, wherever he was on Christmas morning, wholly incapable of seeing or feeling the magic.

Sophie jumped on my lap, bumping the camera, her face bright with excitement. "Let's call Daddy!" she said. "Let's tell him he came. He needs to know Santa came." Her skin was warm from the fire. She was already lanky and had lost some of her baby fat. How could he possibly miss this, miss her? The reason I'd stayed in the marriage was to witness her being loved by her father. And now that was slipping away.

I bounced Sophie on my knee. "Absolutely. Let's call Daddy and tell him Santa did not forget you."

## ANOSOGNOSIA

Anosognosia is a phenomenon that commonly occurs in people with bipolar disorder and schizophrenia. They simply cannot believe that they have a serious psychiatric illness. Anosognosia is more commonly known as "nonadherence."

I was in denial about the seriousness of David's condition as well, but part of my confusion arose from David's insistence that he was not sick and did not need treatment.

Why can't a person see what is apparent to those around them? The National Alliance on Mental Illness says this is a core feature of the neurobiology of these conditions. "Frontal lobes organize information and help to interpret experiences. In conditions like schizophrenia and bipolar disorder, frontal lobe difficulty is central to the neurobiological processes that underlie the disorder. Psychological denial is not the reason for the lack of insight in these illnesses."

More than forty states have passed laws defining assisted outpatient treatment (AOT), also known as outpatient commitment. AOT status requires a person to engage in treatment and gives the state authority to bring a person to a treatment center. All these laws specify a process for assessing whether an intervention is appropriate.

In Oregon, intervention is allowed only if it can be clearly shown that the person meets one or more of the following criteria:

1. is a danger to himself or herself or others,
2. is unable to provide basic personal needs,
3. suffers from chronic mental illness or has had two hospitalizations in the previous three years, and/or
4. will continue to physically or mentally deteriorate without treatment.

NAMI has active support groups across the nation providing opportunities for engagement with doctors who are interested in the issue.

# Chapter Eight

Three years passed, years in which David and I moved through our lives with Sophie as our only contact. The cycle had begun to seem normal, or at least tolerable. "She's got tennis on Wednesday, piano lessons Thursday, and a sleepover at Maddie's house Friday," I said, as David gathered his things for another Saturday away from us. "Let me know which days you can drive her."

I had learned to operate within the confines of a dead marriage. I stuffed away my emotions as David stuffed more manila files into his briefcase.

I'd bought the Valextra leather case for him as a wedding present, but he'd only started using it after his favorite, beat-up case was stolen. When I'd bought it, it had reminded me of him, stylish and streamlined. Now, the weight of his briefcase reminded me of the haphazard way he seemed to be approaching his work these days—stuffing too much into his already overloaded life. I knew better than to suggest (again) that he go paperless. I knew better than to make suggestions about hiring more subcontractors and a secretary. I had enough work complications of my own, getting used to a new shift at 101.9, KINK-FM. I had transitioned from political talk radio to KINK in 2002, and now it was the number one radio station in town.

David stomped upstairs. "I'll let you know, okay?"

Sophie called to me from outside. "C'mon, Mama. Let's get in the pool, already!" I went outside and feigned a cannonball, much to Sophie's delight.

A man dressed in a stuffy gray suit and a white shirt appeared at our gate holding an envelope. "Is Mr. Krol here?" he asked. His hair was as black as a crow's and covered in the kind of grease men used in the 1950s. It stuck to his forehead in an odd formation, like a puzzle that had been glued in the wrong pattern.

I tried to sink lower in the water, embarrassed to get out of the pool in a bikini. "Uh, yes, he's inside in his office."

"If I could just come in for a moment." His eyes were gray, and he had sweat on his upper lip. Something about this guy gave me the creeps.

I stayed at the edge of the pool, showing only the top of my head. Sophie was splashing behind me. "Um, well, perhaps you could come back at a different time? I believe he's on a conference call with an important client."

He shifted his weight to the other foot, eyeing the opening in the gate. Clearly the guy wasn't leaving.

"David," I called, "there's someone here to see you." The door was open. Surely David could hear me. Sophie sensed my anxiety and looked at me nervously. She stopped kicking, measuring up this strange man dressed in too many layers on such a lovely day.

We waited. Goosebumps flashed over my body. My towel was several feet away.

Suddenly David burst out onto the deck, grabbed the man's elbow, and marched him down the stairs toward the street. "For God's sake," I heard him hiss, "it's Saturday!"

Their voices rose and fell. A car door slammed. Then the engine started and the man's car barreled back down the street, past the "Children Playing" sign that was always out on weekends and what must have been curious stares from our neighbors.

David returned, his face flushed.

"Who was that?" I wrapped Sophie in a towel first, then myself.

"It's none of your business," he said. Sophie exchanged a worried glance with him. "He is a client. You do your job; I'll do mine."

"David," I pleaded. "You'd tell me if something was wrong, wouldn't you? You'd let me know if you needed help?" I stood in front of him, shaking, hoping for something, anything.

"God, you are such a drama queen," he said, rolling his eyes. "Soph, get dressed. Let's get some ice cream."

*It is his business,* I decided. *If he doesn't want my help, so be it.*

I never did find out who the man was or why he had come. But that day I knew without knowing that David had never stopped keeping secrets from me. He lied while he looked me in the eye.

Another year passed. David and I moved in totally different orbits. We were roommates now, not lovers. I washed his clothes; I did his dishes; I made his bed and cleaned the house. We left notes for one another regarding Sophie's care. It was far from ideal, but in a strange way, I'd come to terms with the dysfunction of two emotionally and physically divorced people living together to raise a child. When he finally moved the last of his books into his own room downstairs, I was actually relieved.

But there was more. David had stopped eating the food I cooked six months earlier. It was an odd new habit I thought he'd adopted out of defiance. He'd refused my cooking, refused to sit down to family meals, refused anything but frozen pot pies. He'd go to the grocery store and come back with two bags filled with the green cardboard boxed pies. The same food, the same smell, night after night. I'd watch him open the door to the microwave, retrieving another scalding chicken pot pie. He shifted it gingerly from side to side until he could deliver it to the counter, where he grabbed a fork and began spooning chunks of chicken and gooey crust into his mouth.

I poured myself a glass of water. "David, we're having dinner in an hour. Chorizo. Used to be your favorite."

"Nah." He stabbed at the pie for another chunk. "I like these—they're really good." His face, normally chiseled and tanned, looked puffy and yellow. His white shirt, the same cotton European cut he wore when I first met him, only now in XXL, was buttoned the wrong way. He noticed me watching him and waved me away. "WHAT?"

"I'm worried about you, David. You look so stressed out." I put the glass in the sink and leaned against the counter. "Is everything okay at work?"

He cleared the last of the gravy from the aluminum holder and threw it in the garbage can. "Nothing out of the ordinary." He refused to meet my gaze.

"Okay, I'll say it." I pushed myself away from the counter and faced him head on. "What are you doing? Trying to kill yourself? Nobody can survive on pot pies, David. This is the second one you've eaten today." And the eleventh he'd eaten that week.

He ran his fingers through his hair, and his nostrils flared. "So what? They taste good." He pulled his shirt down over his belly.

When I first met David, he'd just finished a month cycling in the California desert. The first time we'd slept together, I remember running my fingers down the toned muscles of his back, feeling the suppleness of his skin. I'd loved his smell, his entire way of being. So much had changed.

He burped and left the kitchen.

Later, I watched him rolling on the Persian carpet with Sophie, her giggling over his attention, then lazing on his stomach. Her head was turned sideways on his chest, completely relaxed in pajamas the color of cotton candy, her blonde hair pulled back in a ponytail. She looked ethereal next to David's large frame. His eyes were closed in a rare moment of peace, his hands folded gently over her back.

In some ways, it was all I'd ever wanted: that scene of my daughter being loved so completely I knew she'd grow up with her self-esteem intact. And yet, it was not enough for me. I had compromised my own needs, physically and emotionally, for too long.

The phone rang as I rinsed Sophie's plate. "Sheila," the voice said, "this is Shannon Presser."

I wiped my hands on a towel and moved quietly from the kitchen into the bedroom, focusing all my attention on the call. Shannon was Sophie's school administrator.

"Hi, Shannon, what's up?" I was concerned by her tone. Shannon was a wiry, energetic woman who had built the most successful Montessori school in Oregon from fifteen families to several hundred.

"This is very uncomfortable for me to say. I don't know how to frame it, so I'll just go ahead. Sandra, Sophie's after-school art teacher, came to my office this afternoon. She was very upset."

I sat on the bed, prepared for some news of Sophie, something terrible. Maybe she'd drawn or said something profoundly troubling or revealing. David and I had been fighting so much lately, arguments that could spin out of control over anything. In the past, I had trained myself to walk away, to make sure Sophie was nowhere in earshot. But these days, he followed me, antagonizing me. I had even looked up the contact information for a divorce lawyer, preparing myself for the inevitable.

"Go on," I said.

Shannon lowered her voice, almost to a whisper.

"Sandra says David asked her out on a date."

"What?" My eyebrows lifted, my eyes widened, and my lungs filled as I took in as much air as I could possibly get.

"What, when? When did this happen?"

Shannon spoke louder now, with more authority. "Sandra said David had been talking to her quite a bit about Sophie's artistic ability. Sandra offered to give Sophie private tutoring since she's so talented. But then, out of the blue, he asked her out. He said you two were getting a divorce."

The heat suddenly felt too high in the house. I was sweating. My ears buzzed. I heard a rush of air come out of my lungs, a sound mixed with so much sadness it softened Shannon's tone. "I'm sorry," she offered. "I hope I did the right thing by telling you. If you are divorcing, we should be prepared. You know, to watch for any signs in Sophie that might be troubling."

"Yes, yes, of course," I said. "I will let you know, Shannon. Thank you for calling."

My head swayed, or was it the room? I tried to stand and could not find my legs. I lay back on the bed, barely breathing, a throbbing pain at the base of my heart.

There was a part of me that had always known he would take a lover—he'd never admitted to the first affair, and I'd stayed despite his infidelity. We'd eventually moved into our dull separation without ever signing a legal agreement: separate beds, separate rooms, separate lives. I didn't ask where he spent his nights. He did the same for me. Now our arrangement seemed humiliating, laughable. At work, I was so capable, so driven. I was able to get to the crux of a story quickly, to weed out the extraneous and find just the facts I needed. Yet at home, I was awash in a jumble of chaos, incapable of doing what I needed to do. Leave David.

Sophie's art teacher? A woman in her twenties? I wondered how many times Sophie had been present at other flirtatious moments in her father's life, moments that made her feel uncomfortable for reasons she couldn't yet understand. The phone call had cleared my mind. We had both known we were divorced, in spirit, physically and emotionally. The only thing left was to pay the lawyers.

The following week, as I formulated the plans for how I would tell David I was leaving, it finally happened. Oprah would have called the phone call from Sophie's school my "moment," the time we finally confront what we've known all along. I was done. Our marriage was over. As it turns out, David was also on the brink.

He was late again, the third time that week he'd forgotten to pick Sophie up. He was supposed to be taking her to a birthday party across town, another nine-year-old who would be waiting for all her guests to arrive before the fun began. Sophie was an hour late.

Finally, David ran up the front steps, breathing hard. "Fucking traffic," he said, his face dripping with sweat. His pupils were dilated. I took a step back from him.

"If you're not going to be on time, I'll take care of her on my own." I grabbed my purse.

"The fuck you will," he exploded. "You fucking bitch, don't you ever threaten to take my daughter from me." His eyes were pinched so narrowly I could barely see them. His white shirt was untucked, and there were large sweat rings under his arms. Everything about him stunk of craziness. I recoiled, shocked by this unfamiliar person.

Sophie ran to her bedroom. I went up and tried to calm her. "Hey, sweetheart, I'll drop you at the party. Let's get out of here. What do you say?"

Sophie's anger turned my way. "Why can't he just be normal? He's never on time. He's not nice anymore." She gathered a big purple box with a bow on it in her arms and wiped away her tears. "And I am so sick of you fighting."

"I know, baby. I'm sorry." My purse felt heavy on my arm. I could hear David slamming cupboard doors and pacing the kitchen floor.

We sneaked out the back. I dropped Sophie at her party and drove home. David was fixing himself a sandwich when I walked back in the house.

"I want a divorce." I said it in measured tones, trying not to let my voice rattle. "I'm leaving you." My shoulders straightened. I was lighter, liberated by my own truth. Why had I waited so long to say those words? This was easier than I expected. Just then, his body slammed to the floor, a collapse that looked exactly like it does in the movies, where the person's eyes roll back in their head, and then slowly, they fall sideways. He barely missed the dining room table going down. It was a dull, unforgiving thud on the floor. His eyes were closed, but he was breathing.

I sprinted to a neighbor's house, a friendly doctor who never seemed in a hurry. As I ran, I replayed the image of David's sprawl; it reminded me of the many yellow outlines I'd seen on the nights when I covered murder investigations. The tape outline always looked fake. People don't really fall that way, do they? Actually, they do. One arm was higher than the other, one knee bent as if scaling a climbing wall. He was that taped outline, a human being in limbo, not dead, not alive.

I reached the neighbors' house. "David collapsed," I panted. "Please help!" The friendly doctor's wife, also a doctor, looked up in concern.

Dr. Benson turned from the sink. He had a head of broccoli in his hands. "Is he breathing?" He wiped his hands quickly on a white towel and slipped on a pair of flip-flops. Their lives looked so normal—the baby in the high chair, a toddler tugging at Mommy's leg.

"Yes, he was breathing." I was barely able to catch my breath. "But his eyes fluttered like he might have had a seizure."

"Call 911," Benson said to his wife. We ran back to the house together.

Two neighbors heard the commotion and followed us into the house. David was still sprawled on the hardwood floor, unconscious but breathing. Benson kneeled by his side, took his pulse, and opened David's eye. Then both of his eyes flashed open. "What the hell?" David asked, staring at our neighbor.

"Hey, David, you gave us all a good scare," Dr. Benson said. "Don't go moving yourself right away. Answer some questions for me. Did you hit your head going down?" The doctor touched him gingerly, on his shoulder and then his head. I stood back, relieved he was in good hands.

David shook his head no. "I don't think so. My elbow hurts."

The ambulance drivers knocked on the door, breathless from running the flight of stairs. Benson explained the situation to them; they loaded David in a gurney and told me I could drive to the hospital behind them.

It was in the emergency room, when David was tethered to beeping machines, that he finally realized he was trapped.

"Get me out of here," he yelled, ripping the monitors from his chest. The young doctor was exhausted from the pace of the ER—a stab wound, a broken hip, a homeless guy who sliced his foot open, and a baby with a raging fever. The doctor ran his hand through his disheveled hair. "You walk out of here, sir, and none of the bill you've racked up today will be paid for by insurance." The ambulance ride alone would be hundreds of dollars.

David's eyes looked like those of a caged animal. He'd always hated hospitals from the multiple surgeries he had had to fix his cleft palate as a child. "You don't have to stay here, you know," he hissed at me. "I'd prefer you leave."

"I know," I said, dreading the outcome of what would be expensive, and useless, testing. "But I'm staying anyway, David. You need help."

I knew it wasn't his heart, or his lungs, or a tumor in his brain that was making him sick. It was something more pervasive, and more deadly. He was slipping away from me, and Sophie, and anyone who could help him.

I walked away from the emergency room thinking that David had fooled the physician. It was only later, as I read through David's medical documents, that I learned differently. "Admitting physician Dr. Replogle suspects bipolar affective disorder largely based on presentation."

After David's first visit to the emergency room, it didn't take long for him to leap from partially functioning to full-blown madness. The ensuing eight weeks were the most horrifying of my life.

## CARE FOR CAREGIVERS

Spouses of the mentally ill, unlike other relatives, tend to get less support and feel less connected to each other and to family members. They face additional financial and social problems. Many people decide that they are not able to endure persistent symptoms or cannot live with someone who is unable to sustain a healthy relationship.

To watch someone you love slip away is torturous. To watch that person resist intervention, stubbornly refuse treatment, and show callous disregard for his life partner is even more difficult. I wanted David in Sophie's life, not just every other week, but every day. But when I recognized that my own ability to cope was slipping, I felt as if I needed to save myself in order to allow Sophie one functioning parent.

I may have been better able to weather the storm of David's illness and its impact on our family if I had asked for help earlier, or known where to go to find it.

I have since found that there is support out there.

In 1979, families frustrated with the lack of services, treatment, research, and education available to them founded the National Alliance on Mental Illness (NAMI). It offers education and support for family members of people with mental illness. Many people report finding a "safe place" in the communities of people NAMI supports. NAMI's family-to-family group meetings are designed for adult loved ones of individuals living with mental illness. The meetings are facilitated by relatives of people with mental illness who have been trained to provide critical information and strategies related to caregiving.

You can obtain information about your local NAMI office by calling 1-800-950-6264 or by going to www.NAMI.org.

# Chapter Nine

August 2006. Ninety degrees, suffocating by Portland standards. Star, our yellow Lab, panted heavily, leaving drool marks on the hardwood floors. Max, a West Highland, napped nearby. The sun shone brightly through floor-to-ceiling windows. The pool looked cool and blue, but there were dishes to load, a house to clean, and dogs to feed, and Sophie needed a ride to summer camp before I headed off to work. I was pissed at David for refusing to get air conditioning. The linen suit I wore had sweat stains under the arms. I'd begun looking for apartments and was saving up the down payment for a house. I had an appointment with a divorce lawyer. But I hadn't said a word about these plans to David. As much as I wanted to leave him, I also didn't want to be responsible for destroying his life. He seemed so fragile, as if one line might suck the last of his life out of him. In a weird turn of events, David's frailty now held the marriage together.

David stood near me while I loaded the dishwasher. He stared out at the weeds in the garden, where he and Sophie had excitedly planned to "grow huge, monstrous tomatoes and corn." Dried clods of dirt covered the spots where she'd carefully planted her seeds.

David's big hands seemed to be the only thing holding him up. He leaned against the granite kitchen countertop, putting what was left of his weight on his hands. In the few weeks since his hospitalization, he seemed to be vanishing. I guessed he'd lost fifteen pounds. Green boxer shorts hung limp and low around his hips. He slumped from the weight of being alive. His beard was an unkempt inch of scraggly hair.

He stank of alcohol and something that reminded me of dental fillings. Ever since he'd started taking antidepressants, the stench of metal seeped through his pores. After being hospitalized, David had talked a friend of his who was a primary care doctor into giving him the meds. When I asked the doctor's name, or where his office was, David refused to give me the information. The whole thing seemed dangerous and unprofessional. But I also hoped the meds might help stabilize David.

At night, he said he lay awake, sweating. I changed his sheets daily, trying to keep the stink from sinking into the walls. Ribs showed through his skin, and he seemed not to care when his boxers slipped further down his waist. Sophie had actually been the one to pick those shorts out, guessing that he would love the color, green, and the red pheasants flying up toward the waistband. David used to love watching wild birds in flight.

She'd used her allowance to buy the boxers, then stuffed them in a red stocking along with a plastic bag of gummy bears. "I love them!" David said on Christmas morning, pulling the boxers on over his jeans and doing a dance that made Sophie laugh.

David spoke slowly, quietly. "I heard voices last night."

"What do you mean?" I didn't look up. I tried to focus on getting the dishes done before work, anything to calm the chaos. There were fifteen minutes left to get the house clean, drop our daughter at summer camp, and get to work. I put another dish in the dishwasher. Rinse, load, repeat.

"Last night I heard voices telling me to jump off the bridge," he said in a monotone. He was no more dramatic than if he were talking about how much it costs to fill up his truck with gas. "I heard it as plain as day. Jump from the Vista."

The china breakfast plate I was drying dropped to the floor, breaking into four large pieces. Bizarre—I never believed the movie scenes when people dropped things in response to being shocked by dizzying events. Now, I recognized myself inside a cliché.

David stared down at the pieces, studying the shattered pattern on the floor. "Did you mean to do that?" he asked.

After that day, David's behavior spiraled down. It was at its worst at night. I dreaded the darkness and the sounds he would make as he battled his demons. He paced in tight circles and muttered to himself. "You can't leave. I'll leave first. You can't take her."

I tried to comfort him. "David," I said, "I won't take Sophie from you. You can see her every day if you want."

He crumpled to his knees and cried. "I have fucked this up. It's entirely my fault."

I lifted my hand to his back, rubbing large circles.

"Please don't," he said, pulling away abruptly. He never could stand to be touched. He rose to his feet unsteadily and then fell to his knees crying loudly, a moaning sound that reminded me of the wolves in Yellowstone. I reached out my hand again, but he rolled his eyes. "Don't bother."

Later that night, I heard him turning on lights, banging cupboard doors in the kitchen. The television turned on and then off. In time I would learn that hating to be touched was part of his illness. So is not sleeping and sensitivity to light and sound.

As his nights grew increasingly restless, David didn't complain. At all hours, lights turned on, then off; the toilet flushed. I heard him making himself a drink. I listened to these sounds in total despair, wishing I could wrap Sophie in her pink blanket and whisk her off into the night. Instead, night after night, I lay awake, piecing together the puzzle of who David was, just as he was falling apart. The monstrous, dark mystery living in our home was finally in plain view.

He'd always been moody, like a storm brewing, harmless at first, but then menacing. There used to be enough warning to get out of the way. I'd sweep Sophie out the door to the park or the movies or shopping. Then the storm would lift, and he'd wake up and announce he was taking Sophie mushroom hunting or skiing or gliding.

"Let's get out of this house!" he'd say. "It's *gorgeous* outside." He was sorry, so sorry, for being such a difficult person to live with. It was going to be different now. He was changed. He would tell me funny stories about his day, sing while he did the laundry, and even make his famous dish of rice and beans for dinner. It might last a couple of days, or long enough for a short excursion. Sometimes, his mood changed between the time he'd made the plans and when he got his coat on.

David must have sensed his mind slipping as he became more ineffective and confused. His anger, in hindsight, was undoubtedly the panic of a man about to go under and take his family with him. But he never let on, and if I inquired whether there was something I might do to lessen his obvious stress, David shoved me away rather than tell the truth. From a distance, I tried to piece together what had gone wrong. He'd become busier than he could manage alone. He'd refused to hire an assistant or a full-time accountant. Sometimes I'd overhear him juggling six or seven different remodels and two commercial jobs at once.

He was fueled by endless energy, but it was odd energy, erratic and irritable. One day, I saw his work truck flying down Burnside, David holding two phones to his ears. He was driving with his knees. He didn't notice my car, stopped at a traffic light. He was hurtling down the street at sixty miles per hour. I barely recognized that man, that stranger who flashed past me, caught by a red light camera in my mind.

## CAREGIVER DENIAL

When I think back on the ways in which I denied the onset of David's mental illness, I am overcome with heartache. Imagine what it was like for him to experience the fear of losing control of his thoughts and emotions and the additional guilt of involving his family in a downward spiral.

People may hide or deny obvious changes in their patterns and behavior because they are in enormous pain due to the social stigma associated with mental illness. We were both unwilling to look squarely at the problems unfolding in our home, both attempting to preserve our own sense of self-esteem and both failing the reality test.

People with bipolar disorder commonly shock and surprise their loved ones with grandiose ideas, excessive spending, sexual indiscretion, and irritability. Those periods can alternate with normal behavior and severe depressive episodes. I have heard many people with bipolar disorder say that a much better description of mania is "mixed depression."

People who have severe depression feel miserable. They have no energy, and life seems meaningless to them. They feel "frozen" or incapable of doing anything to make themselves feel better. Some people believe that they must have done something to deserve such punishment. The irritability and the unwillingness to share the interior of one's mind can be especially alienating for caregivers.

David's preoccupation with noise, light, and sound was not at all unusual for a person suffering from a mental illness. Instead of confronting his increasingly unusual behavior, I attempted to "fix" the situation: moving from a perfectly fine home, choosing to ignore sexual indiscretion, and moving away from him physically during times of greatest stress.

In his book, *Scattershot: My Bipolar Family,* David Lovelace writes, "Depression is a painfully slow, crashing death. Mania is the other extreme, a wild roller coaster run off its tracks, an eight ball of coke cut with speed. It's fun and it's frightening as hell. Some patients—bipolar type I—experience both extremes; others—bipolar type II—suffer depression almost exclusively. But the 'mixed state,' the mercurial churning of both high and low, is the most dangerous, the most deadly. Suicide too often results from the impulsive nature and physical speed of psychotic mania coupled with depression's paranoid self-loathing."

# Chapter Ten

In September 2006, I finally called for help. I couldn't care for David alone anymore. His anger was explosive, his behavior so erratic that I feared for my life. He was suspicious and paranoid in a way I'd never seen before. He smashed a hole through the basement wall one night as I left for a fund-raiser. He hadn't slept through the night in weeks. He was provoked by the slightest change in noise, smell, and light. He refused help, and I knew the law well enough to know you can't commit someone in Oregon without his or her consent. I believed he would never harm Sophie—but me? I could not be sure.

And now David was missing. He had taken off from the house, alone on a walk. He couldn't contain the manic energy he had in his body, so he'd walk and walk and miss appointments or forget to pick up Sophie at school. This time he hadn't come back, and I was worried. *He should be in a hospital,* I thought.

His sister, Jill, lived two and a half hours away, in the beach town of Astoria. "Jill, I need your help," I said over the phone. My voice cracked, but I held back the tears. She had enough worries of her own, as a single mom with three kids and no job, her nursing degree months away. I didn't know where else to turn. "David is getting worse. He left this morning at eight for a walk, and he's still not home."

"Oh, you poor pet," Jill said. "I'm finishing finals this week. I'll get there as soon as I can." I imagined her hanging up the phone and wondering how in the hell she would manage to help when she could barely hold her life together.

I pulled on a jacket to go find David. I'd be late for work again. I hadn't told anyone about my problems at home. News spreads like a virus at work, and I couldn't risk losing my job when I needed it most.

My mind raced with images of David passed out on the Wildwood—a nearby woodsy trail and one of my favorite city hikes. My head flipped through gruesome possibilities. I tried to think back to the last time I'd taken a long walk. March? *This must be how it feels to be at war,* I thought, *when you lose track of the hours and days and months to the fear and chaos around you.* My friends had stopped calling for our walks. I never knew whether David would be there to take care of Sophie, and at nine years old, she was still too young to leave home alone.

And now David was missing, again. As I searched, I wondered if he'd just decided to take off. Maybe he'd bought a plane ticket to Canada, or Mexico, or Brazil. He hadn't gone to work in weeks. His wallet and phone, which had begun to seem like unnecessary accessories, were still on the kitchen counter. The faster the images filed through my head, the quicker I walked. I checked my watch. Four hours. He'd been gone four hours.

It startled me to see a tall frame come round the bend near the Japanese gardens, approximately a quarter mile from our home. For a moment, I didn't recognize him, the boyishness of his face, the changed expression caused by what I later realized was a full-blown manic attack. His wrinkles and dour expression seemed erased, replaced by bright, wide eyes and a smile that was uncharacteristic. "David?" I asked, relief washing over me. "Are you okay?"

He was sweating profusely, his hair wet and shiny, his eyes bright blue again. He smiled broadly, happy to see me, another hiker on the trail. I couldn't tell if he even knew who I was.

"You were right about this park," he said. "It's beautiful. Why haven't I used it more? Why haven't I been walking every day? It feels great to walk. It feels like everything is golden, like there's this halo of something so good, so promising, you know what I mean?"

His words spilled out so fast they were hard to understand. "The only problem is, I'm really thirsty. I've been walking for like, an hour, and I'm really thirsty." He looked at me, smiling widely, beaming even. "Isn't this fantastic?"

David never said "fantastic." He rarely said anything was "great." He was in trouble. Mania. The other side of depression. The skin on my arms chilled, even in the heat.

"David," I said, "you've been walking for four hours. You've got to come home." I touched his wet T-shirt. "Come home."

"Oh, don't worry about me." He grinned. "I'm the best I've ever been. Really, this feels great. You have a good day now."

He looked at me, empty, another stranger talking to someone encountered on the trail. Then he turned and strode off, tall and brisk, a man in training, an athlete at the top of his game. I would later learn this was the height of David's first manic episode, an episode brought on by weeks without sleep, our impending divorce, and the lethal nature of an illness unchecked.

I fell to my knees and cried out loud. Everything I'd tried to hold together was gone. Maybe he wouldn't come home. Maybe he'd just keep walking. How would I break this news to Sophie? To my boss, my coworkers? A hiker passed me by, saw me in the dirt, crying, my hands covered in soil.

"Are you all right?" he asked.

"No, but thanks for asking. It means a lot." I sniffed, wiped my nose on the corner of my hoodie, and rose to my feet. "I'll be fine, really."

In a moment the hiker moved on. When he was gone, I realized how the whole scene must have looked to him. He probably thought I was the crazy one.

Jill finally agreed to stay with us for a few weeks to help get David stabilized. She pulled up in Old Yella, the Mercedes David had given her when her old car stalled on the busy highway between Portland and the coast. The backpack slung over her shoulder looked like it had been through a war. She liked it that way. Jill was blithely unconcerned about her appearance. She wore baggy men's cords, an old sweater, and men's shoes. Her red hair was frizzed at the ends, but her complexion and her eyes were always bright.

"Sweetie," she said when she saw me, "you look exhausted."

There was so much to do. Work. Sophie. David. The frayed edges of my life felt like fire, growing fiercely out of control. I opened the drawer to get a baggie to pick up the dog poop Jill had stepped over on her way into my home. The box was empty. I had to go to work.

"There's soup in the fridge for lunch," I told Jill. "Call me if you find out anything, would you?"

Once at work, I settled into my desk to prep for my on-air shift. I'd been working at Portland's number one radio station for four years, and the work was everything I wanted: demanding, exhilarating, and fun. Moving from television news to radio hosting was the best career choice I'd ever made. I'd cut my work hours and looked forward to working with my on-air partner. I was encouraged to let my personality come through during the broadcast. And as an unexpected bonus, it never mattered what my hair looked like. These days, visual anonymity was a good thing.

The phone rang between live breaks. Jill was hysterical. "He did it, Sheila; he did it; he tried to kill himself! He cut his wrist. He used a razor. It's not bad, but he tried."

Her words disappeared into the phone, and a surge of blood rushed into the back of my neck. "I'm coming home now," I heard myself say. "No, wait, is he in the hospital?" I couldn't think straight, couldn't figure out how to manage the crisis with my cohost pointing at me through the studio window, his finger in the air, giving me one minute to prepare for our live broadcast. I pressed the red talk button to interrupt him. "Sorry," I said calmly, "I've got an emergency at home."

I ran two stoplights to get home. A note on the counter read, "Took him to St. Vincent."

I called Sophie's babysitter and told her I would be late, and not to worry. I turned the lights off, crazily conscious of David's reminders to save energy. How could he be so lucid about some things and so crazy about others? It's as if some of the files in his brain were corrupted, while others remained completely intact. They'd commit him now. I knew it.

As I locked the door behind me, I wondered if David would ever come home again. They could force him into lockdown, or a residence where Sophie would have to empty her pockets before going in. I'd been avoiding this moment, convincing myself that he would be fine and so would Sophie. But he needed help, with a full-time staff, in a hospital. I felt as if I were going to throw up. The traffic to the hospital was bumper-to-bumper. Every single car in front of me seemed to be there on purpose, prolonging my agony.

I rushed in the front door of the hospital. The woman at the reception desk registered my anxiety and then continued to talk on the phone.

"Can I help you?" she finally asked.

"My husband was admitted earlier today," I said. She looked up from her papers, bored. "For a suicide attempt."

Something in her eyes changed. "What's his name?"

"David Krol."

"Krol?" she said. "What a weird name."

I wanted to slug her. "Can I please see him?"

Her pen ran down the names on the list. "He checked out," she said. "Treated, evaluated, and released."

I pushed back a scream. "How does someone who just attempted suicide get treated and released in the course of an afternoon?"

She shrugged her shoulders. This was not her problem. I pulled out my phone to call Jill. Shit, she didn't carry a phone, one more example of her resistance to a modern world. David's cell phones were still on the counter at home. I tallied the cost of the ER with every other bill dangling from my consciousness. *I should take a leave of absence from my job.* I didn't know how I'd keep Sophie fed and housed without a salary.

I drove home in a jam of other commuters puzzling over their problems. My exit came and I passed it, heading to the babysitter's. I'd pick up Sophie, and we'd leave. We'd get a little condo in the Pearl District, where lots of single Portland moms seemed to make it work. We'd reinvent our lives and let David destroy his. We'd wait it out until he finally got help. My fingers shook on the wheel, and my head felt light. I realized I hadn't eaten all day. No groceries at home.

I pulled up at the babysitter's and saw Sophie sitting in the window, illuminated by a reading light. She was pensive, worried, her face tight and lacking expression. Her skin had always had so much color: pink cheeks, pink lips. In this light, she looked drained, haunted. She saw my car and stood up. A faint smile passed over her face. The weak wave she offered crushed my heart.

"Sorry I'm late, sweetheart," I said, hugging her tightly. I opened my wallet to find cash for the babysitter; she preferred to be paid under the table. Sophie held onto me a beat longer than usual, her long arms holding my waist tightly. She sighed once we were in the car. "I hate eating dinner there. It's frozen this or frozen that. Where were you?"

Her voice was as close to crying as I'd heard in a long time.

"Daddy had to go to the hospital." I tried to say it without hinting about the panic I felt inside. I turned the car on. "He's okay now, sweetheart. Let's get you home."

Sophie sat back in her seat, looking forward into the dark neighborhood. She turned, opened her mouth to say something else, and then stopped herself. I guessed she didn't want to know more than she could handle.

When we walked in the door, David was standing over the stove, stirring chicken noodle soup. The sleeves of his plaid shirt covered what must have been the bandages from his suicide attempt. He looked up as if nothing had happened.

"There's my girl." He dropped the spoon in the soup. "I've missed you, Sugar Dugger." It was a nickname he'd given Sophie as a toddler. Sugar, dugger, booger. They used to make rhymes together, competing to come up with nonsensical words that made Sophie laugh. When he lifted her under her arms to pick her up, his sleeves shifted to expose his wrists and the bloody bandages.

I stood in the doorway, aghast. I might as well have been invisible to him.

"What happened, Daddy?" Sophie asked. "There's blood on your wrist. Are you okay?"

David let her down. "I hurt myself at work, Sophs, no worries. Just a little cut from the skill saw." He'd avoided acknowledging me until now. He tried to look in my direction but couldn't meet my eyes.

Sophie led him to his chair. "Here, Daddy, sit down. You should rest."

Jill came up the stairs, taking in the tenderness of a child caring for her parent. Her eyes filled with tears.

After I'd tucked Sophie in, I came out to the living room where David sat, frozen. The soup was still in the stove, bubbling in an overheated mess. I turned off the stove and then sat back down with him. "Tell me what happened."

He couldn't lift his head. "I don't know," he said. "I'd been walking through the woods, and I just got this idea about how much better everybody would be if I died. So I came home and tried to find something to kill myself, but the only thing I could find in the garage were some old razors, and they were really dull. So I had to saw and saw and saw." He made a sawing-like gesture over his wrist. I swallowed hard, trying not to interrupt.

"It's not like it is in the movies, where you just make a slit and then it's over. I barely got through my skin, but there was so much blood, it scared me." His voice had turned small, and his eyes were wide, like a child who'd just discovered the danger of fire.

I waited to speak. There were far more effective tools in that garage. Skill saws, drills, axes—the number of deadly tools in that garage numbered in the dozens. It didn't make sense, David rummaging through the plastic bins to find a rusted razor blade.

"How can I help you?" I leaned forward, hoping to make contact someplace deep inside David, somewhere familiar and safe.

"I don't know," he said, avoiding my eyes. "I really don't know what's happening to me."

"What did the doctor say?" I asked.

Jill entered the room and sat down. She spoke up when David wouldn't answer. "He said that David wasn't a risk to himself or others. That he likely did this because he's upset over the divorce. That we need to give the antidepressants time to work."

My voice broke. "Did you tell them he's had thoughts of jumping off a bridge?" I turned to David. "Did you tell them the truth?"

"No," he said.

"Why would you lie?" I asked, accusingly.

"I just answered the questions the way I knew I should in order to go home." He said it as if he'd just aced his SAT. "I hate hospitals. You know that." He pushed himself off his chair. "I'm going to bed."

Tears formed in the corners of his sister's eyes. "I'm so sorry," she whispered. "I had no idea."

The next morning, I sat outside Sophie's summer day camp in my car, the engine still running. My nail polish was chipped. Dark rings circled my eyes. Adele was the only person I could think to call; she was David's older sister, a psychologist in Montreal, and she loved David dearly.

"Sheila, he's decompensating," Adele said. "I talked to him on the phone last night, and he alternates between hysteria and delusion." She seemed shocked by this turn in her brother. I wondered if she knew more than she was telling me. As a psychologist, she must have known what was happening to David.

The car idled in the parking lot. Young children played in the playground, blissfully unaware of my presence. I remembered Sophie at that toddler stage, all blonde hair and rosy cheeks, always singing, singing.

Adele was David's closest ally in the family, the person who understood him the most. She'd taken him in every time his father turned him out; they'd traveled together, smoked pot together, and laughed at one another's jokes. They saw each other too infrequently these days, but Adele was David's most trusted confidante.

"Sheila," she said, "you've been amazing to stay. But it's making him worse. You need to leave. Get out. Let him clear his head."

Adele's words landed hard. For so many years, I'd felt obligated to David for Sophie, and then, after realizing the folly of that idea, I'd felt obligated to David's illness.

His sister had essentially set me free. But instead of relief, a wave of worry washed over me. What would become of him now?

## GUILT

We've all heard the term "survivor's guilt," which refers to the guilt people feel after surviving a plane crash or a traumatic incident in which other people lose their lives. Survivor's guilt also afflicts relatives of people with severe or disabling illnesses. Survivors blame themselves for having their health when their loved ones become incapable of caring for themselves.

Nearly all relatives of people with mental illness feel guilty, according to marriage and family therapist Rebecca Woolis, the author of *When Someone You Love Has a Mental Illness*. She notes the effects of guilt as including the following:

- depression and lack of energy for the present,
- dwelling on the past,
- diminished self-confidence and self-worth,
- less effectiveness in solving problems and achieving goals,
- acting like a martyr in an effort to make up for past sins,
- being overprotective, which increases your relative's feelings of helplessness and dependence, and
- diminished quality of life.

Woolis says that developing new ways of thinking about the situation takes time, patience, and a willingness to discuss your situation with others. She notes that many of us prefer to handle problems within our families alone or believe that we may appear weak or wrong if we ask for outside help. This approach leads to a great deal of unnecessary suffering for many families.

Our culture is ready to help when a loved one suddenly develops cancer or is in a devastating accident. Friends drop by casseroles; people write, call, and ask questions about how they might help the family. But our country's prejudice and ignorance about mental illness make it very challenging for family members to seek help when a loved one is suffering from a psychiatric disorder.

It is crucial that Americans begin to view mental illness as just another sickness of the body. We do not hesitate to ask for help when our loved ones exhibit signs of diabetes. The brain is just another organ, vulnerable to illness and capable of recovery. Feeling guilty about a loved one's affliction of the brain serves no one, and as with other medical problems, treatment must be sought in order for anyone to get better.

# Chapter Eleven

It never occurred to me that our situation could get worse, but it did. David's father, who had been sick with heart disease for several years, suffered another heart attack. His mother called to say Lew did not have long. She pleaded with me to have David call. She knew very little of David's condition.

Two days later, he was packing a bag for Canada. He had only underwear and a pair of jeans in his duffle bag. "You'll need a jacket," I said softly. "You don't know how long you'll be gone."

He turned and left his bedroom without speaking. I wondered if he'd remembered his passport, his toothbrush, and his cream for the rash on his hands. I wondered if he'd crack up. Jill promised me she or her son would drive, so David wouldn't be behind the wheel.

Sophie asked to see her grandfather one last time. Everything in my body rebelled against the idea. I didn't want my daughter to leave, but it seemed terrible to deny her this time with David's family. I took Jill aside and whispered, "She is in your hands." Jill silently agreed.

I held Sophie tightly before letting her pick up her backpack full of stuffed animals and clothes. I wanted her to feel safe, to understand on the deepest level how much I loved her. She took it for a moment and then said playfully, "Uh, Mom, you're squishing me."

I kissed the soft skin on Sophie's cheek. Her cheeks were always flushed, more so when she was in hurry or exercising, but even now, preparing for a road trip, the blood rushed to her capillaries in her cheeks and she glowed. Her lips looked just like David's, blood red and formed in the shape of a heart. When she was born, David said her lips were the biggest thing on her face. I missed them both, missed the days when all of us would have been packing to head to Canada. "Call me, whenever, however, a thousand times a day if you need to, okay, baby?"

Sophie rolled her eyes. "Mama," she groaned, picking up a backpack three times her size, "I am not a baby."

David stood, gaunt and exhausted just from the idea of traveling. I wanted to tell him goodbye then, that I wished I could have been a better wife, more understanding, or generous, or whatever it was that he needed. I had tried, but I was done trying. The tightness I felt in my jaw was the grief of letting him go, surrendering finally to what I wasn't capable of. I could not care for him any longer. I barely knew him. Jill gathered all of them up, a whirl of backpacks and duffle bags, and they were gone. The house was suddenly so quiet I could hear my own breathing.

While David, Sophie, and his family were in Canada, I spent my evenings viewing two-bedroom condos, the kinds of places I would have lived in when I was twenty. I could hardly imagine Sophie hauling her suitcase through a hallway of strange smells, of broccoli, garlic, and too many people living in such close proximity.

I'd fallen in love with our home before I'd even stepped inside. The architect had built the house himself, a modern, sophisticated hideaway on a dead-end street near Portland's famous rose garden. It was perched up above the rest of the homes, like a tree house in an old growth forest. Sophie spent her summers in the pool and her winters hoping for enough snow to sled on the steep hill above our place. The apartments the broker showed me were small and confining. I said no to every option.

When David and Sophie had been gone for three days, a particularly depressing rain drenched the city. I agreed to meet a friend for a drink; it had been weeks since we'd seen one another.

The bar where we met was moody, with low lights and a mix of "Pearl people," young urbanites from the trendy Pearl District who had abandoned the notion of the house on the hill. I could be pretty anonymous here.

"So," Jill said, twirling her glass of champagne by its stem, "tell me everything." Jill was a journalist too, a friend who never wasted a sentence.

"Remember when you told me I'd know for sure when I was done?" I asked.

She nodded.

"I'm finished."

I looked up to see a man walk through the door, stomping off the rain from his shoes and lifting his head toward us. I'd seen him before, at a fund-raiser for children with cancer. He was tall and lean, with salt-and-pepper hair and striking blue eyes. He wore a tailored white shirt, distressed jeans, and a black leather belt with silver rivets just like one I'd seen on Billy Idol. He stood straight, like a ballet dancer, and grinned widely when he recognized my friend.

"Oh, no," I said when he started to walk in our direction. "Do you know him?"

She turned. "Hey, Colin. How are you?"

He leaned down to kiss her on the cheek. "Can I join you?"

Before I could say no, he introduced himself by holding out his hand and smiling. "I'm Colin MacLean. Have we met?"

His straight, broad shoulders reminded me of Woods, my college boyfriend. *Excuse yourself*, I thought. *Get up and walk out the door, away from the confusion and magnetic pull of this stranger.*

"No, we haven't met." I held out my hand. His fingers were long, and the silver cufflinks on his shirt were cast in the shape of small dice. His hand folded around mine gently, a first touch that made the hair on the back of my neck stand up.

"I'm Sheila," I said.

How could I even begin to entertain the possibility of Colin? It seemed unfathomable. But the emptiness of David had starved me, physically and emotionally. I had shut off the bone-rattling weariness of a dead marriage for too long, suffering from a kind of loneliness that could make anyone bleak.

Colin sat down across from me. He looked me straight in the eyes when he spoke. It was as if I was being seen for the first time in a decade. Ten years I'd spent in a troubled and complicated marriage. I wanted desperately to feel something other than the dead weight of responsibility and sadness. Colin's presence sent a surge of erratic energy through my body, a wave of attraction and guilt like a defibrillator waking up my heart. I knew I was in over my head, and I stayed anyway.

We talked about being out on "First Thursday," a monthly event in Portland when the galleries stay open and artists and musicians bring their wares into the street. I hadn't even remembered it was First Thursday—it had been so long since I'd been aware of anything except David and the troubles he caused.

"I love it," I said. "But it's way too crowded. I can hardly hear myself think."

Jill looked at both of us, grinned, and excused herself to the bathroom.

Colin's eyes were steady and calm. "Well, maybe," he said, "we should continue this conversation over a quiet dinner."

## MENTAL ILLNESS, THEN AND NOW

There have been enormous strides in the understanding of mental illness. In the early 1800s, when "proper" and (initially) "humane" mental hospitals were founded, it was believed that the buildings' "high walls would grant a sense of safety" and that the "well-ordered routines of a hospital would restore a sense of order and normalcy." And, in these hospitals, "medical reassurance constituted an early form of psychotherapy."

For nearly two centuries, mental hospitals maintained a level of care and success which, many would agree, was not perfect but which served patients at least somewhat sufficiently. In the 1970s, legislators began the massive program of returning psychiatric patients to the community under the pretense that they would be discharged to a network of group homes and community care clinics. It fell apart. Lack of money, and the reality that the private sector couldn't make a huge profit off of the care of the mentally ill, doomed those projects.

Edward Shorter, the Jason A. Hannah Professor of the History of Medicine at the University of Toronto, writes, "Psychiatry's dirty secret is that if you had a severe mental illness requiring hospital care in 1900, you'd be better looked after than you are today." He also notes that "despite a flurry of media hand-waving about new technologies in psychiatry, the average hospital patient probably does less well now, despite the new drugs, than the average hospital patient a century ago" and that "care of very ill psychiatric patients has gotten much worse."

Many psychiatric units now offer stays of seven days, far too short to stabilize most patients and keep them safe. Very few services are available in the community, and adequate group housing is in short supply.

Many patients today find themselves on the street, homeless, or with no care at all. More than 50 percent of the nation's prisoners suffer from a mental illness.

# Chapter Twelve

The next night Colin and I had dinner at a Cajun place on the east side. The lighting was low; the booths were cozy and warm. We both ordered martinis, straight up, two olives. My head went light early; I let the warmth from the cocktail sink deep. There was a nice hum about the place. The bar was busy, but not overly busy; the acoustics were leveled out so that you could actually talk. The food I saw coming out of the kitchen looked fantastic, colorful, and plentiful on the plates. I was surprised by my own good mood.

Colin talked, and I had to remind myself to look at his face generally and not keep getting lost in his eyes. I'm not a sentimental person, and I was aware of the superficial things I found myself thinking: *He's gorgeous. Great hair. Nice teeth—so white.* I watched his lips open and close and entertained thoughts that were entirely inappropriate given the complexity of my life.

He'd been divorced four years and had two daughters, one nearly six, the other eight; he couldn't help but smile when he mentioned his girls. He took out a picture from his wallet, but the lights were too low for me to see their faces very clearly. I nodded appreciation, moved by how tenderly he placed the photo back in his wallet.

"Adorable." I stopped chiding the schoolgirl in myself and let my shoulders fall, listening to him chat about his work (high-tech), his kids, the toll of a bitter divorce. It felt good to fall silent; I talked all day for a living. I liked his voice—deep, but not too baritone, and he enunciated his vowels and consonants like a trained singer.

He also straightened his silverware. That combined with his precise look—shaven except for a soul patch, baby blue shirt tucked neatly in black Italian pants, shined shoes, moisturized skin—were distinct clues to perfectionism.

Was he too controlling? Was he a player? I was performing mental gymnastics to accommodate the position I'd put myself in. I imagined myself bolting to the door and then fantasized about reaching over to touch his hand. The kind of normalcy Colin seemed to embody was so infectious. I placed both of my hands at my side. Slow down.

"So, what's your story?" he said, unaware of the minefield he'd just entered.

"Ahh, where do I start?" I said, editing myself. "One daughter, Sophie. She's nine."

"How long have you been divorced?" he asked, toying with the toothpick in his martini.

"I'm not divorced."

There was a long pause on both sides of the booth. I couldn't lie; I'd rationalized a life for Sophie that didn't include divorce.

"Wow, you seemed really unmarried last night." He looked at my ring finger.

"Yeah, I took it off three years ago."

I'd had one brief but intense affair within those three years. Richard was an out-of-town businessman, someone whom I knew could be discreet. He was passionate and smart, and he helped me reclaim buried desire. I explained the relationship to Colin with as much brevity and honesty as I could. "He was not a long-term boyfriend," I said. He was an ember to a much larger fire.

Colin nodded. There were deep wrinkles around his eyes, and I liked that he'd let his hair go salt-and-pepper. But there was something deeper about Colin than his drop-dead good looks. He seemed completely comfortable with himself; his gaze and his breathing were steady and deep. I'd been around David's volatile energy for so long I'd forgotten what it was like to be with someone so calm.

"We pretty much live separate lives," I said, surprising myself with my own candidness.

"Three years is a long time to be separated," he said.

"Tell me about it," I said. So that was it. I gathered my purse and started to stand.

"Wait, whoa, wait a minute." He reached for my hand. "Please sit down."

"I'm really sorry," I said. "I shouldn't be here. My life—or what's left of it—is totally screwed up." There was a part of me that couldn't believe I'd shown up in the first place. What the hell was I doing here? Why would I want to take on more complication now?

He looked at me without flinching. "And?" he laughed. "Does that mean you skip dessert?"

After hot fudge brownies and coffee, we stood outside the restaurant, one of those places that plops itself down in a residential neighborhood and manages to thrive despite its less-than-perfect location. People's homes were lit up with evening activities. In some windows you could see the glow of the television. From others, you could hear the low thump of music.

It was ten thirty, the time when many couples look at each other and either find comfort or something to ignore. David and I had taken the routine to a whole new level of ambivalence. How lovely it would feel to be touched again by any man, but especially this one. The loneliness and restlessness I'd felt for so many years welled up inside me.

"Um, I should go," I said.

"I'd like to see you again." Colin leaned into me, almost pressing me up against my car door.

The whites of his eyes were even brighter in this light.

*Oh, for God's sake*, I found myself thinking, *this ridiculously strong attraction is purely biological.* I put my forehead on his chest and allowed myself to appreciate his smell—the cleanest, freshest masculine smell I'd smelled in a long time. I tried to place his shampoo, his lotion, whatever it was that made this man so enticing, but no labels came to mind. He leaned down to kiss me, hovering just above my lips until I couldn't stand it any longer. I pulled him in and kissed him long and hard.

The combination of feelings was too much to process out loud. Colin's kiss had amplified every emotion world-weary adults are trained to be wary of. The dopamine raced through my body, electrifying the moment. I wanted the simplicity of romance and the exuberance of desire. I wrapped my arms around his waist. He was built like a lean pyramid, wide shoulders, narrow hips, the kind of body swimmers develop after months in the pool. He looked down at me and smiled.

The leaves above us crackled when the wind blew through them. I'd always loved fall for its profound changes in color and temperature. There was something shifting in the air.

David called from Canada when I was packing boxes in Sophie's room. I'd found a loft in the Pearl District that would do—temporarily. It wasn't the greatest place to raise a nine-year-old, but it was close to work, there was lots of light, and the rent was affordable. I planned to move in with Sophie until we could find a small house I could afford.

David's voice sounded higher than I'd ever heard it, supercharged by nerves and grief and the side effects the drugs were having on his body. He was angry with his father.

"I tried to talk to him," he said. "He's just the same—judgmental, unforgiving. Christ, he's the most stubborn man I've ever met."

David's father was notoriously moody; sometimes David would make the long drive to Canada only to have his father retire to his room upon his arrival.

"I am so very sorry. Your dad is a really good man in his heart," I said.

Then, David began to wail. I could hear him open the door to the outside, pacing the big green lawn his father had insisted on keeping, even with advanced heart disease. David's mother would need her only son, but he was of no help now.

"You can't leave me," David cried. "I can't take it. I can't."

"David, we don't need to talk about it now," I said. "This isn't the time."

He let out a sound like an animal's cry, a combination of grief and longing and bone-chilling madness.

"David, please, you're scaring me. Is Sophie okay?"

He sniffed, the door creaked back open, and his voice was nearly normal again.

"Sophie, your mom wants to talk to you."

"Hey, Mommy!" Sophie's voice said into the phone. "I miss you soooooo much."

"How are you, sweetheart? Is Aunt Jill taking good care of you? Are you and your dad okay?"

I asked the questions as if they were code, a secret way for her to tell the truth. What was happening up there?

"Oh, yeah, Daddy's really sad. But we went to Grandpa Lew's favorite beach, and Dad built a big fire. You know how Dad gets carried away."

David had always been a bit of a pyromaniac. He loved watching flame dance. He built big fires in the winter and huge bonfires on the beach, but I always wondered what it was about the flame that seduced him.

"Sophie, promise me you'll stay with Aunt Jill during this trip," I said. "I don't want you alone with Daddy."

"Why not?" she said, innocently.

"Because. Because, honey, he's too sad to take care of you alone."

My legs were falling asleep, the circulation cut off by sitting for so long on a hard moving box. My shoulders ached; I arched my back to try to find some relief.

"Okay. We're going to have dessert now, Mommy. I love you. Gotta go, bye!"

The phone went dead. Jill would drive Sophie, David, and her son home the next day, and then I could take Sophie to the new apartment.

I pushed myself off the box and picked up another knickknack from her dresser. The photo, bedazzled in white and red jewels, showed Sophie as a toddler, dressed in a big sun hat and baby blue sundress. We were vacationing that year at my sister's second home in Capitol Reef National Park, the place where the lightning show and new love had electrified our romance.

Sophie was resting her chin on David's head, completely relaxed, looking intently into the camera. He was staring into the camera as well, not smiling, disturbed. No, distracted. He looked completely distracted, as if his mind was racing away from the moment. There was a pink and blazing orange sun setting behind them, but David was completely unfazed by it. The photo had always stood out to me, maybe because Sophie's gaze was so intense, and maybe because I could see the beginning of David's illness in that shot.

*Did he always know he was different?* I wondered. *Did he know that he harbored the beginning of a mental illness? Did his family know and minimize its importance, or even worse, keep a diagnosis from me?* I often caught David mumbling, a habit I used to think was charming. Other times, I'd catch him staring off into the distance, troubleshooting what I thought was a problem at work. Had he always been working to sublimate his feelings of anxiety and madness? Had the mere act of living been a burden, one made worse by a child, a family, a mortgage? My heart ached for him, for the man in that photo, the David I'd fallen in love with.

The phone rang again, startling me. David's voice was filled with rage. "You know what?" he screamed. "Fuck you and your fucking life. Go ahead and leave. I could give a shit." He started to hang up, and then he screamed so viciously it scared me to my core. "You're a real bitch, you know?"

I held the phone in my hand, stunned by David's vicious attack.

Who was he? I was too paralyzed to move. I must have sat for hours on that box, its seams cutting into the skin of my legs.

No sooner had David returned with Sophie than we received news of Lew's death. I had prepared myself to tell Sophie that we were leaving, and now there was another crisis that made me feel miserable for even considering my own needs. David didn't even bother unpacking his bag—he returned home to attend a small funeral for his father. First, the divorce. And now this.

I weighed my plans for moving. How would Sophie remember this? Mom left Dad the weekend after Grandpa died? Heartless. And yet, I knew if I didn't leave soon, I might not survive. I was losing weight, emotionally drained, emptied of energy and joy. The night with Colin had changed something for sure. He had reminded me what it was like to be alive, not just living, not just going through the motions.

But the notion of abandoning someone who was doomed now loomed over every choice I made. I knew if I left David in this state he wouldn't make it. I'd held on ten years. Surely, I could wait a few more weeks until he was stronger.

David returned from Canada more distant than ever before. He ignored me when I spoke to him about the details of the funeral, of Sophie's life, of his grief. He paced the house at all hours of the night. He refused to eat anything I'd cook.

After David's mother settled Lew's affairs, she agreed to come to Portland to help take care of David. I rushed from work to pick her up from the 6:10 train. Alice was a willow of a woman made even frailer by the death of her husband. As I drove up, I could see the tan slacks that bagged around her and the red scarf around her head that covered thinning, stressed hair. She was standing on the corner by the train station in the red coat I'd bought her eight years earlier for her birthday. She was in her early seventies now. She was still gorgeous, with the bone structure of a movie star and a mind that was lightning fast.

She was also English, no nonsense, brisk about her business and the order of life. "Hello, dear." She kissed me on the side of the cheek. "Thank you for picking me up." She folded her scarf into neat triangles before placing it in a plastic bag inside her purse.

As we drove, the wiper blades thumped against the windshield. I tried to give her the most direct version of what had happened. "It's been really bad the last year, Alice. David refused to get help."

She blinked when I told her this.

"I think he's been sick a long time."

"Well, it would seem to me losing your father and your marriage all in one month might send any of us a little crazy." She sighed. "Psychiatrists, all just a bunch of nonsense, if you ask me. Suggesting you look at your navel for the answers to problems. I understand David's resistance completely."

Psychiatrists, nonsense? Alice had just dismissed Adele's field of expertise and given me far more understanding into David's refusal to get help.

She looked out the window at the homeless people lining up outside the soup kitchen. "What a shame," she said absentmindedly. There was an order Alice expected from the world, and it occurred to me that the world often disappointed her. We drove the rest of the way home in silence. I clutched the steering wheel until my knuckles were white.

We drove past the Pearl district, where I'd met Colin for the first time. How odd it must have been for her to learn the details of our crumbling marriage now. Ten years she'd missed. David never really shared his life with anyone. As she straightened her back in her seat, Alice's way in the world reminded me of my marital obligations.

We pulled into the driveway, and I said, "I'm really sorry about Lew, Alice. I liked him very much."

She opened the car door, got halfway out, and then turned. "I know you did, dear. He liked you too." She paused. "Everyone goes through hard times in a marriage. It wasn't always easy. But you work on it; you work *for* it. That's how you have a good marriage."

Before I could respond to Alice's philosophy on how to make a good marriage, a good life, she opened the door to my house and hauled her bag upstairs.

That night, David came to my bedroom. "Can I lay down with you?" he asked.

"What is it?" I slid to the opposite edge of the bed.

"I think about us all the time," he whispered. "I let you go, didn't I. I let you go?"

He touched my arm, then my face. "Please don't, David." I turned away from him. My body ached, but not for him.

"I don't know if I can make it without you," he said.

I was so tired and irritated by his erratic nighttime sojourns. I whispered, not wanting to wake his mother. "It seems to me if you'd wanted to save our marriage you might have made an effort to get help, to see a doctor, before now."

"I was fucked up." He sat up in bed, his hair askew and his beard much longer than I'd ever seen before. "But I'm getting better now, I am. I'm going to go to counseling, too. I'm not giving up on us, Sheila; please don't give up on me." His eyes were glassy, bloodshot from lack of sleep.

I sighed and sat up to face him. My jaw was tense; I'd been grinding my teeth at night. "David, maybe you haven't realized how I've been suffering too. This isn't a life for me—it's not one for Sophie. I don't want to have her grow up thinking she doesn't deserve affection and respect from her husband. I don't want her to believe adults sleep apart."

I hugged him, and my heart broke for the little boy in him, the kid who'd been shipped off to boarding school, the kid who was bullied every day because he was shy. He'd turned the anger inside and never really let me in.

"No, no, I won't go." He started to raise his voice. I knew his mother would hear us fighting.

Maybe it was the lack of sleep, or the anxiety I had over worrying about Sophie's safety. I was really, finally done. I wanted to jolt him into reality, into seeing the seriousness of our situation. "I'm seeing someone else," I said. "Just a couple of times, but I like him."

David laughed a mocking laugh. "How charming," he said. "Is he younger than me?"

"Why does that matter?" I said. "Why does any of it matter? You never cared before." We hadn't slept together in two years, and neither of us questioned one another about how we survived the physical isolation of a marriage that existed solely for our daughter.

The beige-and-black law offices of Jody Stahancyk were designed in tones meant to neither soothe nor evoke emotion. Jody was Oregon's best-known attorney, a big woman, six foot two, with a voice that boomed through the hallway. The stories of her courtroom antics were widely circulated. She could intimidate judges. She could make male lawyers cry. I'd heard all the stories, but I really needed her help. It had been a long shot to get in, and I'd obviously waited far too long before calling, but she'd agreed, thanks to a series of interviews I'd done with her when I reported for the ABC affiliate.

We talked about shoes for ten minutes. Her daughter knew of a place in Chicago that sold designer brands at cost. How much was this costing me? I'd heard stories of people not being able to afford her after the first meeting.

When she finally asked, "What can I do for you?" I wasted no time.

I told her about David's illness, how I didn't want to make it worse by getting a contentious divorce. "I want to know the best way to work this out. And I know this sounds absurd, but I really don't even want him to know I've seen you."

She peered at me over red horn-rimmed glasses. "How long have you been married?"

"Ten years."

"Then you'll give him half of everything you own. Do you have savings?"

"Yes, a 401(k), a pension, a few hundred thousand dollars in savings and from investing in apartments," I said. My own shoes were bought on closeout from a warehouse sale. I'd worked so hard to save. Now I was going to give away half of it. "And the house."

"Do you both own the house?" Her female assistant, a young Asian lawyer dressed in a beautiful black suit, took notes as we talked.

"No, David didn't believe in buying on credit. I bought it. It's in my name."

"Well, whatever you do, don't leave the house," she said flatly.

I sat back in my chair, floored. "What do you mean? I'm packed. I've signed a lease on an apartment. I'm halfway moved in." My silk blouse was stained with sweat.

"Well, unpack, and get back in that house. If things get ugly, and you've abandoned your primary residence, that house will be his, along with half of everything else you own." She started scribbling on a paper and then addressed her assistant. "Krista, get Sheila the papers for a no-fault divorce. Fill them out for her. We'll have an asset sheet drawn up tomorrow."

She turned to me. "Here's how it's going to go down. You're going to buy him out of the house and offer him half of everything you own. He gets to keep the assets from his business." She looked up, struck by her own curiosity, "He does have assets, doesn't he?"

"I don't know."

"Are you an officer of his company?" She leaned back in her leather chair, which looked custom-made to fit her frame.

"No, I've never signed checks; I know nothing about how he runs his financials."

"Try to find out in the next few days, would you?" She smiled. "On the one hand, your ignorance may have protected you from some nasty corporate debt. On the other hand, your ignorance could cost you mightily if he's run up a bunch of personal debt. Does he have credit cards? A mistress? A secret place in Vegas? Is he a drug dealer, a drug user? You need to know these things."

This was her territory. There wasn't a scenario or scheme she didn't already know forward and back.

"No, none of that," I said quickly. I had long suspected his infidelity, but I didn't know anything for certain about David's private life.

Two more hours passed in her office as I laid out the entire story of our marriage and my worry about preserving what little mental health he still had. I was spent, as if the energy had been squeezed out of me in drops, question by question. At the end of the session, she handed me some chicken scratch on some paper.

"Okay, this is a rough guess, but based on what you've told me, here's how you'd make the split." She handed me the paper. The numbers looked completely devastating. My savings would be virtually wiped out. In my twenties, I'd worked two jobs, anchoring and reporting. In my thirties, I'd invested in apartments with an attorney friend of mine. All the missed nights from Sophie, all the weekends showing and renting apartments—it was all for nothing.

"What about custody?" she asked. "You want your daughter full-time?" I had never, ever considered taking Sophie from David. Ever.

"Absolutely not," I said. "Sophie is all that David has left. I want her to be with him, at least half of the time."

"And can he take care of her?" she asked.

My shoulders fell. "I don't know. I really don't know anymore." As bad as David's condition had become, he managed to hold it together around Sophie. He was his best self with her. It was an irrational assumption, but I believed he would never harm her intentionally.

Jody's phone was lit up on all five ringers, people on hold, other divorces, other marriages crashing in around her, and yet she was perfectly composed, booming orders to her assistant like a four-star general in a theater of war. "Okay, that's a good start," she said, wrapping up. "Look, I do this all the time. You are in a better position than

98 percent of the women who come through here. You're a smart cookie. You'll earn it back. You've got your kid. We can keep you out of court. You can count on me. Now, go convince David to settle this quickly."

I shook her hand, the firmest shake I'd encountered in weeks. I liked this woman; I didn't care what people said about her. She really did pull out all the stops for her clients.

Before I left, she added, "We'll help you file the divorce. The media doesn't have to know."

This was the news I welcomed most. I'd read other local personalities' divorces unfold on the pages of local gossip sites. None of them had Jody as a lawyer.

"Thanks, Jody," I said, the bones of my knees knocking. Standing next to her I felt pathetic, incompetent, tiny.

She softened. "Remember to breathe, would you?"

Brian Goff is a gifted therapist in Portland, Oregon, whose specialty is suicide. He's seen more than 500 significantly suicidal patients. Goff says, "A large percentage of survivors I work with say they regret the choice of attempting suicide. Rarely have people actually wanted to die. They just didn't want to live the way they were living."

Goff has worked at the forefront of several therapies that offer promise for the most deeply troubled patients. Intensive therapies, such as dialectical behavior therapy (DBT) and cognitive behavioral therapy (CBT), have reduced rates of repetition of deliberate self-harm. Goff cofounded a DBT clinic and has used that technique successfully with hundreds and hundreds of patients. Now, he's combined what he sees as the best elements of both in a treatment that uses mindfulness blended with cognitive behavioral psychotherapies.

Goff begins with this premise: people want to live a life worth living. And if they can be given the tools to help them ease the struggle of their present condition, they can begin building a life worth living. The new hybrid therapy developed by Goff, acceptance and commitment therapy (ACT), focuses on modifying the functions rather than the forms of symptoms, using acceptance and mindfulness strategies.

"Western medicine moves the locus of control so that the solution is no longer inside of us," Goff says. "Someone else will take care of it. ACT puts the construction of one's life and the reorientation of one's experience back in the hands of the individual.

"We teach people to experience their thoughts as thoughts. When they think, 'I'm going crazy,' we teach them to change the thought to "I'm having the thought I'm going crazy." Thus participants *develop a different relationship with* the thoughts, feelings, and bodily sensations that would normally form a toxic spiral, deepening hopelessness and the sense of entrapment and opening the way to another suicidal crisis."

With ACT, people learn to move beyond the thought that "my situation is hopeless" by changing it to this: "I notice a thought that my situation is hopeless." "ACT therapists are giving people tools to put these thoughts in context," says Goff. "So much of traditional CBT focuses on symptom reduction. So often, people are doing the things they do to avoid unwanted internal experiences (i.e., thoughts and feelings) rather than doing things that are important and meaningful to them."

In ACT, there is something more worthy of one's time than reducing discomfort (which often backfires like trying to get out of quicksand): that is, learning to be flexible enough psychologically so that you can do the things that feel meaningful, vital, and important to you. It is often said, "Living well is better than feeling good."

Goff asks his patients a theoretical question that provides insight into the behavioral component of suicidal ideation: "If I had a magic wand and I could do something, anything, for you, would you say, 'Please kill me'? In all the years I've asked it, I've never heard 'Yes, please kill me,'" Goff says. "The answer is, 'Cure my Parkinson's.' 'End my depression.' 'Save my marriage.' 'Prevent my bankruptcy.'"

"Most people who suffer from mental illness begin with a host of vulnerabilities: environmental, genetic predisposition, early trauma, nutritional deficiencies etc.," says Goff. "You inherit certain qualities of your internal world, among them sensitivity, reactivity, the ability to return to a normal mood."

Goff says with the right mix of circumstances that are toxic—physical or sexual abuse, neglect or a detached parent, early childhood trauma, environmental toxins—you are much more vulnerable to mental disorders. In an ACT approach, the focus is not on reducing the frequency or changing the content of inner experiences, but rather on changing the patient's relationship to the behavior. ACT is successful in the psychological treatment of a wide range of problems, including drug dependence, chronic pain, epilepsy, depression, social phobia, work stress, and borderline personality disorder.

# Chapter Thirteen

The night of the party, October 8. The temperature inside the car had dropped. Colin and I were still parked outside the party, in the same parking place in northwest Portland, but the world and my view of it had made a cataclysmic shift. I had begun the evening of October 8 thinking that maybe David was stabilizing. The divorce papers were drawn up, tucked away in a drawer until he appeared well enough to make decisions for himself.

I'd begun the evening thinking that Colin and I might be right together. We'd seen one another several times since our first date, and with every coffee or quiet dinner, I'd come to realize Colin *was* one of the "good guys." I would have preferred a carefree romance and to have been more settled when we met, but I also felt instinctively that I should not pass up the best thing that had happened to me in years. It was as if I'd been drowning, and Colin had revived me.

Now, according to the officer on the telephone, David had broken into a home and stolen a gun. It was completely clear now that David was psychotic. I could no longer deny how seriously ill he really was or believe that he would somehow, magically, get better. The party inside the restaurant was still rocking. I could see dancers bobbing through the windows, but it seemed like a world I'd never be able to rejoin. Not now.

Colin hadn't moved during the entire retelling of the story. I half expected him to drop me off in front of my home and wish me luck with my problems. Instead, he cradled me in his arms. "Sweetheart, you've been through so much," he said. "Let me help you."

I wiped the tears from my eyes and imagined what I must have looked like to him, with my mascara-smudged mug-shot face and my legs shivering with cold. Those girls inside the restaurant party were unburdened, many of them daughters of Portland's most wealthy philanthropists. I'd needed to escape the party immediately to go to David. But now, I realized, Colin deserved this time, this retelling of such an important part of what I'd been holding inside. Given the seriousness of the story, I expected him to call the date our last.

"What are you doing with me?" I said. "Go, have fun."

"I don't have a say in whom my heart chooses," Colin said. "And it's crazy for you. It was from the very moment I laid eyes on you." He smiled and put his thumb on my chin.

I stopped talking. The tension in my throat broke, and I cried, "I've never been so scared in my life." I had never shared this level of intimacy about my marriage with anyone in my family, or with any of my friends. I had been too ashamed to tell those closest to me what my life was really like, how difficult it had become. Somehow, I knew instinctively that Colin was safe territory.

"It will be okay. You'll be okay. So will Sophie. I promise you."

Colin started the car. "I have the girls all weekend. If you'd like to drop Sophie by while you deal with things, I will entertain her like the so-called Disneyland dad that I am." He squeezed my leg. "Okay?"

"Okay," I said. "Thank you."

"Now, let's get you to the police station," he said, pulling carefully into traffic.

"No," I said. "I've got to go home. David's mother should know."

## MINDFULNESS

Mindfulness helps people cope with mental illness. The origins of mindfulness meditation lie in a Buddhist tradition dating back more than 2,500 years, but many therapists are now seeing it used successfully to treat patients with a wide variety of problems, including chronic pain, depression, and suicidal ideation.

Mindfulness has been described as "a particular way of paying attention: on purpose, moment-by-moment, and without judgment."

Early sessions of mindfulness therapy concentrate on learning to focus on sensations, such as the breath. Later, patients extend mindfulness to thoughts and emotions, especially as they are experienced in the body.

In group mindfulness therapy sessions, participants learn to tune in to small experiences and aspects of their surroundings that would usually pass unnoticed and to work toward increasing the presence of nourishing activities in their daily lives (activities that lift mood and increase energy). An important aim of the therapy is to improve positive well-being, not simply to reduce negative emotions. Finally, participants learn to identify patterns of emotional response and negative thinking that act as warning signals for potential relapse and to help one another develop crisis plans, incorporating actions to take in the event of future depression, hopelessness, and thoughts of suicide.

For patients with suicidal ideation, riding the wave of their thoughts can be liberating. "What's going on here? What is this? Do I recognize this? Is an old tape playing? Do I need to engage with it?"

Two controlled clinical trials have now demonstrated that mindfulness-based cognitive therapy (MBCT) can reduce the likelihood of relapse by about 40 to 50 percent in people who have suffered three or more previous episodes of depression. In the book *The Mindful Way Through Depression,* authors Mark Williams, John Teasdale, Zindel Segal, and Jon Kabat-Zinn outline why mindfulness can be so helpful for people with depression and reveal that, by cultivating the awareness-of-being mode, we can:

- get out of our heads and learn to experience the world directly, experientially, without the relentless commentary of our thoughts.
- see our thoughts as mental events that come and go in the mind rather than taking them literally.
- start living here, in each present moment.
- disengage the autopilot in our heads.
- sidestep the cascade of mental events that draws us down into depression.
- stop trying to force life to be a certain way because we're uncomfortable right now.

Unfortunately, many people attempt to learn the skill of mindfulness while they are in the middle of a full-blown mental health crisis. That is why the most successful programs involve early intervention and treatment.

# Chapter Fourteen

Alice seemed discombobulated when I woke her. She looked around the basement bedroom, trying to familiarize herself with the objects in the room.

"Alice, he's missing," I said.

She sat up, suddenly alert and on duty again. "Who, David?" Her face was ashen, drawn. She shook her head, trying to assimilate everything happening around her.

"He has a gun." I told her the story of the phone call, the police officer. "You'll have to get dressed. We need to drive to the Columbia Gorge, where they are looking for him. It's near Multnomah Falls. A forty-minute drive."

"Of course, I know where that is." She rose in a flannel nightgown. My heart ached for her—an old woman, terrified from losing her husband, and now, possibly her son.

"I'm sorry, Alice." I handed her a robe. "I'm sorry it turned out this way." She still didn't seem to quite realize where she was. She wobbled and then sat back down on the bed. The death of her husband had been a terrible blow.

"Well, we'll just, we'll just find him, then." Something tripped in her voice, and the brisk, efficient Englishwoman was gone, replaced with hurt and vulnerability. "Won't we? Find him? I'm sorry, I had a glass of wine with dinner." She sat on the side of the bed, her hands on either side of her temples. "I must not have heard him go out."

I calculated how much time we had left to deal with this crisis before I would need to pick Sophie up from her sleepover the next morning. She usually liked to stay for a big breakfast. No need to tell her anything yet.

We were halfway to the sheriff's office when my cell phone rang. I answered it, hoping for a miracle.

It was the same officer who'd called before. He sounded tired. "Ms. Hamilton," he said, "don't come to the sheriff's office. Go directly to the Mt. Hood Medical Center." My hand clutched the steering wheel; this was it—they would tell me that David was dead, or that he shot someone. I braced myself for the worst.

"Is David okay?"

"For now. He went back to the house where he stole the gun. He turned on the gas and tried to kill himself there. Then he went to an abandoned house up the road, where he tried to cut himself. Somewhere during the night, he fired off two shots; maybe as a test, who knows? It appears he's taken a bunch of pills, too."

He was talking fast; too many images were jumbling in my mind. David trying to light a stranger's stove? Firing shots into the sky? This wasn't making sense.

"How did you find him?"

"He went back to the original house again, and the owner brought him to the hospital. Apparently he knew the woman whose gun he stole."

The officer had no idea how confusing the information was, how much of a mystery I'd found myself in. I stammered something nonsensical.

"She called the police. She's the one who took him to the hospital. Do you know where the hospital is, Ms. Hamilton?"

My reporting career had prepared me for this disaster in ways I never imagined. I'd been to the Mt. Hood hospital twice before: once to report on three climbers who had been plucked from a crevasse on Mt. Hood, and the second time to report on a young snowboarder who had been rescued after getting caught in an avalanche. "Yes," I told him, "we're almost at the exit." I held the phone inches away from my ear, as if dampening the volume might help me avoid this reality. Alice's eyes were wide as she waited for me to fill her in.

"I don't even know if I've got this right," I said to David's mother as I turned the car into the hospital. "David is here. He's okay. He knows the woman who brought him here."

"Thank God," Alice said, staring out into the darkness. There were two emergency room technicians sitting on the back bumper of an ambulance when we arrived. One was smoking; the other was staring off at the moon.

The ER was empty, except for a small woman with blonde hair sitting in the corner. She looked frazzled; her skin was nearly translucent under the fluorescent waiting room lights.

"We're here to see David Krol," I said. "We're his family."

The clerk checked her charts and then motioned toward the other woman sitting in the waiting room. "Yes, there's another family member already here. She checked him in."

My startled look must have given away my shock. "Did she say she was family?" I asked, not keeping my voice down.

"Yes, she did," the clerk said, "but she couldn't show proof of relation, and Officer Rodale said she was the person who phoned in the call, so we thought something might be up. We haven't allowed her to go back just yet."

I stared at the woman in the waiting room, a mystery figure in a ninety-pound frame. She wore a coat that was way too large for her, one of those green barn jackets you see horse people wearing, and English riding pants and boots. Her blonde hair was long with touches of gray, frizzy and unkempt. She tapped her leg nervously as she waited in the corner. I exchanged glances with Alice and then walked to the corner where the woman sat.

"Hi, I'm David's wife, Sheila," I said. "You are?"

"I'm Diedra Collins," she said quietly. "I'm a good friend of David's."

I sat down across from her. "I've never heard him mention you. How long have you two known one another?"

I was trying to be polite, to piece together the story as I might if I were gathering facts for a news story. Go slowly, find the "who-what-where-when-why."

"I'm an architect," she said. "We knew each other years ago when I worked in Portland. I just reconnected with David about a year and a half ago." A year and a half, about the time David really started missing his evening pickups for Sophie. I nodded, hoping she'd provide more details.

"I was out at the barn when he first came tonight. It's about an hour from my home. I had no idea he'd gotten in my house. He knew where I kept the gun," she said, staring at the carpeting on the floor. "He knew I kept it under my pillow." She twisted her keys, and tears filled her eyes.

The woman was clearly a long-time lover. This was not about me, nor this waifish woman David turned to in desperation. He was sick. He needed help.

"Excuse me, will you?" I said. "I'm going to check on David."

Alice and Diedra exchanged confused looks with one another and then started to chat quietly.

I pushed open the doors to the emergency room. A couple of nurses sat at computers, bored, tired. I found David in the third treatment room, sleeping on his side. He was in a tiny blue paper-like hospital gown, tied at the back.

He was still tanned from the earlier days of summer; his skin had always been so beautiful. His feet and ankles hung over the edge of the bed, and he snored lightly. I sat at the foot of his bed for a minute, trying to conjure up something for him other than pity.

I'd fallen so hard for him in the beginning. I thought his intellect and wry sense of humor would cast their spell on me forever. Once, in a coffee shop, I'd laughed so hard at something he said that I reached across the table and kissed him. He'd pulled away and scrunched his eyebrows, embarrassed by the public display of affection.

The first time I'd walked into his home, I'd been charmed. His art collection charmed me. The chickens had charmed me. I'd hoped his love for Sophie might keep him whole, even if I couldn't.

Now, a lifetime later, sitting at the foot of his hospital bed, I'd run out of hope—and solutions for David. A doctor popped his head in from behind the curtain. "He's pretty heavily sedated," he said. "It may be a few hours before he wakes up."

"Yeah, he hasn't slept in weeks," I said. "So what happens next?"

The doctor was completely bald, with muscled, tan arms, the kind of guy who goes into medicine because he works hard, plays hard, and climbs mountains on his days off. He had dark brown eyes that seemed to tolerate little distraction. He shifted his weight in his running shoes as he talked. "It's a little out of our hands at this point. The county takes over from here."

"What do you mean?" I asked.

"Once someone has made a serious suicide attempt, the county demands a hold and a court-ordered evaluation. Someone will be contacting you to tell you where he'll be transferred." He kept eye contact, a very precise delivery of information he'd obviously given before. "It's roulette on the weekends. There are so few mental health beds available. We may have to keep him here until one opens up."

I'd reported on the overcrowding in Oregon's mental health system for so long. Now, it was my turn to feel the repercussions of years of funding cutbacks. "So, are you talking hours or days?" I looked through the curtain to see a police officer sitting outside in the hallway. I realized David was being monitored—David, the big bear, the guy who would never hurt anyone. *You've got it wrong; you've got him wrong*, I thought. *He's not like the rest of them.*

The doctor shook his head and smiled. "Sometimes weeks."

My mouth fell open and my eyes did a double-take. "You're kidding."

I knew he was not.

"The process is pretty ugly," he said. "Since he's asleep, maybe you could use this time to do the same."

The curtain moved, and Alice walked in. "Hello," she said to the doctor. "I'm David's mother. Is he going to be okay?" She held out her hand and tugged on the hospital gown, trying to cover David's backside. I felt a pang in my throat; I couldn't imagine the hurt of seeing your only son wounded, vulnerable.

The doctor kindly repeated everything he'd told me. He excused himself when a second man in a police uniform showed up.

"Ms. Hamilton," the officer said, "could I have a moment with you?"

I nodded and excused myself, leaving Alice alone with her son.

We stood in the hallway outside David's room. "We're going to need to get a report from you. If you don't mind." He pulled out a notebook similar to the one I'd used on so many stories. I'd been on the other side of crime and drama so often, asking the questions. I didn't want to make his job harder.

"He was supposed to be at home with his mother," I said quietly. "She fell asleep, and he went out."

"Where were you?" He leaned against the white wall. The other officer moved in his chair to eavesdrop.

"I was at a birthday party with a friend. Your sergeant, I think, he's the one who called me."

"Do you know the woman whose home he broke into?"

"It was his girlfriend," I said. "And no, I didn't know her." I looked at the tile floor, wondering how much bad news had been broken in this very spot, how many lives had been shattered outside this hospital room.

The officer bit the underside of his lower lip.

"Ms. Hamilton, we never found the gun," he said. "We found the place where he went after he got the gun. It's an old abandoned house just up the road from Ms. Collins. There were some empty bottles, and it appears he tried to cut himself again, but we never found the gun, Ms. Hamilton. It worries us."

A wave of nausea moved through me. I stammered, "Maybe when he wakes up he'll tell us where it is."

"Ms. Collins doesn't want to file charges against him. It's unlikely the county would move forward on its own. But you need to find that gun, for his sake, Ms. Hamilton. For your sake, too."

The next morning, I drove across town to pick Sophie up from the sleepover. I dreaded the next step and tried to imagine all the ways in which she might react. She was deeply intuitive and would immediately sense something was wrong if I didn't tell her. She was also still very much her daddy's girl and would be devastated by David's hospitalization.

At nine, Sophie was tall for her age, and her teachers said she was a natural leader, a gifted athlete, creative. She aced her studies without even trying. But at this stage, Sophie did not want to stand out. As a parent, it was a worrisome time. She had recently started dressing like everyone else at school, talking like everyone else, and eyeing herself critically in the mirror. She straightened her hair, begged to wear lip gloss, and wanted to grow up more quickly than I would have liked. I knew she'd return to her fiery, independent self soon enough; I just didn't want her confidence disrupted.

Sophie was in the "tween" years, as parenting magazines called it. I was also in between—caught between my protective instincts and the knowledge that she deserved and needed the truth. Sophie wanted to be like everyone else at this stage in her life. The news I was about to deliver would change everything.

The scene at the sleepover was casual chaos. Cereal bowls filled with Sugar Pops lined the coffee table. Sophie lounged in front of the television, looking a disheveled and tired kind of happy. "You ready to go, sweets?" I faked my smile.

"Nah, Mom, not yet, pleeeeze?" She tilted her head sideways. She was sitting in an oversized recliner watching an episode of *SpongeBob SquarePants* that she had to have seen a dozen times.

The kids had every line memorized, and they still loved him. I wanted to give in, to postpone the inevitable.

"C'mon, Sophs, let's get you going. It's already ten thirty." I started gathering her things.

"I had soooooo much fun," Sophie said, smiling. "We stayed up till, like, midnight."

"That sounds like fun," I smiled. "Tell everybody thank-you."

Sophie was polite in a genuine way, saying her thank-yous and goodbyes and making eye contact even when she was sleep deprived. She held her pillow close to her tummy as we made our way to the car. It reminded me of the way she held Bear. She was nine, such a tender age for a girl. Had David thought of what this would do to her?

I turned the key in the ignition and started driving.

Sophie was quieter than usual, and I hoped she was just burned out from the night before. But soon enough she turned to me. "Mom, what's wrong?" she asked.

"How do you know something's wrong?"

"Because you didn't correct me when I said 'like,' and you're not mad I stayed up so late." She looked out the window on a bright, hot day.

I spoke slowly, trying to pay attention to the driving, at the same time measuring my words so I wouldn't sound as scared as I was.

"Daddy is in the hospital," I said.

She reacted before I could continue, turning in her seat so the seatbelt strained against her shoulder. "What's wrong? Mommy, what happened?"

I couldn't tell her and drive at the same time. I pulled over in front of a row of houses where people were doing normal Sunday activities—pancakes, television, church. I hated David for robbing Sophie of her innocence. Her disheveled look had gone from happy to distraught, her chest rising and falling so rapidly I worried she might faint.

"Soph, he's very sick, but not like cancer or a broken leg. He is so sad, honey. He needs some time in the hospital for the doctors to take care of him."

Sophie pinched her eyebrows together and said, "Sadness isn't a sickness, Mom."

My heart broke for her. "Sophie, honey. It is a sickness when someone gets so depressed they don't want to go on living."

Sophie sighed and hit her leg with a clenched fist. She played nervously with the seat until it was reclined all the way.

"It's your fault, you know," she said, turning away from me. "Daddy doesn't want a divorce."

I drew in several deep breaths before I spoke. I'd protected Sophie from the negative details of our marriage in order to protect her relationship with her dad. I wasn't going to change that strategy now.

"Sophie, you can't understand now; you're not old enough. But we've known for a long time that we needed to separate, even before Daddy got this sick."

She tried to sit back up in her seat and screamed, "Why can't I just have a normal life? Why can't you two get along? What's wrong with you? Why did you even get married in the first place if you didn't love each other?"

I couldn't hold the tears back anymore. "I'm so sorry to put you through this, sweetheart. I tried, honey, really, I tried for a long time. I did love Daddy, very much, for a long, long time. I just can't be with him anymore."

Sophie flopped back down on the seat and did her best to turn her entire body away from me. "I've got a headache," she said.

I took her straight home and let her stay in her room the rest of the day. My afternoon would be filled with phone calls from counselors, David's family, the police, the girlfriend, and my link to the mental health system, Robert Stellar.

Robert Stellar was a short Italian man with hairs sprouting from his nose and ears and a deep olive complexion. I heard his voice on the phone and recognized it immediately: there weren't many New Jersey accents in Portland, and his was still thick. A mental health supervisor for Multnomah County Court, he'd once won a contest at our station and sat in on the show. He'd been mesmerized by the radio business. Now I needed to learn everything I possibly could about his business.

He told me he was calling on behalf of the county. "I'm sorry if this is awkward. You were so nice at the radio station, I thought I could help you."

I sat at the kitchen table with a cup of coffee. "Thanks for anything you can do."

Stellar explained that he would be the county representative overseeing David's commitment hearing and that he would monitor David's progress during hospitalization.

The heat from the day was beginning to rise in the kitchen. I'd always wanted air conditioning; the summers in Portland were getting hotter and hotter. David said it felt fake against his skin—he was so sensitive to air and textures and light and sound. He couldn't take air conditioning, or cotton, or traffic noise, or bright light. Now, I viewed those eccentricities in a different light, as part of his illness. My yellow Labrador was splayed on the hardwood floor, seeking relief by keeping still. Sophie's West Highland, Max, sat near me, sensing my anxiety. He whined, missing David.

Robert explained the details of the county mental health rules: once someone has made a serious attempt on his life, the county intervenes, evaluating that person for thirty days in a mental health facility. The problem was, there were waiting lists a mile long for the facilities, and families were not allowed to take their loved ones to a non-sanctioned facility, meaning moving David would not be allowed.

"There's a good one at Good Samaritan hospital," Robert said. "And another one in Gresham, but I assume you're going to need something close to your work."

"That would be helpful." My voice was thin, broken even. The images flashing through my mind were not pretty—David in hospital gowns, David cutting himself in an old abandoned shack, David wandering through his girlfriend's home, the doctors shooting him full of sedatives. It was hard to believe that was the man I married.

"Sophie would really like to see her dad," I said.

"Why don't you give him a couple of days?" Robert asked. "He was probably going downhill for a really long time. He may need to get back on his feet before he sees her again."

Sophie would not accept that answer. She'd seen the side of David that was sad, yes, but never unstable. That was not her dad, not then, not now.

"I'd like to see him today, if it's possible." A bead of sweat trickled down my chest. I would need to miss work again.

"That would be fine. Why don't we see what happens with a transfer later this afternoon, and I'll call you again."

"Robert," I asked, "when will I get to talk to a doctor?"

"As soon as we get him checked into a facility," he answered.

David's sister Adele would be arriving later that afternoon. Somehow, I felt more prepared to deal with the mental health system with her by my side. She was a psychologist in Canada, and although the two health systems couldn't be more different, she would have good ideas about David's care. I wondered whether she'd diagnosed David and, if so, why she hadn't ever told me about his illness, when she had first seen it, how serious she thought it was.

We met in the hallway outside David's room at Emanuel Hospital, the second place he was taken while he waited for a permanent room.

David looked close to death. His eyes fluttered in a deep state of dreaming, but his breathing was so shallow his chest barely rose and fell. His skin had a yellowish tint to it, as if the drugs might not be all that good for his liver. He'd suffered from hepatitis C after traveling to Africa, and drugs affected David in the strangest way, as if his damaged liver just bounced the toxins back out through his skin.

He hadn't shaved, and his beard was starting to come in full again, this time with patches of gray instead of dark brown. It was shocking to see him age so quickly, as if a shrinking, aging machine had taken over his body. I felt completely helpless. I left Adele in the room and went home to be with Sophie. My last glimpse of Adele that night was her sitting next to David holding his big hand in hers. Tears rolled down her face. Maybe she felt as hopeless as I did.

## SUICIDE AND PSYCHOTROPIC DRUGS

Psychotropic drugs affect your mood, behavior, and perception by changing the way your brain functions.

One class of psychotropic drugs, known as selective serotonin reuptake inhibitors (SSRIs), are prescribed for a variety of symptoms, including depression, bipolar disorder, attention deficit disorder (ADD), attention deficit hyperactivity disorder (ADHD), and schizophrenia. In addition, SSRIs are used to correct low levels of serotonin in the brain.

Although SSRIs have been used to successfully treat many patients, they can be disastrous when prescribed to people with bipolar disorder. In a study of thirty-eight bipolar patients treated with an antidepressant, 55 percent developed mania and 23 percent turned into rapid cyclers. The group prescribed antidepressants also spent "significantly more time depressed" than bipolar patients not given the drug.

It may seem paradoxical that a treatment that is therapeutic for depression can worsen the course of bipolar disorder, but there are numerous studies to back up this claim. Researchers find that "there are significant risks of mania and long-term worsening with antidepressants" among bipolar patients. Use of antidepressants may "destabilize the illness, leading to an increase in the number of both manic and depressive episodes" and "increase the likelihood of a mixed state," in which feelings of depression and mania occur simultaneously.

Once antidepressants induce rapid cycling, it abates in only one-third of patients over the long term, even after the offending antidepressant is withdrawn. Forty percent of patients who have worsened in this way continue to "cycle rapidly with unmodified severity" for years on end. Antidepressants can induce a "chronic, dysphoric, irritable state" in bipolar patients.

In a large study by the National Institute of Mental Health, "the major predictor of worse outcome was antidepressant use."

These patients were nearly four times more likely than the unexposed patients to develop rapid cycling, and twice as likely to have multiple manic or depressive episodes.

SSRIs carry mandatory warning labels about potential increased suicide risks for children, usually those being treated for ADD or ADHD. Increased suicide risk in adults is also a factor with SSRIs, but warnings are not as widespread, which has led to many unnecessary, avoidable deaths. It is important to understand the risk to people who may appear to be depressed, but, in fact, suffer from bipolar I or II.

# Chapter Fifteen

I hadn't seen Colin since the birthday party. Part of me believed that I should cut it off. The other part longed for a partner again, a person to laugh with and to share the interior of my life. Balancing a new relationship was a ridiculous feat given what I was going through, but I had a powerful intuition about why Colin had entered my life when he had. I was not meant to live ridden with anxiety. I was as worthy of love as any other human being.

I think back on those early days of knowing Colin and wonder how I *knew*—knew that he was kind and compassionate and that he would be there for me not just in crisis but in the daily ups and downs of life. With all the betrayal, and the unmasking of David as a man I barely knew, how did I dare even trust a man I'd known only a few weeks?

Despite the sickening feeling that David had become a completely different person than the one I fell in love with, I felt intuitively that his isolation and dishonesty had contributed to his breakdown. If he'd loved openly and honestly, and shared with me his private horrors early on, our life together could have been saved. In David's mental breakdown, I saw what becomes of one who keeps his heart on a short lead. Yet I wasn't ready to give up on love. In fact, as my marriage crumbled, I felt more open and vulnerable than I had in years. I was humbled by Colin's courage in dealing with what was an untenable beginning to a relationship. He was sturdy and reliable at the time I felt the most unsure. The least I could do was see if my hunch about him was correct.

I punched in his number.

"Hey," he said, "I've been worried about you. Can you meet us for a quick bite?"

"Us?" I asked tentatively.

"My beautiful, lovely daughters," Colin said. "Meet us at Twenty-third and Lovejoy. Santa Fe—the taco joint. See you there in half an hour."

I hesitated and then whispered the mantra that helped me through so many of the decisions I made during the first few months with Colin. "Stay open." The phrase struck me then as it does now—oddly simple and profoundly powerful. I replaced my T-shirt with a long-sleeved sweater and ran a brush through my hair.

Colin introduced me as a friend. His girls were largely oblivious to me as they doted on their dad. One tied pigtails in the top of his hair. The other sat on his lap. The oldest, Charlotte, was eight. She had her dad's beautiful blue eyes and dark brown curly hair.

The youngest, Olivia, was a tiny, lithe, blonde five-year-old, smiling sheepishly from her dad's lap while she took bites of a bean and cheese burrito. He was patient, cutting Olivia's food into tiny bites for her and filling the guacamole cup three times.

I mostly listened to them talk about school and their teachers. I looked for any clues they might be irreversibly scarred from divorce. Nothing out of the ordinary. They had big appetites, reminding me to pick up more groceries for Sophie and all the relatives staying at my house.

Colin held the girls' hands as we crossed the street for gelato. The girls sat at the ice cream bar while we talked at a table nearby.

"It's really good to see you," he said. "How are you holding up?"

I wanted to bury myself in his shoulder and surrender all my worries to him. Instead, I faked a smile.

"It's good to see you, too," I said, telling the truth. It was good to see him. Just being here with him made me calmer, more centered. "I'm doing okay, I think. The bureaucracy is unbelievable. We don't know when David will get into a treatment facility, and we can't really move forward until the county tells us where to go." I bit the inside of my mouth. I didn't want to worry him, but I also didn't want to hide something so important. "They never found the gun."

Colin interrupted, "They don't know where the gun is? You mean, he could go back up there and get it?" His eyes were concerned, his brows narrowed. Colin, I knew by now, was not a man prone to dramatics. "Do they think he hid it, or dropped it, or what?"

I knew what he was thinking—that David could escape and hurt me, or Sophie. Even Colin or his daughters.

"I don't know, but we're doing everything we can to find out," I said, underscoring the need for concern. "His girlfriend is looking for the gun. But she's on twenty-five acres up there; it's not like carefully manicured trails or anything. It is deep brush and trees. It could be anywhere."

"Wow," he sighed. "This is unreal, isn't it? I don't know how you're doing it, Sheila." He held my hand across the table. I suppressed the anxiety and fear and put on a brave smile.

"Would you consider staying with me?" he asked. "Just until we know you're safe."

"No, thanks," I said. "I'll be fine. Really, we'll be okay."

The girls turned from the bar with gelato mustaches and smiles on their faces. "We're done, Daddy," Olivia said. "Can we go?"

Colin threw me a conflicted glance, his fingers lingering around my hand. I squeezed his hand back, careful not to show how frightened I'd really become. Colin cleared the gelato cups from the bar, tipped the waitress generously, and then carefully folded a paper napkin before he dabbed the gelato mustaches from his daughters' lips. "There you go," he said gently. Seeing that familiar gesture of affection and caring, one I'd seen so many times when David dabbed Sophie's upper lip, made me shudder.

"I really want you to stay in touch with me," Colin said. "Okay?" I nodded, grateful, but wondered whether I was complicating my life rather than straightening it out. I watched out the window as they headed to the sidewalk. Colin instinctively reached down to grab his girls' hands before reaching the intersection.

David was transferred to a psychiatric care facility two days after his suicide attempt. Robert Stellar, the caseworker, had obviously pulled strings to get David to a facility so quickly, and one that was so close to my work. He called me whenever there was a new piece of information, anything for me to hang on to. David would be transferred while I was at work. His sister could stay with him during the transition. I could visit when I got off. I signed off wondering if listeners had any idea how much stress I was under, whether my voice sounded broken and scared, or whether the years of training really could mask my anxiety.

I parked in a space in front of the hospital. Outside, three young skateboarders dressed in baggy shorts and T-shirts loitered around the entrance, skating, stopping, starting over. There were good stairs, handrails, and smooth cement here: *A skater's paradise,* I thought to myself. The worlds outside and inside a hospital could not be more different.

The receptionist gave me directions to the psychiatric center. It took up one wing of Good Samaritan hospital. Robert had prepared me on the phone for what I'd encounter once I got to the psychiatric center: A small box on the wall with a button. You push it, and the people inside look at you through a camera to determine if you are safe. Two sets of heavily locked doors open. Then you surrender your purse, your shoes, and your belt. Only then can you see the patient.

The communal room was bare of windows, no pictures, no art anywhere. (Glass is considered dangerous.) Four tables were set up on one side of the room leading to a kitchen. There were small seating areas for families to visit, the kind of furniture you see in group homes that haven't been updated in a decade. The room was full of the stink of Brussels sprouts just cooked, the clank of people cleaning up from dinner.

The muted, bland colors on the couches would make anyone depressed. A couple of families sat with patients—you could tell which ones were the patients because they were dressed in cotton scrubs. One man shuffled past, disoriented and mumbling. He took tiny steps, a couple of inches at a time, as if he were recovering from a stroke.

My throat tightened. I couldn't swallow. What kind of place was this? How could someone possibly get better here? The lighting was horrible, artificial, dim. The staffers sat behind heavy shatter-proof glass laced with wire. They were completely walled off from the patients. After they'd taken my purse, no one had even attempted to show me where to go, or let me see David's bedroom, or even tell him I was here. My palms were sweating.

*Breathe, breathe, and breathe*, I told myself.

A young woman, who looked like she weighed about eighty-five pounds, eyed me from the corner. She was curled in a fetal position, her mouth slack-jawed when she looked my way. The scrubs hung on her emaciated body, and her feet showed bones covered by thin, dry skin. She growled as I walked past.

I looked to the other side of the room: there was David rounding the bend. He was completely shaven again and clean, cleaner than I'd seen him in months. His wrists were bandaged, but his arms were still tan from gardening. He stood across from me awkwardly, as if we were strangers meeting in an airport. He swallowed. His mouth sounded dry.

He wore blue scrubs with black slippers and a plastic tie around his waist that replaced his leather belt. "Yeah, I've always wanted to be an MD," he said with his hands turned up, showing off the outfit.

I laughed, confused. I hadn't expected this. Could David be better already? His eyes were clear again. He wasn't shaking. It was as if he'd come up from a long slumber and looked and felt better. His hair was combed back, and even though he was thin, he looked like he might survive.

He led me to a furniture grouping, four chairs divided by a low table. He sat, clasped his hands between his knees, and hung his head.

"How are you feeling?" I asked.

"I don't know anymore."

"Have you seen a doctor here?"

"Not yet." He shook his head. "Sometime tomorrow afternoon."

I wondered what he would do until then, in this bare and dismal place. He hated to sit still; it made him antsy and nervous. He was used to handling a dozen jobs, flying around in his truck, juggling two cell phones and the demands of clients. Hospitals are always boring, but this was even more so. There were no books or magazines and no recreation room. There appeared to be *nothing* for him to do here. This place looked like *One Flew Over the Cuckoo's Nest*, only smaller.

"Is that for the kids?" I asked, noticing a table in the corner set up with crayons and coloring books.

"That's for us." He raised his eyebrows. "They invited me to color this afternoon."

Tears filled my eyes. I remembered my friend Claudine telling me once how she'd never asked a question David didn't know the answer to. Whether it was politics or religion or history or mathematical theory, David was a walking encyclopedia. Full of stories. Full of life.

"This won't work," I said, unable to control my tears. "This place is horrible, David. You are not as sick as these people, David. We have got to get you out of here." I was protecting myself again. Denial.

He grabbed my arm across the table and looked me straight in the eye. "I am these people," he said. "This is where I belong."

"No, no, you aren't!" I objected. "David, you are not doing a shuffle and talking to the sky. You are not so emaciated you can't think. Well, you are skinny, but you are not . . ." I broke down crying. "You are not *as sick as they are.*"

David had always been different—and I'd finally accepted that he was mentally ill, but the full impact of what that meant was now making its way into my consciousness blow by blow.

David kept his voice measured and low. "Yes, I am," he said. "I am, Sheila."

I rambled, desperate to reframe his story: "You do not know that, David! You just lost your dad; we're going through a really terrible time, you and me. But that doesn't mean you can't get over this. With medication and rest, you can repair yourself, David. But not here, not here."

He sighed, suddenly looking tired again. It was as if I'd caught him at his best for a few moments, and now that person was gone, replaced by someone who needed to go back to bed. I tried to reach him the one way I knew I always could.

"Sophie misses you, David," I said. "She misses you so much."

"Ah, the Sophster," he said, as if he were being reminded of an old friend. "How is she?"

"She doesn't understand, of course. But she needs you, David; she needs you home."

"Yes." Suddenly he stood, even though I was nowhere near finished talking. He clearly was. "Please give her my love."

Then he shook my hand. We might have been complete strangers.

"Thanks for coming," he said politely, and then he turned and walked into a bedroom several feet away.

I followed him. I couldn't just walk away without reaching him, without telling him that I'd help him to get better, that Sophie would, too. That we'd find a way to make him healthy and whole again. But could we?

The room was bare—there were no windows. It was the size of a prison cell. There was a bed and a chest of drawers. He lay down facing the wall.

"I'm really tired," he said, without turning over. "Maybe you could come back another time."

I sighed, tension building in my throat. I was the imposter in a world he'd already accepted as his own. Did he know something about the interior of his mind that I didn't? Had he really left the world—my world, Sophie's world—so far behind?

"Okay, David," I said, patting his arm. "Okay, I'll see you tomorrow."

I wandered through the room back to the security area and knocked on the window. A couple of people behind the desk talked to one another. I knocked again. The dark-haired woman looked up, annoyed, and then continued her conversation with another nurse.

I knocked a third time, annoyed. Being a nurse in a psych ward had to be tough, but these two nurses were taking complacency to a whole new level.

"Are you leaving now?" she asked, looking up from her conversation.

"I'd like to talk to David's doctor first, if that's okay."

She looked at a book below her. "David? What's his full name?" she said.

"David, David Krol."

"How do you spell that?"

I sighed. Of course they don't know who their patients are. Of course they don't know who the patients' doctors are. This was a high-priced holding cell for people hell-bent on killing themselves. My blood pressure rose. My chest rose and fell quickly.

"How many clients do you have here tonight?" I said.

"Twelve," she replied.

"Then would it be possible to learn their names?" I asked. "They have names, you know. They are hurting out there. And here you all are locked behind your glass cages. David has been here since nine o'clock this morning and hasn't seen a doctor? What am I paying for, anyway? Imagine him in the emergency room for nine hours without seeing a doctor!" They were underpaid and overworked, I knew. But they had stopped caring, letting the system turn them into cogs, to the point at which they were hurting, not helping, their patients.

The woman straightened her back. "The doctor will be on tomorrow," she snapped. "If you want to come back during business hours, you are welcome to talk to her then."

She clicked the glass door closed. The other nurse came around with my purse.

"Visiting hours are over," she said, coldly. I suddenly realized the fatal error I'd made. In showing how angry I was over what I realized was inept and callous care, I made the staff my enemies when I needed them most. But I was too tired to try to fix my mistake, and I walked quietly out the door, hearing it shut with a firm swing behind me.

## INVOLUNTARY HOSPITALIZATION

When a loved one needs immediate psychiatric intervention or help, but they don't agree with that decision, caregivers may come up against the issue of involuntary commitment, also known as civil commitment. Involuntary commitment occurs when a judge decides that a person is mentally ill and mandates treatment, which can include psychiatric hospitalization. If a loved one resists outpatient care and cannot agree upon a plan for his or her safety, sometimes involuntary commitment may be necessary; David's second suicide attempt triggered an involuntary commitment.

Dr. Xavier Amador, Ph.D., has devoted his life and his practice to understanding mental illness. He has a brother with schizophrenia and knows the trauma of mental illness firsthand. Amador's book *I Am Not Sick, I Don't Need Help!* outlines techniques to prevent involuntary commitments for people with psychiatric disorders. Among those techniques is a four-step process for creating a treatment agreement that keeps the patient out of the emergency room and out of an unwanted court-ordered hospitalization:

1. Listen.
2. Empathize.
3. Agree.
4. Partner.

"Finding common ground with a person with mental illness can be very difficult. She doesn't think she needs medication or therapy. You think she does." Amador says that common ground can exist even between the most entrenched oppositions. When faced with the frustration of trying to convince your loved one to get help, remember, "the enemy is brain dysfunction, not the person."

Amador says there is no universal checklist you can use to tell you when you should call for help. However, there are certain circumstances that always warrant commitment. When someone is obviously about to hurt himself or endanger someone else, the imminent danger of harm signals the need to call in outside help. In fact, this is the most common legal standard for committing someone, against his or her will, to a hospital.

Then, there are three ways to seek a commitment for a loved one: go together to an ER, call your local crisis team, or call your local police. Many police departments and psychiatric emergency rooms work in partnership to keep mentally ill people who commit minor offenses out of jail.

# Chapter Sixteen

The next morning, as on so many of these recent mornings, I dropped Sophie at school and drove home in a fog. My blood sugar felt perpetually low, my body heavy with fatigue, dulled to the piles of work all around me. The dogs were hungry; at least I could feed them. I pulled the huge bag of dog food from the bin, and it felt like it was going to overwhelm my body, crush me underneath it.

I sat in front of the bin and let grief wash over me. I forced myself to crawl to the hand-woven carpet David had given me for my birthday four years earlier, and I let myself lie down.

He'd bought the rug when we were in Costa Rica, and he tromped all through the streets with that thing lugged over his shoulder. We couldn't locate a place to mail it, so he carried it everywhere, into little shops, to the beach, back to the hotel. We finally found a place to ship it home. It probably cost us more than if we'd bought it in the States. He was so headstrong in everything he did.

That reminded me of Jody, the divorce attorney. The divorce had been the last thing on my mind that week, but now I sat up and considered my list of "Crucial Things to Do." Jody had told me to find a copy of David's company charter. I dragged myself up from the carpet and willed myself upstairs. David's office was on the top floor of the house, where the heat rose, and I stayed out of his space as much as I could. I couldn't think straight with all his crazy piles, piles, and more piles. He never threw anything away. Sometimes, I'd find files that were fifteen years old, dated back to when he first started building.

"David," I'd say. "Let it go."

He'd shake his head. "Nope, not yet."

His drafting board had a half an inch of dust on it; the first time I saw him standing at that board, I realized I'd fallen in love with him. I'd surprised him at his home, but he hadn't heard me come in. I climbed the stairs to his office to find his back to me, deep in concentration, puzzling over a set of plans on his drawing board. He stood back from the plans, and then moved forward, interacting with the design as if he were an artist and it was his painting.

On that day, which now seemed like another lifetime ago, the window had been open to a view of the elementary school across the street. Sounds of children wafted into the room. He wore a white button-down cotton shirt with the sleeves rolled up, and his hair was typical, mussed, thick dark brown.

He turned to see me and didn't jump or even act surprised. He put his drafting pencil behind his ear before he reached around to kiss me. I thought he was the one person I knew best, that the normal walls and barriers between human beings wouldn't be there for us. He was different, yes. But I understood him. And I loved him so much.

Now, a decade later, I opened drawer after drawer of his chaos. I couldn't find anything in this mess. In hindsight, I knew the disorganization was a symptom of the illness. I pulled open the bottom two drawers of his desk. Inside were dozens of white envelopes with his name on them. Strangely, they were unopened. I looked at the return addresses—Multnomah County Court, Clackamas County Court, Yamhill County Court.

Bills? Lawsuits? Worse?

My heart beat as if it were hooked to an electrical prod. I forced myself to focus on my breath, right now. I asked myself to survive the moment, just this one, and I'd never ask for anything again.

I tore into the envelopes, ripping them open one after another. At first, I thought they were misprints—how could David owe so much and not mention it to me? Clackamas County Court claimed he owed $2,600 for failing to appear in court for a ticket. Multnomah County wanted him on a $1,200 violation that had been ignored for eighteen months. How did I miss this going on? I ripped another envelope, and my index finger started to bleed. I opened letter after letter without stopping to find a bandage, leaving bright red stains on notice after notice about his seriously delinquent debt. One of the notices, from a roofing contractor, had both of our names on it.

How dare David hide these from me, hide my responsibility, take my good name from me! David had always retrieved the mail first since he worked at home. I thought it was polite that he sorted my mail from his and left mine in the foyer. I ripped open more envelopes. There was a warrant for his arrest. Jesus. My heart was going to explode. I'd never had a panic attack before. It was as if a stranger had entered my home and forced himself on me. I ran from his office to the garage, where he kept another old filing cabinet. I pulled open the top drawer and dozens more unopened envelopes fell out. This time there were thirty or forty. The second drawer wouldn't budge; when I finally yanked it hard enough, dozens more envelopes fell onto the floor. The third drawer was also stacked full. I couldn't swallow. I was covered in sweat.

The extent of his deceit now hit me hard, took the wind from my lungs. His business was tens of thousands, maybe hundreds of thousands of dollars in debt. I couldn't breathe; I couldn't get my breath under control. I threw the envelopes in a pile and cried. Some of the dates on the envelopes were three years old, a timeline to the worsening of David's illness.

Now that day in the swimming pool last summer took on new significance. David probably had several bill collectors like the greasy-haired man with the gray suit and scuffed shoes. Our independent way of living had protected his secret. We had separate bank accounts, separate phone lines, separate lives. I had made sure the mortgage, the utilities, and Sophie's school tuition were paid on time. I had trusted that David knew what he was doing with his business, that the juggle of construction credits and debits, although highly precarious, would work out in his favor.

The first time he asked for financial help with his business, I ignored my own internal warning system and bought his excuse that it was just a "bridge loan," money he'd use just until his punch lists were complete and his many clients paid. A hundred thousand dollars was a lot of money. It meant taking out a second mortgage on the house. But I loaned David the money. The debt was in my name.

## NEW BREAKTHROUGHS IN THE UNDERSTANDING OF PSYCHOSIS

At the University of Maryland, Dr. Robert Buchanan is testing anti-inflammatory action in schizophrenic patients using a combination of aspirin, omega 3 fatty acids, and fluvastatin. The trial is being conducted to determine whether psychosis might be caused by inflammation in the brain.

Researchers reporting in the journal *Biological Psychiatry* have observed the role inflammation plays in the onset of psychosis. Dr. Tyrone Cannon says, "Inflammation is increasingly recognized as a contributing factor to the emergence of progression of disease in every organ in the body." In people who develop psychosis, markers of proinflammatory cytokines, or substance secreted by certain cells of the immune system, may predict the rate of gray matter loss among the individuals who convert to psychosis. The research suggests that activation of microglia, a type of cell that acts as the first form of active immune defense, is involved in tissue loss.

Neuro-inflammation may tip people over from an at-risk state into psychosis. The authors of a 2010 review of the literature suggested "it has been established that pro-inflammatory cytokines induce not only symptoms of sickness, but also true major depressive disorders in physically ill patients with no previous history of mental disorders." There is even some evidence for a connection between inflammation and depression-related suicidality. Researchers don't yet understand precisely how inflammation could lead to depression, but they are testing anti-inflammatory strategies in the hope of finding one or more that works.

A study reported in March 2015 linked psychosis in bipolar disorder to a gene variant associated with higher levels of a protein thought to play a role in cognition and psychosis. The protein is found at high levels in the brains of people suffering from infections. Scientists hope to develop anti-inflammatory drugs that can safely cross from the bloodstream into the brain and affect the pathways beneficially.

# Chapter Seventeen

The radio station where I worked was in a relatively plain, older building and had been there for forty years. The station was a ratings blockbuster, with awards lining the hallways: best program director, best morning show, best reporting, best everything. You wouldn't have known it by the look of the place.

A peace sign still hung above the receptionist's desk. Every cubicle was littered with something irreverent or funny—off-color bumper stickers, photos with rock stars, recent articles clipped from *Spin* or *Rolling Stone* or *Paste* magazine. My cohost saw me walk in and said, "Welcome, mein Freund." I'd managed to juggle David's two weeks of hospitalization without missing more than a couple of days of work. But I had the foreboding sense that I would need more time off in the future.

I gave him a huge hug. He put his hands on my shoulders and squinted at me. "You okay?" he asked, tilting his head to one side.

"Nope," I said, "but let's pretend I am."

We entered the studio together, a room filled with thousands of CDs, even though we ran the music off a computer hard drive. My cohost sat on one side of the studio; my desk and computer were on the other. We spoke with eye contact and hand signals, and it all sounded like two friends sitting down for an afternoon chat.

"We're on in five," he said, smiling, holding up all five fingers on his wedding band hand. No wonder his wife adored him.

The schedule, or "clock" as we referred to it, kept us on track. At the top of the hour, news and information. Then music. Commercial break. More music. More talk. The news. "Here are a few of the stories we're keeping an eye on for you—on Wall Street . . ."

I finished the five-minute newscast, conscious of two clocks, the station's and mine. I'd been piecing my life back together in off-air time, the five- to seven-minute intervals when I could call David at the hospital, or pay bills, or deal with the question of where Sophie and I might eventually live after the divorce.

"I'll be back in four minutes!" I said, and then I ran next door to my production office, where I interviewed authors, artists, and politicians.

I punched in the number for James McCall, one of David's oldest friends in Portland and one of Portland's most brilliant defense lawyers. He wasn't the ambulance-chasing type; he took big cases against corporations or government when people were harmed.

He'd know what I should do.

"Hey, Jim," I said, taken aback by the energy in my voice. I'd slept so little lately, but adrenalin and fear are powerful drugs.

"Sheila!" He always sounded so cheery when we met, as if the weight of his clients' problems never permeated his optimism.

"How's the Hermiston case going?" I asked. Most recently, he'd been representing twelve workers from the Army's chemical depot near Hermiston, Oregon, who were allegedly injured during a chemical leak. He hadn't taken a penny and wouldn't unless the government compensated the men for the injuries to their respiratory systems.

"Let's just say they have the best attorney in town," Jim said with a smile in his voice. "Hey, I'm so sorry to hear about David. My ex seems to get all the news before I do. I'd like to go see him, if it's possible."

"Sure thing, Jim. He'd like that." I was conscious of the clock counting down the minutes until my next on air-break. "I'm at work, so I have to make this quick. David is in trouble, Jim. I found hundreds of unpaid bills he's stuffed away. I don't know how far the trouble reaches. And I don't know if it involves me. I need someone who can help me get to the bottom of this."

Jim paused, then exhaled loudly. "Well, this is tricky. I'm David's attorney, or at least I was in the past. So I must advocate for him. But I understand your dilemma. You need to get a power of attorney from David so that you can understand what you're up against."

"It looks mostly like company debt."

"Are you an officer of his company?"

"No."

"Do you have check-writing ability, or have you ever taken a loan from the company?"

"No." I looked through the window at my cohost holding up three fingers. Three minutes to air. "I've loaned David money, but I've never taken a loan."

"I'll draw up some papers and meet you at the hospital after work."

Two minutes. I talked as I walked back into the on-air studio. "Jim," I said, "I can't thank you enough."

"You take care of yourself, okay, kid, and that beautiful daughter of yours." I wanted to stop, to acknowledge his caring and compassion. Instead, I offered a harried, "Thanks, Jim. A million ways, thanks."

I punched in the phone numbers for Jody Stahancyk, the divorce attorney. Her secretary answered. "May I speak with Ms. Stahancyk?" I asked quickly, looking at the clock.

"She's away from the office. May I take a message?"

"Please tell her to call Sheila Hamilton. It's urgent."

I sprinted to my seat and put my headphones over my ears. The clock ticked, and the red light went on. "There's some new science on coffee—now it's good for you!" I made it through the rest of the stories: A local hospital received a major donation. Two pit bulls were euthanized for attacks against humans. I introduced the sound clip for an interview with Robert Plant, the former lead singer of Led Zeppelin, and then we wrapped it all up with information about his new tour with a group of young musicians.

I took off my headphones and let out a big sigh. "Whew," I said. "*That* was close."

My cohost pulled one headphone off his ear and kept his fingers on the board. "Sheila," he said smiling, "you're a pro."

"At some things," I said. "And at others . . ." I made an "L" with my thumb and pointer finger and put it to my forehead.

He laughed a hearty laugh, his earring catching light as his head shook.

Jody Stahancyk had one of her younger attorneys call me back. I briefly told him the story of David's hospitalization, the enormous debt I'd uncovered, the guilt of asking him to sign the divorce papers now that he was in lockdown.

The attorney sat quietly on the other end of the phone and then spoke in measured tones. "If you are still married, you will be responsible for his personal debts. And it will be very difficult, given the circumstances, to get a judge to grant a divorce now that he's been institutionalized."

So two of us were on lockdown now.

I thanked him for his time and told him I would be in touch.

When I returned to the hospital, the mental health visiting area was busier than I'd ever seen it. Alice was sitting with David, as was Jim McCall. Alice was wearing a gray wool dress with red ballerina flats and a red scarf around her neck. She smiled faintly when she saw me.

Jim was talking with David in soft tones about how to start sorting out his business trouble. Jim, always the gentleman, stood when he saw me. "How are you doing?" he asked, shaking my hand.

"I'm okay, thanks, Jim." I turned to David's mother. "Hi, Alice. Hello, David." It was an awkward, formal moment, reminiscent of how couples must feel in the lawyer's office before they divorce, trying desperately to be polite and functional while their worlds fall apart.

Jim had stacked the legal documents in the middle of the coffee table that separated the chairs. "Shall we begin?" he asked the group.

David turned to Alice. "Mommy, what do you think?"

I was stunned. I had never heard him refer to his mother as "Mommy." I had never heard his voice so soft, or so lacking in authority. I wanted to stop the meeting right then and ask him what drugs he was on, or what had happened to destroy his confidence. Where was the strong, opinionated, brilliant man I had married? Where was the voice that would boom through the house when he called for Sophie or me? I bit my tongue as acid rose up in my stomach.

Alice nodded decisively. "I think we need to get a clearer picture of everything, David."

His face looked soft and more rounded, like a child's. The tremor that had affected his leg and hand seemed to be under control today, but he looked stressed by the number of people, the attention, and the decisions before him. He was still painfully thin for his size, even though the nurses reported that he was eating again. Was it the drugs or the illness robbing him of his manhood? I had heard about people who become mentally ill reverting back to childhood. If I hadn't seen it myself, I would never have believed it was true.

It was only in the reading of David's medical records that I later learned how far he had fallen: "It is imperative that this man be kept in a safe situation until he gets enough relief from the psychotic depression. He has annihilistic delusions, believing that his mind is gone, cannot be recovered, and that things will only get worse for him. He feels an overwhelming unilateral guilt in the loss of his marriage and business. In my interview with him, it became clear that he is so convinced of this that from his perspective it would not make any sense to go on living much longer. He cannot even decide whether his daughter would be better off with him or without him."

Jim knew I was the person who would be responsible for David's personal debts. He outlined the process. "This will be a temporary measure, David. We'll give Sheila the authority to make decisions for you and look after your financial affairs for a period of three months. That should give us a better idea of what we need to do next. Are you sure you are okay with this?"

David nodded yes. He didn't look at me before he signed the document. His signature looked exactly as it had a decade or so earlier when he'd signed our marriage contract—all loopy and slanted heavily to the right. The nurses from behind the glass wall shot me their customary dirty looks. David handed me the papers and said, "I'm so sorry for doing this to you. To you and Sophie."

I swallowed before I spoke. He was so vulnerable here. "We'll work it out, David. We'll take care of everything."

Jim sensed his intrusion and excused himself briefly to the table nearby. Alice excused herself to the restroom. "David," I asked, "why couldn't you tell me your company was in trouble?"

"I thought you'd think I was stupid." He lowered his gaze to the floor.

"But what about your accountant, your taxes?"

"There are a lot of people who owe me money. I just couldn't ask. I couldn't ask for payment."

"What? What do you mean? There are people who owe you money? For how many jobs?"

"I don't know, six or seven." He motioned for a pen and the pad of paper I held. "These are the names. Some of the jobs are nearly finished. Others have been done for a long time but the clients want some minor changes. I just lost track of it all, Sheila. I'm sorry. I feel like a fool."

I was beginning to understand the depth of his illness in terms that now tied David's past to the present. I thought of the story his mother had told me in the kitchen when we first met, how his paper route had turned sour when he became too paralyzed to collect money from his clients. I put my fingers over my mouth, pressing against the sadness welling up inside me. David squirmed on the couch, looking like a kid forced to stay after school. His left leg bounced up and down.

"Do you think I'll ever get out of here?" he asked.

"Of course you will, David. You'll stay for a couple of weeks, maybe. Then we'll move you back home, and you can rebuild your life."

"I just can't see it, you know?" He searched my eyes to make sure I understood. "I just can't see being the guy who picks up Sophie from another person's house. I don't want to do it. I can't."

Jim must have sensed David's agitation. "Everything okay over there?" he asked. David nodded yes.

"You know what's weird?" he said, turning back to me. "They have this manual, this huge physician's manual that talks about all these different psychiatric illnesses. One of the aides here let me read it when I finished the books everyone has brought me."

He leaned forward in his chair as if he were sharing a secret. His eyes widened, and he spoke in low tones. "I'm bipolar. It's true. It's like, check, check, check. Even the strange things I think I'm smelling." He made a sign with his hand as if he was counting off the warning signs that applied to him.

It was the first time I had heard anyone mention a diagnosis. My spine stiffened, and I felt my jaw drop.

"Is that what they say, David? Is that the diagnosis?"

He nodded.

No wonder David felt so paralyzed he couldn't bill the clients who owed him money. No wonder he couldn't sleep, couldn't eat. No wonder he had huge variations in his weight and his energy. People with bipolar II disorder are often highly prone to lying. They experience irritability and anxiety instead of the joyous, manic high associated with bipolar I. They also suffer from maddening swings in energy and focus. They are highly sexualized, and infidelity is common. All the signs were there.

My temples began to throb. A wave of pity and longing for the man he used to be washed over me. I stroked the top of his head and kissed him on the cheek.

"David," I said, "we'll all be here for you, no matter what happens." It was as if a small lens I'd used to view him had suddenly opened wide, and finally, the big picture was in view.

David stood up and shook my hand, as he had the last time. "Goodbye for now," he said, walking toward his mother.

I swallowed hard and tried to compose myself. Jim sat down next to me.

"You're going to need to be tougher than all of us put together." He patted my hand.

"I don't know, Jim," I said, "I don't know if I have it in me."

Later that day, I took the legal papers to David's bank and asked for a printout of all the deposits he'd made in the last six months, all the checks he'd written, and the balance left in his business account. The woman behind the counter looked at the power of attorney document, her eyebrows penciled in and pinched.

She made several long phone calls before she finally pushed a slip of paper under the glass and reported the account balances. Ten thousand dollars remaining—not enough to make a ding in any of his debt.

I remembered attorney Jody Stahancyk's admonition: "Your ignorance may have saved you, but, on the other hand, if he's rung up personal debt, you're on the hook." I raced to the car and called David's accountant.

"Did you know anything about this?" I asked him.

"I had a feeling things were way out of control," he said, Hendrix music blasting in the background.

"Why?"

"Because he hasn't paid me either."

David's mother, his sister, and a friend of theirs were sitting in my living room when I got home. I poked my head in on Sophie. She was listening to her iPod in her room. "Hi, love, how are you?" I asked.

She threw her arms around me, and I could hear the music too loud from the earbuds. Things had settled between us since the scene in the car. "I'm okay, Mama," she smiled. "How are you?"

My heart melted when she called me "Mama." There's something so profoundly personal about that term of endearment. "I'm good, too, sweetheart. Just fine—better now that I see you."

I smothered her head with kisses. "Hey, turn the tunes down a notch, would you?" She rolled her eyes, smiling. If she worried about David every day, every moment as I did, it did not show.

I settled in the living room with Alice and Adele. "I'm in real trouble," I said. "It looks like a large portion of David's debt, his taxes, his county debts, will fall to me and Sophie. I know you want David to be able to stay in the house, but I don't know whether he can afford it. And I don't know where Sophie and I would go, either."

I loved this house, this kitchen, the place we had finally settled into as home. The thought of leaving it now, unsettling Sophie when things were so chaotic, packing her clothes and stuffed animals and moving to a tiny apartment, all seemed incomprehensible. The last few weeks had taken my spirit. I bit my lip to stop it from trembling.

Alice avoided the topic. There was a chicken in the oven, which she must have cooked. The aroma wafted through the air, a mix of rich olive oil, herbs, and sea salt. "What do you say we eat something? You must be starved."

Her denial never waned.

I stayed up reading with Sophie and then tucked her in. "Is he going to be okay?" Sophie asked. I knew from her tone she was not talking about Harry Potter.

"I hope so, baby. We're doing everything we can for him." I kissed her on the forehead, and she turned over, as she did every night, so that I could scratch her back. Her tiny waist and long torso looked so much like David's sisters, all beautiful women.

Their emotional struggles hadn't meant much to me before David's illness; every woman suffers from a bout of sadness and anxiety now and then. But now, I obsessed over his family's propensity for depression and mental illness.

I had more of the story than Alice knew. Adele had given me the complete history. David had been sent away to boarding school in England at the age of ten, a year in which he was brutalized by the other students. He returned home to attend school at a Boston prep school as his father studied at Harvard Business School. The transitions were hard on him; he'd made few friends since the kids at both schools had been together for an extern long time, and David was an outsider.

Although David always did well academically, and his test scores were off the charts, he was kicked out of school because he quit going to class. Next came another boarding school, another difficult transition. David was finally kicked out of the house at sixteen. Michael's sister Adele says her father suffered from erratic mood swings and David was often the target of his anger.

But Alice never let on about any of this, not to me. She never shared the details of David's upbringing that I would later realize were central to his feelings of abandonment. There was so much unsaid about their family's pain—no mention of Lew's erratic behavior or his affair with a family friend, no mention of both parents kicking David out of the house at sixteen. They were a family good at keeping secrets.

His father, prone to shutting himself off in his bedroom during our visits, had given up a lucrative career and a Harvard education at the age of forty-three. He never worked for another person again, instead buying, remodeling, and then selling houses to keep his family afloat between sporadic moves around the world. Adele would later tell David's psychiatrists she was convinced Lew was bipolar, and that her mother suffered from depressive episodes. Adele's mother, however, would never accept the designation of a psychiatric disorder. She was deeply skeptical of the profession and refused to categorize her loved ones' suffering as mental illness.

Watching Sophie sleep, I knew I needed to understand everything I could about the genetic nature of bipolar disorder and the genetic risk of depression, one from his side, another from my own mother. A double whammy from two gene pools. Sophie deserved my vigilance. I kissed her on the cheek and wished her peaceful dreams. When her breath was even and deep, I went to my bedroom and opened my laptop.

Dr. Kay Redfield Jamison appeared in the search as one of the leading experts on bipolar disorder, a condition she has survived since college. She writes intimately about her condition: "About 5.7 million American adults or about 2.6 percent of the population age 18 and older in any given year have bipolar disorder. The disorder typically develops in late adolescence or early adulthood. However, some people have their first symptoms during childhood, and some develop them late in life." I drew in a breath and forced myself to continue reading. The house seemed to go completely still, and every keystroke I made sounded abnormally loud, underlying the gravity of what I was learning.

"Manic depression is far more lethal than the nomenclature suggests. Cycles of fluctuating moods and energy levels serve as a background to constantly changing thoughts, behaviors, and feelings." This is what I saw in the final weeks before David was finally admitted to the hospital: the extremes of the human experience, the breaking of every boundary I'd ever thought existed in David's personality. He had swung from psychosis to a condition that resembled retardation. It was all there in the literature.

I put my hands to my forehead and felt overwhelmed, stupid. How had I missed it? The early years with David were confusing and erratic. I chalked his behavior up to a million different things—moving, too much stress at work, too little exercise. David refused to talk with me about how he was really doing and instead blamed demanding clients, the cold, the rain, me. But in the last three years, it was all there to see. Every question about David's behavior was answered in clinical terms—his seductiveness, his reclusiveness, his frenzies, his abnormal intellect, and his creative side.

I pulled my robe tighter around me and read what I should have been told the first time David attempted to cut his wrists, the first cry for help. "Patients with depressive and manic depressive illness are far more likely to commit suicide than individuals in any other psychiatric or medical risk group. The mortality rate is higher than it is for most types of heart disease and cancer. Yet the lethality is underemphasized, a tendency traceable to the widespread belief that suicide is volitional."

The computer burbled out the time. "It's 1:00 a.m." I dug further.

One study, reported in *The New York Times*, called into question whether nature, not nurture, was the single factor making a person prone to mental illness. "The new report, by several of the prominent researchers in the field, does not imply that interactions between genes and life experiences are trivial; they are almost certainly fundamental, experts agree. But it does suggest that nailing down those factors in a precise way is far more difficult than scientists believed even a few years ago, and that the original finding could have been due to chance."

The article concluded, "The findings are likely to inflame a debate over the direction of the field itself, which has found that the genetics of illnesses like schizophrenia and bipolar disorder remain elusive."

Even if David had a genetic predisposition toward mental illness, he'd functioned, albeit with mixed results, until the strain of our divorce and the death of his father. Dr. Jamison cites the risk factors for suicide: "losing a spouse, living alone, not being married, the death of a loved one."

The stress of our divorce, the lack of sleep, and the side effects of antidepressants that should never have been prescribed created a lethal trifecta in David's body.

I propped another pillow behind my back while reading about the psychiatric topics that I would now need to thoroughly understand: depression, bipolar disorder, suicide. Suicide is now the third leading cause of death in young people in the United States, and the second for college students. The 1995 National College Health Risk Behavior Survey, conducted by the Centers for Disease Control and Prevention, found that one in ten college students had seriously considered suicide during the year prior to the survey; most of those had gone so far as to draw up a plan.

In the next room, Sophie slept. Even though I was no longer in love with David, I adored him for what he gave our daughter. I would always care for him, if allowed.

The house was quiet, except for the low hum of the furnace. Sophie dreamed, but of what? How would I ever really know her mind if I couldn't understand David's? How might his life have turned out differently if he'd allowed true intimacy, a deep connection with someone he trusted? What should I have done differently? I vowed then to teach Sophie everything I had learned and would learn about the nature of mental illness, however confusing and contrary the information seemed. She needed to understand her risk. She would not be able to do recreational drugs, or work in overly stressful jobs, without learning how to cope first. She would need my help, help I would have gladly given my husband if he'd been willing to take it.

The information gave me a sense of confidence. Now that I finally understood what I was up against, I thought I could help David in a way I hadn't been able to previously. I thought it would all work out.

## WORKING ON MENTAL HEALTH CHALLENGES TOGETHER

Organizations around the country are stepping up to support families and instigate changes to the way research is conducted on mental health. However, most data is funded and provided by pharmaceutical industries, and while this is enormously helpful, there are inevitable concerns that big pharma's top priority when conducting research and sharing data isn't necessarily the wellbeing of the consumer.

However, there is one community foundation that focuses solely on supporting research that has no commercial interest or benefit. Dr. Gina Nikkel is the CEO and president of the Foundation for Excellence in Mental Health Care, a nonprofit organization with the ambitious goal of bringing new and effective recovery practices to every community in the country. By joining the efforts of private philanthropists, public policy analysts, and top medical researchers, the organization strives to provide support and tools not just for those experiencing mental illness but also to those who treat them—psychiatrists, psychologists, and other mental-health clinicians.

Nikkel says, "The strategy is threefold: research, recovery, and program development and education. It's clear that we must pay attention to what research actually says, support a wide variety of bio-psycho-social research that is not paid for by a commercial interest group, and join together to fund programs that are trauma informed and promote recovery."

In addition to allowing donors to create their own funds, the organization engages with investment advisors to carefully choose the existing funds it supports. As many charitable organizations do, it invests widely, and seeks improvement through innovative and creative solutions from all over the world. One fund it supports is the Hearing Voices Research & Development Fund, a UK-based nonprofit that brings peer-group support to communites in the

United States. Another is the Bill Anthony General Research Fund, an educational grant focused on research into early treatment methods, better standards for evaluating children, and long-term use of antipsychotics in the treament of schizophrenia.

For more information about these organizations and others, contact the Foundation for Excellence in Mental Health Care at www.mentalhealthexcellence.org.

# Chapter Eighteen

Two more weeks passed. It was a gorgeous Indian summer day in mid-October when Colin called. "Look," he said softly. "You're going through hell. But so is Sophie. You've got to get her out of the house. The Willamette is green again."

In the rainy season, sometimes the river looked muddy brown. Sewer pipes couldn't hold all the rainwater, and sometimes they overflowed into the Willamette. But now, thanks to a lot of work, the river was relatively healthy again. "Please," Colin said. "Please come out on the boat with us."

I hesitated, wondering whether I could, or should, enjoy myself while David was locked up in such a hellhole. But Colin was right. Sophie needed the sunshine and a break from the house, and I did too. Her face lit up when I told her we had an invitation to go boating. She dressed in yellow shorts and matching flip-flops and grabbed a jacket, and we were out the door. Alice and Adele were planning on spending the rest of the day at the hospital anyway.

"I'd like you to meet a friend of mine and his kids," I told Sophie as we drove. "We can get some air."

"Okay," she said. "How old are the kids?"

"Eight and six," I said. "Girls." This brought a smile to Sophie's face.

When we got to the dock, Colin and his kids greeted us. He was dressed as casually as I'd seen him, in cargo shorts, a black T-shirt, and a baseball cap. "Girls, you remember Sheila." The girls wore shorts and flip-flops. They nodded shyly.

Sophie held out her hand, looked him straight in the eye, and said, "Nice to meet you, Colin. You the captain?"

He saluted. "At your service."

The dock was busy with trucks and boats and people trying to get in or out of the water. A heavyset man carrying an ice chest to his boat looked at the five of us together and yelled to Colin, "Man, you've got your hands full!"

Colin laughed. "How bad can it be, surrounded by beautiful women?"

The girls reluctantly donned life jackets and then chatted as we motored down the river, wind in their faces. Colin navigated the busy water conscientiously, taking wide turns away from any boats pulling skiers or where people appeared to be drinking. He stood while he steered the boat, looking backward, then forward, then to the side, occasionally shouting something to the girls. "Look at the bird's nest." Or, "Do you guys see the ducks over there?" He captained the boat to an area that wasn't quite so busy.

Sophie moved from where she was sitting and came to sit next to me. I held her hand while we watched for herons and eagles near the shore. I'd stopped at a sandwich shop on the way and had bought huge subs for each of the girls. We pulled over to a riverside dock and squeezed onto a single picnic bench to eat our snack. Sophie and Charlotte laughed about their enormous appetites. They were a year apart, of similar height and build. *People would guess they were sisters,* I thought to myself.

Olivia picked out her pickles, tomatoes, lettuce, and olives until all that was left was turkey, mustard, and bread. Seagulls picked at the pieces she discarded. The setting sun cast pink and gold reflections off the glass towers of the city; the colored lighting over the bridges illuminated the river in pinks, purples, and blues—a rainbow of light. Colin was proving himself to be a patient, loving father. He made a good living as a high-tech sales manager, but he'd passed up several opportunities for advancement because it would have required him to move away from his girls. Good priorities, as far as I was concerned.

As we drove home, Sophie turned to me, her cheeks pink from the sunshine and air, and said, "Colin and his girls are really nice."

"I think so too, love," I said, squeezing her hand.

We passed the ice cream shop where David, Sophie, and I used to sit outside on summer nights and eat big scoops on sugar cones. Sophie's eyes lingered on the Ben and Jerry's sign as we drove by. "I miss Daddy," she said. The excitement of the day dropped to a soft thud.

"Me too, Sophie. I miss him, too."

I watched her closely as she sat with her thoughts. She'd always been so reserved. Once, as a toddler, a pediatrician had told her she was "brave" because she didn't wail during a needle poke. Sophie refused to cry in doctors' offices after that. She was the kind of kid who, when trying out a new sport or activity, sat on the sidelines until she'd figured out exactly how it was supposed to be done. While other children rushed to the roller skating rink floor, falling and laughing their way to learning, Sophie quietly observed others who did it well. When she finally, gingerly skated out on the floor, she skated slowly and proficiently enough not to fall. She wore her stoicism and cautionary nature like a protective coat, never really letting on how troubled or scared she was by the terrifying events of the past few weeks.

"Soph," I said gently, "you can talk about how you feel. Please don't keep it all bottled up."

She kept her head turned, away from me, toward the light fading over the tall trees that surrounded our home. "There's nothing to talk about," she said.

Diedra, the woman who had checked David in to the ER, called me twice during his hospitalization, once to urge me to learn the location of the gun, and the second time to cry over her fractured relationship.

"I know this is ridiculous to ask of you," she sniffed between sobs, "but David refuses to see me. I've been to the hospital a half-dozen times and stood outside those terrible doors. He won't allow me in." Her voice broke in a thousand pieces. "God, I feel so stupid."

"I'll talk to him," I said. "He needs all the friends he can get."

"And Sheila," she reminded me again, "we need to find that gun."

Later that night, during visiting hours, I asked David about Diedra. "She misses you, David. She cares about you. You should at least see her."

He shook his head, no.

"And she says she still hasn't found that gun. Do you have any idea where it might be?" I asked.

He kept his head down. "Look, I was drunk. Out of it. I dropped it in the darkness. If she can't find it, it's probably gone for good."

Sophie called David daily. Inevitably another patient would answer the ward phone and then wander around from room to room until he or she found the lucky phone-call recipient. Sophie took great delight in guessing how long it would be before someone found him. "Three minutes and counting, Mom."

She'd settle into his big chair for what she hoped was a long conversation with her dad, her feet curled underneath her, hope in her eyes and the tone of her voice. "Can I come see you?" she'd ask. Her face dissolved into disappointment night after night.

"Maybe tomorrow," he'd say. Then, "No, I'm tired, tomorrow." After several weeks had passed, the doctors thought he was finally ready.

"Bring her with you when you come tonight," David had told me. "I can't wait to see her."

Sophie showered, put on her favorite white skirt and yellow top, and brushed her blonde hair until it shone. She was standing in front of the mirror when I found her, looking like a young girl headed on a trip to another part of the world. She stood straight and strong, but her gaze at herself was critical, questioning. "You are beautiful," I said.

She glanced down at her plastic watch. "Do you think he'll remember me?"

I wrapped my arms around her slender shoulders and looked at her in the mirror. "Of course, he'll remember you, sweetheart. He loves you so, so much."

She looked hesitant, then sure. "Okay, let's go then." I explained everything to her just as Robert Stellar had explained it to me. The doors, the glass walls, the drab colors. I thought she was ready.

Her confidence faded when we came to the locked metal doors in the hospital. She glanced from the security camera, to me, to the elevator doors. I grabbed her hand, fearing she might run back to the car. The sound of the nurses unlocking the doors startled her, and she shivered. I'd arranged with David's social workers for her to go through a side door, so the nurses wouldn't open her purse, and so she wouldn't see the security guards in their glassed-in office.

I held her hand as we walked around the corner to the visiting area we'd adopted as David's. When she saw him, she lit up, running toward him as he walked toward us in blue scrubs. She flew into his arms, smothering him in kisses. "Sweetie," he said, sounding just like himself again.

"Daddy!" she said. "I missed you soooooo much." She exaggerated the kisses on his cheeks, his arms, and his head. David held her steadily; he didn't appear nearly as weak as when I last saw him.

"Hey," I said. "You look really good."

"I feel better," he said. "Thanks."

For the first time since his hospitalization, I thought maybe the doctors had finally found a drug cocktail that worked.

Sophie pulled him to the couch and sat on his lap. "So what do you do here, Dad? Are you going crazy without your cell phone?"

I winced at the word "crazy." It didn't faze either of them.

"Well, I read," he said. "And I color."

"What?" Sophie protested. "You color?" She laughed. "You're too old to be coloring, Dad."

They chatted for a bit about school, Sophie's guitar, and the dogs. Slowly, I started to see David's enthusiasm dwindle as it had the first day I'd seen him. His eyes glazed over, even as Sophie sat on his lap. His arms went limp, and, after a time, he wasn't holding her at all.

Sophie looked at me, uncomfortable. "So, uh, Mom, maybe we should be going?"

I searched David's eyes for the answer. They were dead. Again.

"Yes, sweetheart, let's let Daddy get some rest."

She kissed him on the cheek and hugged him around the neck. "I love you soooooo much, Daddy. Please come home soon."

He was looking at something on the wall, something more important than this moment. He limply patted her hand on his neck. "Sugar Dugger," he said absentmindedly.

Once we were safely down the hall, down the elevator, out the door, and in the safety of the car, Sophie let herself react. She looked forward, out the windshield of the car into the darkness of another night. "He's so sad," she said quietly. "He's just so sad."

The next morning, I groggily called Ted Oster, a social worker at the psychiatric ward, the only person there who had ever returned my phone calls. "Ted," I said, "I'm not satisfied with the communication with David's psychiatrist. I've asked to talk to her several times, but whenever I'm there, she's not. She doesn't return my calls."

Ted paused and drew in a long breath. "The care team is dealing with David's family now, Sheila," he said. "Dr. Seder believes you agitate and upset David with your visits. We must advocate for the patient first. And David's family agrees."

I shook my head, disbelieving. "Wait a minute. I have stayed with this man for a decade, and now, despite it all, I am the villain?"

Ted's tone was apologetic, understanding. "I'm sorry, Sheila," he said. "Call me whenever you need. I'll update you as much as I can."

I tried to reconcile the deep hurt and anger I felt from those words. I thought his family understood my intentions, to return David safely to Sophie. Years later, David's eldest sister confided that her family was convinced I was attempting to win sole custody of Sophie. David's family had chosen to exclude me from his care team. The lack of direct communication was hurtful to me and disastrous to David's outcome. They'd obviously gone behind my back to make the decision. I hung up the phone, numb, and stumbled back into bed, desperate for sleep and relief from the pain.

I awoke to Sophie's finger on my face, softly outlining my nose, my eyebrows, and my lips. "Remember when we used to do this, Mama?" she whispered. "Will you draw my face?"

I felt like I'd opened a hotel. David's mother, his two sisters, and two of their friends were drinking wine in my living room. I had hosted company for more than a month. I was wounded by their secrecy, their misguided belief that I would hamper David's recovery. I was the person who stood by him for a decade.

Adele and I talked about it in the living room. She carefully explained that she agreed with the care team, that David really did need a break from me, not Sophie.

"I think it will be better for both of you." She said it with a tenderness that placed the decision in a context I hadn't thought of before. I could be free now. David was in good hands. Everything was under control—Adele would arrange for Sophie's visits, and she and Alice would make the decisions about David's future.

"They're drugging him like he's six hundred pounds and ten feet tall," she said. "I'm going to ask Dr. Seder for a drug holiday. There's no reason for him to walk around stoned all the time."

I nodded. Adele was right—as a psychologist, she should be in charge now. Still, I had the strange feeling of being a stunt double in a movie, watching the hard work being done by someone else. "Are you sure I shouldn't check up on him, make sure he's okay?" I asked.

"Sheila," Adele assured me, "at this point, he'll get better faster without you."

I felt a wave of something unfamiliar move across my chest and shoulders. It was relief. Yes, I felt guilty, yes, I was unsure of what would happen next, but the lightness I felt in that moment was overwhelming and real. I was free.

I tucked Sophie in bed, lying next to her and remembering the night she was born, how I refused to let the nurses take her away. I'd held her on my chest all night long, matching my breathing to her own, in awe of the life David and I had made together. It really was over for the three of us. Everything I'd tried to protect was shattered.

I lay awake, trying hard not to wake Sophie with my crying. At least being involved in David's care, I'd had some sense of control, however imaginary it might have been. Now, I was an outsider, a stranger at the psychiatric ward, a stranger in the home we'd shared together. I was oddly uneasy in my own home. I'd been keeping Colin up to date by phone on the details of the crisis unfolding. He'd reminded me to call whenever I needed to talk.

I carefully tiptoed out of Sophie's bedroom. Adele and Alice would both be there in case Sophie awoke. I washed my face and made the five-minute drive to his home, an old Episcopal church that he'd lovingly restored. The rain came down in big splats outside. I was drenched from the outside in.

"Come in, come in," he said, pulling the wet jacket from my shoulders. "Let me get you some hot tea."

The kettle whistled as I warmed my toes. Colin put it down in front of me and then leaned down and kissed me on the neck. His breath was warm, the blanket he'd given me soft and cozy. He sat down across from me. "So?"

"So where do I begin?" I asked.

"Wherever you need to, Luv."

We talked for over an hour, through two cups of tea. His long fingers held his cup loosely; nothing I said seemed to scare him off.

We talked of his life growing up in Hawaii, an upbringing that wasn't as idyllic as it sounded. "Not when most of your memories are formed at the end of a barstool." The persona of the eligible bachelor fell away as he told me how difficult it was to live in a huge house, waiting for his girls to come every other week. Colin was, like me, human and lonely.

The marble granite on his kitchen counters gleamed. His appliances didn't have a single spot on them. There wasn't a dish or a pan in sight. In any other household, this uncanny sense of order might have made me suspicious or nervous. But given what I'd been going through, Colin's sense of order calmed me and made me feel grounded. In spite of the mess I was in, I was falling in love with him.

The crisis had reopened an emotional conduit that I'd shut down for years, except to Sophie. The loneliness I felt was in the marrow, isolation so deep and painful I was desperate to have the touch of someone who really cared for me. I didn't hesitate when he invited me upstairs.

Colin led me to his bedroom, where his huge poster bed looked too pretty to mess up. The pillows were straightened as if a designer had been there moments before. "You sure you're not gay?" I joked.

"Wait until you see the shoe closet," he laughed, pulling me down beside him. He cradled me tenderly, whispering, kissing me with long loving kisses. David had refused to have sex with me when I was pregnant, a time I loved my body and its overflowing hormones. It had devastated me. Then there was his affair. It had been a long time since I'd been touched, held.

I forgave myself for needing Colin in that moment, needing him much more than he needed me. Of course, it was misguided to start a relationship in the middle of a crisis. Of course, people would talk.

I didn't care. I shut off my brain and breathed in the goodness of this new man. Colin smelled the way he had the first night I met him, like a clean start.

The week of October 20, David began calling me, panicked. "I've got to get out of here, Sheila. I'm going crazy." There was that word again, "crazy." The irony of what he'd said was lost on him. He sounded more anxiety-ridden than ever—I could imagine him pacing the drab hallways in his blue scrubs, worried that a mental hospital would be his home forever.

"We'll get you out," I promised. "We'll get you back to the house, and the dogs, and Sophie. David, everything will be okay."

"Do you really think so?" His voice was childlike, as if he really didn't know the answer to his question.

"Yes," I said, not knowing what else to say. "Yes, it's going to be okay."

David told me about the daily interviews he'd been having with counselors. "The drugs aren't working," he said. I would later learn the doctors had tried many different meds: lithium, which David didn't tolerate, and later Depakote and Seroquel, mood stabilizers that are known as "maintenance drugs."

"Just give it more time, David," I said. "Be patient. It took you a long time to unravel. Give yourself time to build back slowly."

"I'm running out of time. I can't stand this place any longer." He sounded like a prisoner, a man forced into a colorless world—the same dull uniform, the same dull walls without windows every day. "I hate the food, the nurses, the way they talk to me here." He started to cry. I hurt every time I heard David cry. Someone in the background interrupted, asking him to get off the phone. He ignored them.

"David," I said, "you'll get out when the counselors can tell you are ready." I softened my voice. "Show them you are ready." My throat tightened up again, guilt pressing against my consciousness.

"I wish I could fix this for you, David," I said. "But you've got to do this for yourself."

One week later, the counselors reported a "remarkable turnaround." David stabilized on the drug regimen, they reported to his family. He no longer had suicidal ideation. The olfactory hallucinations were gone. He'd told the counselors about a plan for recovery on the outside that included moving back to Canada for a time to help his mother with small jobs. He'd gained back some of his weight. He was ready to be released. He assured the counselors he did not know where the gun was, that he had dropped it in the thick brush and it was likely unrecoverable.

His mother said she could care for him. She signed an order agreeing to monitor his activities and packed a fresh set of clothes so that he wouldn't have to come home in scrubs. Sophie wanted to be home when her dad arrived. She cleaned her room and set out all her favorite stuffed animals on her bed, a welcoming parade of the things she loved most.

Adele, meanwhile, returned home to Montreal for a couple of days to care for one of her patients. She called and asked if it would be okay if I let David stay at the house for a few days. I was nervous with Adele absent from the picture, but at that point, I would have done anything to help David recover. Alice would be supervising Sophie's evening interactions with David. I would still be with her during the day. I said yes and packed a bag to stay at Colin's house.

## "MAGIC BULLETS": PSYCHIATRIC DRUGS

Award-winning science and history author Robert Whitaker is determined to solve a puzzle: why has the mental illness epidemic grown in size and scope, even as the country spends billions of dollars every year on antidepressants and antipsychotics?

Whitaker points out that as the psychopharmacology revolution has unfolded, the number of disabled mentally ill in the United States has skyrocketed. Mental illness now disables 850 adults and 250 children every day. According to Whitaker's book *Anatomy of an Epidemic,* "Those numbers only hint at the scope of the problem, for they are only a count of those who have become so newly ill that their families or caregivers are eligible to receive a disability check from the federal government."

Psychiatrist Daniel Carlat says that psychiatry has largely forsaken the practice of talk therapy for the seductive and more lucrative practice of prescribing drugs. Although we know that many people are helped by psychiatric drugs and will personally attest to how the drugs have helped them lead normal lives, there are a host of deeply troubling consequences to a culture that favors prescriptions over therapy.

In his book *Unhinged: The Trouble with Psychiatry—A Doctor's Revelations About a Profession in Crisis,* Carlat says psychiatrists have settled for treating symptoms rather than causes, embracing the medical rigor of DSM diagnoses and prescriptions in place of learning the more challenging craft of therapeutic counseling.

"Overprescription" was a word I didn't know existed until I saw David catatonic in a hospital, drooling, physically unable to move his limbs. The approach was not "What are the factors that contributed to this man's breakdown?" but instead "Try a drug, any drug."

Carlat writes, "In any field of medicine, patients become desperately ill and die before their time, despite the best efforts of doctors. This is as true in cardiology and oncology as it is in psychiatry. Whether we are talking about depression, schizophrenia, or bipolar disorder, the new drugs introduced over the past fifty years are no more effective than the original prototypes—such as Haldol for schizophrenia, lithium for bipolar disorder, and Nardil for depression." He continues, "Why put patients through months and years of weekly therapy if simply taking pills worked as well if not better? As it turns out, we were wrong in two ways. We both exaggerated the effectiveness of the new drugs and gave psychotherapy a premature burial."

# Chapter Nineteen

The phone rang as I was curled up on Colin's couch, in front of a fire, prepping for an interview I would do the next day. My laptop was on my lap as I scanned previous interviews with General Wesley Clark, who would be coming into the studio to talk about the Iraq war.

"Thanks, thanks for all you've done," David said over the phone, his clear, strong voice giving way to emotion. "Really, Sheila, there's a place in heaven for you."

Odd. David didn't believe in heaven. Or hell. "Thank you, D. Was it good to see Sophie again?" I said. "Are you feeling okay about being home? Did you make yourself a fire?"

He avoided the questions. "You and Sophie. You're very tight now, aren't you? This has really brought you closer, hasn't it? You love her so much. You are such a good mom."

I sat upright. He'd never spoken to me so kindly, so intimately, especially on the phone. He hated phones. Sophie and I had always been tight. I struggled to make sense of what he was trying to say. I asked tentatively, "David, are you okay?"

I imagined him sitting in his chair in the living room, looking out at the huge deck he'd rebuilt around the pool. He liked looking at reflections in the water, so he lit the deck for dramatic effect. He'd even strung a zip line so that Sophie and her pals could scream from the top of the house to the pool. I'd hoped he'd built a fire; it was his thing, a fire every night after October 1. He paused a long while before answering.

"You know you're going to be okay, no matter what," he said. "Sophie and you will be fine."

"We can all get through this, David," I said. "Please give Sophie a big kiss for me tonight, would you?"

"I will. I promise. Thank you, Sheila, thank you for everything."

The conversation struck me as odd. It was intimate, personal, and so calm, his tone filled with forgiveness and understanding. *I should check on him. No, he's fine.* His family wanted me to leave him alone. Give him his space. *Yes, he'll be fine.* But I couldn't shake the tone of his voice—*Why did he sound so different?* Maybe the medications had changed him.

The next morning, I tiptoed out of Colin's home around five thirty to make the drive home to see Sophie. The day was off to a glorious beginning: there was crispness in the air and red and gold color in dying leaves. Fall. My favorite season for change. I took the familiar winding turns leading up to my house and saw the usual early morning rumblings. Our neighbors, the Shillers, were early risers. Lights and TVs were already on in their house. I imagined Debbie hard at work on her StairMaster before waking up her daughter for school. Patty Benson was on her morning walk. I thought of Sophie, still sleeping, how she liked to be awakened by someone (preferably me) lightly scratching her back. I'd pack her favorite lunch of salami and Brie, with flat crackers, cut-up apples, and kosher pickles, all in separate bags. I'd caught up on the laundry—there would be matching socks to offer her.

Slowly, I was patching our life back together. I took the last curve and had the same reaction I'd had ten years earlier, when I had come home to find my car stolen. David's white work truck was not where it had been parked the night before. I inhaled, held my breath. We'd taken the keys to his car from him, and his employees had the only other set of keys to the truck. Where was he? My jaw tightened; my senses sharpened; the exhale never came. I sprinted from the garage to David's mother's bedroom, panicked.

"What is it?" she said, startled, sitting upright.

"Where's David?"

She looked around the room, confused, not yet sure of why I was asking. "He's upstairs, asleep," she said.

"Then who has his truck?" I asked. *Get on the road, track him down. Find him.* Everything I'd ever learned from reporting on child kidnappings ran through my mind. The first hour is the most important. Somehow, those lessons seemed applicable now.

Alice's face lost its color. She looked thin and drawn in her flannel pajamas. I saw the realization come over her, and it hurt. "Oh no," she whispered. "One of his workers brought back the keys to the truck last night. I didn't think . . ." Her voice trailed off in a distant direction, to a place she had been just a few months before.

I pushed down my worst fear, my instinct. *The gun,* I thought to myself as I skipped three steps on the way upstairs into Sophie's room. *He knows where the gun is.*

I stopped myself outside her room and stabilized my breath. "Good morning, sweetheart." I kissed her on her head.

She opened her eyes and gazed at me, sleepy. "Hi, Mama, why are you waking me up so early?"

"Sweetheart, I'll need Alice to take you to school, if that's okay. I've got to find Daddy."

She sat up in her bed, now wide awake, filled with a dread I knew too well. Her long blonde hair was tangled, and she had sleep in the corners of her eyes. "Is everything okay?" she asked, knowing the answer wasn't yes.

I hugged her tight to my chest. "He's not here right now. It looks like he took his truck out. But I promise, I promise, Sophie, we will find him."

She leapt from her bed, opening drawers and pulling out one

sock with monkeys on it and another with bright yellow smiley faces. She grabbed Bear from the bed—she was getting ready to come with me.

"Baby," I said, sitting her down on her powder pink and lime green comforter, "I need to go alone."

"But I want to go with you," she said, her lip quivering, the oddly matched socks hanging from her hands, Bear tucked carefully under her arm. "He didn't even say goodbye."

I knew. I knew where he was. Back to the beauty and stillness of the Columbia Gorge. Larch Mountain, where Diedra lived. I'd been polite, even nice to her because she loved David, too. I answered her calls when she was crying. I encouraged her to keep searching for the gun David had hidden.

I'd already taken the I-84 exit toward the gorge when Diedra called my cell. She sounded hysterical—a neighbor had found David's white Toyota work truck several hundred yards from her driveway.

"I'm out riding my horse," she said. "They told me the windows of his truck are bashed out. Something's wrong." She dissolved into tears, then loud, long sobs.

"I'm fifteen minutes away from Larch Mountain," I said. "Give me the directions to your home." I was certain I could find him. I knew him better than anyone. Of course, I could find him. I had to. I felt responsible for David's well-being in a way that no one understood. Perhaps it was driven by guilt, or my own false sense of importance in David's life. I'd never stopped loving him.

The road leading to Larch Mountain is a scenic route: it's a narrow, two-lane road that once was the old highway. The road winds along above the Columbia River and a massive gorge, carved out 15,000 years ago by the floods and melting of the Ice Age. Cyclists and hikers from all over the world come here to see an area untouched by McDonald's or Walmart. Officer Rodale had told me people come here to disappear. The closer I got to Diedra's home, the heavier my heart felt inside my body. Now I dreaded the idea that I might find David.

David's work truck was parked haphazardly on the side of the road not far from Diedra's house—a style of parking I'd seen from him more frequently in the past few years. Sometimes he'd be so distracted, he'd leave the driver's door open, his briefcase inside. Other times, I'd find the lights on, the engine still running.

I pulled off the side of the road and sprinted from my car to his truck. Glass littered the side of the road. Both windows were busted, gone—it looked like someone had rifled through his dirty tool compartment to find nothing.

There was a liter of vodka on the front seat, half empty.

The keys were in the ignition.

His red Columbia Sportswear jacket I'd bought him several Christmases earlier was on the passenger seat. He loved that jacket. It was too cold to be outside without a coat. I lifted the coat. Underneath, lying on the seat resting flat and wrinkled side by side, were two photos of Sophie and me. He'd fished them out of photo books years ago and carried them everywhere, even once retrieving them—along his drenched wallet—from the Columbia River. The pictures were worn, ruined in my eyes, but he'd told me he liked them best. I wore no makeup in that shot. Just me, caught reading a book, smiling up at him.

I picked up the photo of Sophie. She was seven, standing tall on David's shoulders, mouth open and arms up, skimming the ceiling of our home, her face full of excitement. "Tall girl," I heard myself say.

"Tall girl" was a game they'd played nearly every evening in our home, until Sophie had become too big for David to walk around with her on his shoulders. I held the pictures to my heart as it heaved up and down. "David, please, please for Sophie's sake, please, no," I whispered.

The sense of knowing made it impossible to breathe, to speak. "David, please say you didn't," I repeated to myself again and again, scrambling on my hands and knees from the driver's seat to the glove compartment. Inside, his wallet, containing four crumpled dollars.

His debit card was gone. I dug further. A bottle of aspirin, some old papers, a cleaning bill, a receipt.

I stopped searching. The road was empty; the gorge was still. *Remember this,* I told myself. *October 25. One day you will want to remember the temperature, the way the air smells, how the day was clear, with amber sunlight shining down. One of the most beautiful places in the world.* The road, with its curves and spectacular vistas, was empty. I picked up David's coat, hearing the echoes of so many cops at so many crime scenes I'd covered, rattling on about the "moron who touched this or that." David's coat, the prints on his vodka bottle. It was all evidence now.

I had so many photos of him wearing that coat; he wore it everywhere once it turned cold. He never lost it, never left it behind. He loved that coat.

I ran up his girlfriend's gravel driveway and then reminded myself she was gone. Back to his truck. I screamed, "Somebody, please help!" I recognized my own panic; the uselessness of my cries for help—intuition told me it was all for nothing.

I sat back in the driver's seat of his car and hugged the cold steering wheel. My body shook; I wore only a Patagonia shell. "David," I cried. "Jesus Christ, David."

I knew he had come to finish something he'd started six weeks earlier. Everything in between—the diagnosis, the drugs, the weeks incarcerated with bad food, broken crayons, and empty bookshelves—had only made him more determined to carry out his plan. It would not be like David to leave a note. He never wrote letters. His penmanship sucked.

I left his coat and his truck and everything he'd left behind just as I found it. I got back in my car and drove away from the certainty of his death. I would pick up his mother. We would figure out what to do next.

I don't know how fast I was driving. I do not know how I navigated the turns; I do not remember whether I listened to the radio. I do not remember the other cars on the highway that morning with me. The Columbia must have been running wild—on any other day, I would have noticed.

I do remember sobbing as I passed the exit by Sophie's school, imagining her working away on her report on Sequoia trees or African elephants, opening up her lunch and either being delighted or disappointed, picking out the food she didn't like and setting it aside on a paper towel. I remember wishing I'd be pulled over so I could tell a cop what had happened and they would take me, sedated, to a hospital.

I somehow found my way to Sophie's school, winding in and out of the side roads as if it was all new terrain. I recognized the signs of shock in myself and went to Sophie anyway. She was waiting for me on a bench in the hallway. Her hands were quiet in her lap, carefully holding a freshly painted picture. It was a giant Sequoia tree, the tree we'd studied together, marveling over its place in American culture, a sturdy tree that could survive nature, but not man. It was endangered now—and Sophie had chosen it for that reason. Her fingers were slender, delicate, holding onto the parts that weren't wet, careful not to smear the paint. I noticed how sturdy and straight she'd painted the trunk, a strong base for branches that looked like gnarled fingers. David would have raved over it, clearing the front of the fridge to make more room for another masterpiece. "It's perfect," I said, before hugging her close to my chest.

Later, Colin picked Sophie up from our house and took her and his girls to dinner. "I'll take good care of her," he promised. "Please, don't worry. We'll get through this." I hugged him, wishing I could stay and avoid the inevitable.

Two hours later, Alice and I were back at Diedra's mountain property, uncomfortably sitting in the living room, shivering. The cabin was small but elegant. My eyes wandered, imagining David's life here. There was the loft where they slept together, covered in Pendleton blankets. There were the architectural plans and the Indian dream catchers and all the reasons he came here when he felt so alone. David had always traveled—away from us, not closer.

"We should call the police," I said to Alice, who sat in a rocking chair with a blue-and-red blanket over her knees. "They can help us."

"I'd rather he be dead," she said, "than captured again like a common criminal. I will not see him returned to that place." She'd hated the hospital as much as I had. But how could she possibly believe that? Was it because she'd come so close to her own death after feeling such despair? Was she crazy?

I started to argue and then stopped. She looked so confused, her face twisted in pain, a sweater hanging around her bony shoulders. Her pupils were dilated, the whites of her eyes bloodshot. She wasn't making sense. Maybe she was in shock, babbling, in denial.

Diedra's face was puffy and blotchy from crying. "Would you like to look for him?" she asked me.

We stood on her porch. I was at least a foot taller than she. Her property was thick with trees and lush fields and acres of places to hide. I tried to think like David might. "Did you two ever walk together?"

She nodded, pointing to the left. "Yes. This way."

We walked down the gravel driveway, past his truck, another five hundred yards or so to an open meadow, with long grasses and oversized sunflowers slowly dying after a long summer run. "He told me you were in an open marriage," she blurted. "That you'd both decided to stay together for Sophie, but you weren't together any longer." I bit my tongue. There was enough truth in that version that I could imagine David promoting it. None of it mattered anymore—somehow I knew he was gone. I could feel loss as thick and heavy as each breath I took.

I was out of my own body, shivering from the shock of what I believed. I stepped over a log. I watched myself make this awkward walk with a woman I didn't know and listened to her talk about a man I thought I knew so well but realized I barely understood. I stepped over another log and then under a rusty barbed-wired fence. What would we do if we found him? I couldn't come up with a plan. We continued walking, confused, shocked—two strangers who had once fallen for the same man.

Into the gulley. Up again, down again, through another barbed-wire fence into another meadow. This land went on forever, thousands of acres of wilderness. He could be anywhere.

"He was just so lonely," Diedra said. "He told me how much he loved you. That he'd screwed it up. That he couldn't start over. He'd done too much damage."

I turned to look at her but didn't speak. Over her shoulder, a view of the Columbia Gorge opened up that took my breath. The river cut through the gorge with a line so jagged and perfect only nature could have made it. The shadows cast down from the deep canyons were vast. There were at least six different shades of green, gold, and red before me. I imagined David looking out at this view, his arms folded across his chest, at rest.

"I'm glad he found you, then," I said. "I'm glad he found this place."

Her face softened, some of the grief released or at least tempered. "Thank you," she whispered. "I don't know why you are being so nice to me."

"Because you helped him," I said. "Can you show me where he was that first night?"

We walked to the abandoned home where the police had found David's bloodstains the night he was admitted to the hospital. It was a 1920s house, long abandoned. Vandals had spray-painted the side of the home and chopped away portions of the wood exterior.

I pulled back yellow crime scene tape and squeezed myself through the broken door to get inside. It was dark and dank; the sour smell of methamphetamine permeated the wood walls.

The home was destroyed; it now looked more like a barn, or a clubhouse for wayward bikers. I imagined the drunken demolition parties people had thrown here. The dirty floor was littered with bottles and broken glass.

"This is where he tried to cut his wrists," she said, pointing to dried blood on the dirt floor. There was barely enough light to see. A white wooden chair—the chair where David had sat alone with a rusty razor blade—looked like a bad prop for a horror movie. I imagined him alone that night, sawing away at himself with another dirty, rusted razor blade—angry at his own incompetence for not being able to get the job done, disgusted by himself and his surroundings, all the while reveling in the dark drama.

My eyes stung from the smell and my tears, and I could not breathe in this sickness anymore.

I ran as fast as I could out the door, past the crime scene tape, out past the long yard that had been abandoned years earlier. I stood in the center of the road looking back at this stranger of a woman walking calmly toward me. I did not know if I would ever wake up from this horrible nightmare. "I'm going for help," I said. "I don't care what Alice says. We've got to find him. We've got to get help."

Alice stayed with Diedra. I jumped in my car and drove as fast as I could toward Portland. And I called Pat Kelly, a detective I'd known for years.

## THE CONTINUUM OF MENTAL HEALTH

Think back on your own mental health history. Have you experienced a divorce, the death of a loved one, a financial setback such as the loss of a job? Have you moved several times or experienced physical disability? All of these stressors can have a significant impact on mental health. We may move from feeling quite optimistic and forward thinking to a period in our lives when we are anxiety ridden, unable to concentrate, and less willing to spend time with friends and family.

A friend asked me the other day, "Do you think anyone can get a mental illness?"

"Yes," I answered. "In the same way anyone can get liver disease from drinking too much." Our brains are a living organ, which need to be cared for just like our hearts, our kidneys, and our livers. Providing early education on keeping our brains healthy is one of the most important steps we can take in acknowledging the continuum of mental health. As one doctor told me, "Putting the head back on the body where it belongs."

In 2013, Tom Insel, the director of the National Institute for Mental Health, told a TED audience, "Thanks to early detection, there are 63 percent fewer deaths from heart disease than there were just a few decades go. Could we do the same for depression and schizophrenia? The first step in this new avenue of research is a crucial reframing for us to stop thinking about mental disorders and start understanding them as brain disorders."

Just as we all fall somewhere along the heart health continuum, so do we fall on the mental health continuum. The promising recognition of that reality allows this question: "How is my own brain health, and where am I along the continuum?"

# Chapter Twenty

Pat Kelly was a middle-aged Portland police officer who had risen through the ranks of his division to become commander of the Sex Crimes Task Force.

We'd met when I was a reporter for the local television station. He'd helped me on several stories, giving me the inside scoop on which ones would break big and which would fizzle.

Pat guided me through the maze of politics at the "cop shop" and chatted with me whenever our paths crossed, at parades or crime scenes. But the bulk of our relationship had been spent on the phone with one another, to talk news and city gossip, and later to talk about our families and friends. I supposed we were kindred souls, and both of us found comfort in knowing we cared about one another.

His heart was almost too tender for his current job: he investigated the worst kind of crimes against children. Sometimes after a particularly rough case, he would call me from his police car and say, "I just needed to hear your cheery voice."

My cell signal came in as soon as I reached the I-84 freeway. Pat answered the phone on the first ring. "Well, hello, you!"

"Pat, I need your help," I said. I pulled to the side of the road and recounted everything I knew, from the beginning of the day to the abandoned truck to the coordinates of Deidre's cabin. I told him why David's mother didn't want a search team involved—because she feared that he would be found and returned to the psychiatric hospital. I shared with him my intuition that David had taken his own life.

"Oh, Sheila," he said softly. "You may be right. But, right now, we just don't know. He may still be out there." He paused. "We've got to get a search team mobilized." His tone changed from personal to professional. "Go home. There's nothing you can do there now. Be with Sophie. I will call you as soon as I get up there."

I was sitting in the dark in my own living room when he called back with an update. The cell phone startled me.

"How are you?" he said, and then he responded to his own question. "Wait, I know the answer."

"Hi, Pat." My voice sounded exhausted. "Thanks for your call. Any news?"

"I think we've worked out a compromise that will work for David's mother," he said. "We need to start small so that she doesn't get more upset. The search is not large enough to alert the TV assignment editors."

"Thank you, Pat." I held the phone close to my ear, looking out at the darkness and loneliness of the home I'd always loved so much before this. The master bedroom television blared jarring sounds of *SpongeBob SquarePants*. Sophie was sitting in front of the TV in her pink pajamas, too confused to speak, her legs curled up around her for comfort. Max and Star huddled close to her.

Pat said what I'd already been thinking. "Sheila, you need to make sure you and Sophie are safe. We really have to operate as if he's still alive. "

"I know," I said. "I know."

"And he's got the gun," Pat said.

Of course he had the gun. David had known where it was all along. I could not comprehend how someone who was mentally ill could be so calculating in planning his own death. He'd premeditated, plotted, and executed his escape. The thought chilled me to the bone.

Pat's voice brought me back to reality. "Do you have anywhere else you can stay?"

Colin tucked fresh new sheets on a guest bed he'd pulled into his daughter's bedroom. He folded hospital-style corners, pulled two comforters from plastic coverings, and finished making the bed for Sophie. He fluffed new pillows, smoothed the wrinkles on the bedspread, and said, "Will this be okay, Sophie?"

She looked exhausted, her hands still holding tight to her backpack. We'd packed her in a rush, grabbing a toothbrush and toothpaste, two pairs of jeans, hoodies, and a couple of her favorite stuffed animals, Curly and Bear.

She nodded and then asked, "Mama, can you sleep with me?"

"Of course I will, love. Absolutely." I looked at Colin, who was so eager to help, and blew him a silent kiss. "Thank you."

As Sophie and I lay in the darkness, looking out on an unfamiliar street below, I heard Colin locking the doors and setting the alarm.

Before he turned out all the lights, he came back in and planted kisses on both of our cheeks. "I'm so glad you're here," he said, hugging me first, then Sophie.

I wondered if Sophie would resist, push away, but I guess she needed that comfort too. She held on to the hug the longest, then smoothed the blanket of all its wrinkles. Colin's unconditional love of Sophie in those first days of crisis solidified my feelings for him. I'd been longing for a partner, but I hadn't realized how much I'd also missed seeing Sophie cared for by someone who was stable and compassionate.

There were other people who might have put us up for a night—friends with large homes whose offers of help were genuine—but I feared this wouldn't be for a night or two. I listened to Colin performing his nightly rituals before going to bed. The water ran as he brushed his teeth. I could hear drawers opening and closing. He was probably flossing, taking his vitamins. Even in a crisis, Colin was measured and under control. Somehow, knowing that made me feel better that night. I closed my eyes with my arms around Sophie, holding her tight until her breathing evened out and I could relax. My mind raced over the day's events, again and again, like a car on a track. It was like watching a movie, someone else's story, someone else's nightmare.

Colin woke me up by gently kissing me on the forehead. He was already showered, on his way to meet his daughters at their school, a block away. "Good morning, beautiful," he whispered, careful not to wake Sophie.

He had custody of his girls two weeks a month, but every day he walked to school to tell them good morning, and many days, he rushed back from the office to meet the girls for lunch. His hair was combed, his face shone brightly, and he wore a black Italian suit with a crisp white shirt. "There's cereal or pancakes for breakfast," he said hurriedly, kissing me again before he turned to leave.

"Did I dream it?" I asked, already knowing the answer but unable to accept my reality.

"No, baby. No." He kneeled down beside the bed. "Will you be okay?"

Colin's tenderness swept over me, and I wept. In a few short months, he'd shown me so much of his heart, cared for me, and made me feel loved. Only in the consistency of Colin's openness and generosity could I compare how much David and I had missed together.

The crushing sensation in my chest reminded me that there would be countless days of waking up like this: confused, traumatized, unbelieving. I would wake up and remember David's empty, abandoned truck, the keys in the ignition, those photos on the passenger seat underneath his coat as if to say, *I don't need these anymore*. The tears that ran down my cheeks weren't only for me; they were also for Sophie, her loss and her love. Gone.

I tiptoed downstairs to phone my boss, Dale, and tell him what had happened. His family had suffered an enormous blow from the suicide of their son, and he was more than understanding. His tone on the phone was of a man who had been there before. We had grieved as a family for Dale's loss just three months earlier. Now this. "Take as much time as you need," he said, and I knew he meant it.

We both lingered on the phone in silence, unsure of what to say to one another until I offered a simple, "Thanks, Dale. I don't know what I'd do without you."

I hurried back upstairs so I would be with Sophie when it first hit her that her dad was gone. She woke suddenly, her green eyes wide open, staring at the ceiling. "Mommy," she said, "I didn't even tell him goodbye. He didn't say goodbye to me." Her heart-shaped lips quivered, reminding me again of David. Large tears streamed from the corners of her eyes. She was breaking inside.

I cuddled in close to her and held her tight. "I'm sorry, sweetheart."

"Will they find him?" she cried, speaking of the searchers. I hadn't told her about the search, but she must have eavesdropped on every word.

"I hope so, sweetheart. I hope so."

Outside, SUVs and station wagons pulled up in front of Colin's gracious home. Moms and dads got out and walked their kids the rest of the way to school. The children shouted to one another, happy to be in the streets on such a sunny fall day. The bell would ring soon; life would go on without us.

"Am I going to school today?" Sophie asked.

"That's up to you, sweetheart. I want you to do what you want to do."

"Maybe not today. But maybe tomorrow."

"Whatever you decide," I said, kissing her on her forehead, "that's what we'll do. Can you eat something?"

She shook her head no.

"What if we make waffles—at home?"

Sophie sat up. Her eyes were swollen, heartbreak all over her face. "I want to see Star and Max."

"You're right," I told her. "I miss them too. What do you say we go take them on a long walk?"

We made the bed as neatly as Colin would, packed up our things, and headed home.

No one was home when we arrived. Sophie ran up the stairs, happy to be in familiar surroundings. I hesitated, climbing the steps.

The reminders of David were everywhere. The pool where he floated on an air mattress, reading another book. The fridge where he pulled out big slabs of cheese and thinly sliced salami for sandwiches with a cold beer. Even the simple things seemed charged with his presence—the bathroom where he brushed his teeth in the morning, the outlet where he plugged in his phone to recharge. He was everywhere.

I closed the door to the den and his bedroom, not able to bear the smell of his shirts inside, or the mud that was still on his oldest, most worn work boots. I could not bear any of it, because I felt so sure he was gone.

My family came.

A day later, my sister sat cross-legged on my basement floor, amid garbage bags full of the envelopes David had hidden. She moved efficiently, her sharp mind working like a detective, sorting envelopes in terms of urgency and importance. She'd dropped her practice for me, flying to Portland to help me navigate the legal and financial mess.

"This pile is for invoices," she said with her reading glasses low on her nose. "This pile is for claims that needed your attention yesterday." She pointed to a third pile with her finger. "And this pile is for legal action already under way against David."

"Shit," I said. "Before it was just chaos—now it's really scary."

Diane was two years older than I, and a hundred years wiser; she'd devoted her life to Buddhism and was now a priest. Her body looked like mine, lithe with good lines and sharp, intelligent eyes. Her cheeks were prominent, and her chin line was still smooth and radiant. She was growing her hair out after shaving it bald for her ordainment; it was a show of commitment to her holy life. I posted a sign on the fridge that said, "The angel is in," in her honor.

My mother was the next family member to arrive. As soon as she unpacked, she went to work folding laundry. Each new day passed with no news about David; Mom matched socks. Each day the search dogs sniffed and howled and followed bad leads; she folded T-shirts. Every tiny piece of Sophie's underwear was folded and placed back in her drawers. The house gleamed again.

Alice and my mother were very different people. Where my mother was emotional and wounded by my obvious pain, Alice seemed to kick into overdrive, cooking delicious meals from organic ingredients. It was like the frontier, when women would take over as the men were killed off, one by one. But I couldn't function in the house. Once my place of refuge, now my home was a place where I knocked from room to room without purpose. I'd get up to make a sandwich and find myself staring at David's bookshelf. I'd sit to try to answer email and stare at photographs of Sophie and David. I faced David's mother at every turn and felt in her combination of grief and anger my own huge failings. It had been nine days, but it felt like an eternity.

At night, I fled to the warmth and comfort of Colin's home, desperate to find sleep and the strength of his voice. I did not question the way he made me feel, or that I relied on him for emotional support. He was as present and cautious as any human being I'd ever met, and he allowed me to explore my emotions to their full depths.

My thoughts always circled back to David, never far from an internal dialogue of guilt and shame and a strange hopefulness that maybe I was wrong, maybe David's family was right, maybe he wasn't dead, maybe he would be found alive. The fire in Colin's house reminded me of this—if David wanted to survive in the woods, he could.

David was physically the strongest man I'd ever known. He had lived off the woods with his father. He knew how to hunt, which berries and mushrooms to pick, how to build a fire like the Saskatchewans, the tribe his father befriended while working as a forester in Canada. I'd watched him build a snow hut and hike for hours without water or food. Why would a man who had learned so much about how to survive plot to take his own life? It would be one of the great unanswerable questions.

Ten days after David's disappearance, Alice packed her bag and left as quickly as she'd come. I assumed she'd given up.

"You should eat more," she said after our goodbyes at the train station.

"I know, I know," I said. "You too, okay?"

She stiffened when I hugged her. "I'm sorry, Alice," I said. "I'm so sorry."

Alice's forehead pinched, and the tip of her nose grew red, as if she might cry. In all of our weeks together, I'd never seen her break down, never even saw her close. "You know, the night he came home, I told him he should start putting his financial affairs in order."

She tightened her hands around her bag, the veins in her slight hands bulging through. "He made phone call after phone call, and he heard things, things that upset him, from his clients, from his workers. How deep the trouble was." Her voice grew thin. "In hindsight, I should have waited. Let him get on his feet for a few days."

I swallowed. It had never occurred to me that the phone call David had made to me was the last of many—or that he'd tried desperately to gauge whether he'd be able to make a go of a new life. I'd had no idea others had told him the truth—that the company he'd built so lovingly was in shambles, and he would likely face bankruptcy.

I stammered, "You couldn't have known, Alice."

She looked at her watch, then pulled her neat handkerchief from its plastic folder and dabbed at her nose. "Well, I must go now." Alice had tried to make the world as tidy as her home and failed. Now, she would inhabit her home alone, having lost the two men she loved most.

The police search-and-rescue squad had gone back to the mountain several times after its initial search and covered hundreds more miles with Boy Scouts and dogs. Now, the snow was coming, and the department's search budget was dry. Maybe they could search again come spring. David's sisters left the house one by one. Jill had passed her nursing exam and would begin working soon. Adele needed to return home to deal with her own divorce and her patients. My sister and mother flew home, promising they'd check in on us.

One of the most startling things to deal with in the aftermath of trauma is how quickly the rest of the world moves on. The tow-truck driver needed to be paid. The bank called due David's home equity line of credit. My cellphone stopped working due to an unpaid bill. I was in the worst kind of limbo, one in which David had simply vanished, leaving me to tie up a million of his loose ends.

I was struck during this in-between time how Sophie instinctively wanted to re-engage with the people and activities that were *present*. She refused to be stuck in limbo, moving, as my therapist pointed out, like a tree in a windstorm. This was our big storm together, and the only thing that could soften the pain and the process for her was love and a return to the familiar.

I went back to work, desperate for something I knew. Back in my office, I pulled out a legal pad from my file and made a crude list of my priorities. It read:

1. Sophie's emotional well-being (therapist?).
2. Buy a phone card.
3. Go to DMV—David's car.
4. Hire an accountant.
5. Call mortgage company.
6. Call utilities.
7. Meet with investment advisor.

By the time I was finished, I had thirty items that needed to be taken care of immediately. I got started.

Snow fell hard and heavy in November. From time to time, I would talk to the officer from Clackamas County who'd run the search for David, and she'd give me an update. "More than a foot of snow in the gorge," she'd say, then two feet, and then three. Normally Portland doesn't get much snow; it was one of the heaviest winters we'd had in decades. One evening, I awoke from a night terror, my heart beating wildly and sweat covering my body. I'd dreamed of David, lost in the wilderness, barefoot, looking for his Columbia jacket. My pillow was drenched with tears. I knew then that we would find his body.

It was supposed to snow the day I told Sophie I would prepare her favorite meal of crab cakes and risotto for her and our friends, the Wilsons. We planned the meal at Colin's house since I hadn't even begun to decorate for Christmas. Sophie helped smash the crab and mush the cornmeal; we stirred rice and assembled crackers and cheese on big plates. There was snow falling quietly outside, and it was starting to stick. After dinner, we made a huge fire in Colin's living room. Sophie snuggled next to me on the couch. Maddie sat on the other side of the room with her parents, and her sister Jemma was lounging on a long, elegant chaise. Colin, who'd been washing dishes, stepped into the room, the color drained from his face.

"What is it?" I said. "What's happened?"

Colin motioned me to come to the phone. "Take this," he said. "It's important." When we were out of Sophie's earshot, Colin put the phone to his chest and held me tight. "They've found him."

I felt my body collapse against Colin's, the weight of the months falling in on me. He held my arm as I stumbled to his study. *No, not now,* I thought. *Sophie is so happy tonight.*

I raised the phone, and a man spoke. "Ms. Hamilton?" the voice said.

"Yes?" I whispered.

"We had a volunteer search team up on the mountain tonight. Seems like we've been over that place a hundred times."

I was half-hearing the words. The voice seemed distant, distorted, too slow, like a tape played at a quarter speed. It felt like it was pulling me down into quicksand.

"We started back at the house and did a grid search again," the voice said. "And, uh. Well, this is very hard to tell you, Ms. Hamilton, but we found David."

My fingers loosened around the phone. I was going to drop it, drop to my knees. I held on, forcing myself to listen, forcing the reality I'd known for so many weeks to crash down on me.

"I'm very sorry."

"Where was he?" I didn't know how I formed words. A tremor ran through my body. My legs and arms began to shake. Colin's study was the old Episcopal church office—cold tile and a high ceiling. The windows were frosted. I could feel my body freezing from the inside. Colin stood by me, rubbing my back. The blood stopped pumping to my extremities. My fingers felt white, frostbitten.

The voice continued. "He was about five hundred yards north of the house, ma'am, in a heavily wooded area. I don't know how we missed it before. One of my officers said he swore he'd walked through that exact spot a dozen times. But there he was, all right. Sitting right up against a tree, with his legs crossed."

I wanted to stop him, to say, please slow down, it's too much all at once. But this was his trauma too, now, a total stranger and I now bound by a senseless death. I thought I was ready for this call, that six weeks had prepared me for the inevitable. I was not.

"And can I tell you something?" the officer said. "I've come across a lot of suicides in this territory. For some reason, this is a place people come to when they want it over. But this was different. He looked so calm. Peaceful. Really, I am not just saying that, ma'am. He looked like he was at peace. He was looking out at a valley, and he looked like he'd sat there for a long time before he pulled the trigger."

My fingers went limp around the phone; the will that had held me up during the conversation was gone. I could not hear anymore. I could not manage the details of how he'd committed suicide, or why the dogs missed a man's frozen body five hundred yards from where the search started. I could not ask him all the questions that the reporter in me would have asked: What was the caliber of the gun? Was his body decomposed? Was there any sign of foul play?

I whispered, "Thank you." I shoved the phone into Colin's hand. "Take this; please take this."

Colin said something into the phone. I turned and walked away. I didn't want to hear what it was I was supposed to do next, where they would take his body, and what kind of responsibility I had to the police department, or the coroner, or the dozens of people who had aided in his search.

I watched myself walk back into the living room, where Sophie and Maddie's family were talking in low, worried tones, and I watched myself sit down next to Sophie, grabbing her small hands to make sure she wouldn't run screaming into the night. She looked closely at my face, and her eyes widened. Her slender legs were covered with tights that were the color of the snow. Her long blonde hair was pulled back with a red ribbon. I noticed this because David loved her hair that way, out of her face, away from her pretty eyes and her lips that looked like a perfect heart. She moved her face closer to mine, and she tightened her grip on my hands until the blood left them.

I spoke slowly, so I would not babble, so I would not make her more fearful than she already was. The hardest part was hers to bear now. I tried to calm the tremor moving through my body so that I could tell her correctly, tell her the unthinkable.

"Remember when I told you it would be better if we knew, one way or the other, what happened to Daddy?"

Her face tightened, her eyes becoming wildly alert, as if she might bolt from my grasp, away from me. She interrupted, already knowing, already crushed.

"What, Mama, what?"

They were the most dreaded words of my lifetime, and I knew I had no choice but to tell the truth. "They found him, sweetheart, and he's dead. I'm sorry, baby."

I put my arms around her, holding her deep in my chest, trying desperately to cushion this blow. Her body fell into mine, a moment I knew I would have to replay again and again in my lifetime, a memory seared into my brain, deeper than the deepest grief I knew. The shuttle exploding, the Twin Towers falling, all the images of innocence lost I had ever seen—and now this, too. Sophie held my waist, her face buried in my chest.

I had never heard a child's heart breaking. It is a sound so unforgiving I knew I would never stop hearing it. It would ring through my memory at exactly the same pitch, with the same intensity, reminding me of the crippling of her heart.

The deep, grieving wail she let out echoed through the home, into the street, interrupting the silence of the falling snow.

I held her.

## AFTER SUICIDE

In 2013, suicide was the tenth leading cause of death, accounting for more than 41,000 deaths in America. If you have had someone you love commit suicide, you are a survivor. Ann Smolin, C.S.W., and John Guinan, Ph.D., authors of the book *Healing After the Suicide of a Loved One,* estimate that six to eight people are strongly affected by each suicide that takes place in America. That means more than a quarter of a million Americans become survivors of suicide every year.

There are predictable phases of pain that all survivors experience sooner or later: denial, grief, and self-reproach or guilt. Most survivors will re-experience the event through terrifying dreams. The ability to perform one's usual tasks is impaired. And most survivors, write the authors, will torture themselves with repetitive interrogations of "What if . . . ?" and "Why didn't we . . . ?"

The most common refrain I hear from suicide survivors is, "What if . . . ?" What if we'd been able to pick up the phone? What if we'd been there when he stopped by? What if he'd been hospitalized? What if he hadn't been hospitalized?

The truth is that no one can ever be sure that a different choice would have prevented the suicide. The choice someone makes to commit suicide doesn't come to pass because of a series of events. Many families have also shared with me how, after a suicide, surviving spouses and their in-laws blame each other. It is the nature of human beings to try to assign blame, but blaming someone else for a person's choice to end his life is particularly malicious.

Smolin and Guinan suggest that the most direct approach to recovery is to attend a group meeting of suicide survivors. There are chapters in nearly every major city. You can find a group support meeting by going to the American Association of Suicidology directory, or by using the American Foundation for Suicide Prevention (AFSP) website at www.afsp.org.

Other survivors find solace in reading all they can about

suicide. I've listed a complete registry of helpful agencies and mental health organizations at the back of this book. Reading about the suicidal state of mind may help you understand the phenomenon of suicide.

I found the most direct and accessible way of healing was by writing. By having a record of what I experienced and what I was feeling, I was able to discontinue the rumination and replay of what went wrong in the years before David's death. At a time when expensive and time-consuming counseling was not an option, writing saved me from my own negative thoughts. It is my hope that my experience might serve as a cautionary tale for other people who are concerned about a loved one's mental health.

# Chapter Twenty-One

The Kleenex boxes remained unopened.

A week after I'd taken the phone call from the sheriff's office, I was too numb to cry, too numb to do anything but sit in my robe in my living room, staring out at wilted leaves gathering in the bottom of the pool. I'd lost David. Sophie was fatherless. And the ten years I'd stayed to try to keep a family together had all been for nothing.

The phone rang. I answered, zombie-like.

"Hi, sweetheart. We're so worried about you." It was my mom. I hadn't returned her calls since Sunday, the day after they found David. *What day is it?* I looked at the date on the paper. Thursday. *Oh my God. It's Thursday,* I thought.

"Mom, I just need some time to myself. I'll be okay."

"Are you eating? Are you able to take care of Sophie? You know I will get on a plane today and come back there." My mother knew what could happen to me now, the trauma of loss, anger turned inward—depression. My mother had done the hard work of forgiving my father for his infidelity. She'd stabilized on a medication that allowed her to live a normal life.

She was better now—I was not. I knew what she must have experienced in those first few days when she sank into depression, the deadness of winter and the leaves gathering, decomposing. I expected to be flattened by grief in the days following David's discovery. Instead, my emotions were as flat as the gray sky.

"I promise I'll call you," I lied.

She repeated herself, which meant she wanted an invitation. "We'll come right back up when you're ready. We'll help with the funeral."

I did not want her to suffer through this with me. She had suffered enough.

"Thanks so much for calling. You've been so great. I love you."

The wind outside whistled through the trees. I shivered inside my thick robe. My toes curled in my Uggs. The newspaper stared back at me, the crossword puzzle blank.

Sophie walked into the living room, took a huge breath, sighed, and said, "I am so bored. I want to go back to school."

She had taken a shower, pulled on her pink skirt and white hoodie, found matching tights and clean shoes, combed her hair, and brushed her teeth. I'd heard her stirring in the kitchen—I thought she was pouring herself a bowl of cereal, but she'd packed her lunch, which she held tightly in a pink and green lunchbox. I guessed she'd packed slices of salami, a pickle, cheese, and maybe some cookies—if we had any. I imagined how I must have looked to her, with my stringy hair and dull complexion, staring out at the nothingness that follows death. I was usually the one bugging her to clean up.

"Are you sure, sweetheart? Are you feeling okay to do this?" I motioned for her to come sit by me. "It might hit you sideways when you're at school, and you could feel unbelievably sad, or mad, or . . ."

"It's terrible here, Mama. It's boring. And sad. I want to go back to school." She stood her ground, moving her chin sideways in a way only a nine-year-old can. It was 8:15. We had ten minutes to get her there on time.

Something surged through my nervous system—an energy that came from Sophie's need. It was time.

I called the school to let them know she was coming back, rushed to my room, and pulled on a pair of sweatpants and tennis shoes.

We grabbed our jackets from the closet and both ran to the car. For the first time in a week, I was doing something I knew how to do. I took my familiar route, down Burnside, past the Walgreen's where David bought the antidepressants that sent him into his first full-blown mania, past the bank where he bankrupted us. The further I drove, the more I shivered.

Sophie noticed my silence and the way I clutched the steering wheel.

"Are you okay?" she asked.

I gave a fake nod.

"Then could you please turn down the heat?"

I looked at the car heater gauge, blowing hot air at eighty-seven degrees. I was still shivering.

"Oh, sorry." I turned the heat off and bit my bottom lip. "Truth is, I'm not okay. But someday very soon I will be."

The stoplight took forever. I studied Sophie's face: David's lips, his cheekbones, and his fair skin. Her green eyes were clear and bright—she'd stopped crying after approximately forty-eight hours. Her grief cascaded like a tidal wave. Now she seemed focused again.

"Sophie," I said, "your dad loved you so much. It's the one thing that kept him going for so many years. He wanted to see you happy."

Sophie looked at me with a clarity that made her seem much older. "I know that, Mom, and we've got to have a funeral."

"Yes, of course we'll have a funeral—I'll make arrangements today."

The lists of musts swirled in my mind like the yellow sticky notes on my computer: go to the funeral home and have his body cremated, open my home to more strangers and relatives (again), and eat layered lasagnas and casseroles, because all of this is what you do in the week after people die. But what and who is it all for?

"Don't worry, honey," I lied, "I've got everything under control. Where do you think we should have Daddy's funeral?"

We pulled into her school parking lot, and she opened the door. "He hated churches," she said. "Maybe we should have it outside, in the park. You know how Dad loved the cold."

She leaned across the seat and kissed me. When she pulled back to steady her eyes with mine, I felt the goose bumps on my arm grow.

"Don't worry about me, Mommy," she said. "I'm okay."

"Do you want me to walk you in?" I asked, my voice breaking.

"Nah." She gathered her lunchbox and backpack. "I'm not eight, you know."

She was referring to last year, when she'd broken the news to me that she was a big girl and no longer wanted me to hold her hand and walk her into the classroom. Like all moms, I'd loved the daily stroll inside the school, the clusters of tired moms and working dads hurriedly dropping their kids off. I loved seeing the bulletin boards and worksheets and rows of library books, the mismatched socks and round, soft faces, racing to see who could get to class first.

Now I wanted to go back, to reclaim those years, to hold her hand as long as I could. I opened the car door. She waved at me tentatively from the entrance and then blew two kisses goodbye. She lingered at the door for as long as she could, opening it for the toddlers who came crashing through with their parents.

When the final bell rang, she was gone.

I went home, turned up the heat, and forced myself to sit down at the computer.

*David Krol passed away October 25, 2006.*

I couldn't bring myself to write a headline, or a typical obituary full of dates and facts. That wasn't David at all. I typed without editing myself:

*He was forever tied to the beauty and forgiveness of the forest and returned there to find peace. He grew up in the old growth of British Columbia, tagging along behind his father, a forester who taught his only son the spirituality that comes from a deep connection to the earth. David would later work as a logger, a builder, and finally a general contractor employing fourteen of his closest friends.*

*His happiest moments were in the dirt of his Portland garden, where he spent hours of uninterrupted bliss.*

As I wrote, the smell of spring dirt came to me, of garden snakes and Sophie on all fours, crouching low to the ground to pick up a spider or snail, her dad smiling broadly above her. Tears squeezed out the corners of my eyes, and I could no longer resist. I lay on the carpet, weeping. Huge convulsions of sadness came over me, pummeling my body. I wailed so loud my Labrador wandered upstairs to see what was wrong. The wet carpet smelled sour. Star sniffed at my head. I cried for David. For Sophie. I cried because I felt I'd done all I could, and it wasn't enough. Then I closed my eyes to escape myself, my guilt.

The cell phone woke me.

"Hey, you," Colin said warmly. "Have you eaten anything?"

I looked at my watch. It was already one o'clock.

"No," I said. "Not yet."

"I'll pick you up in half an hour."

Colin pulled up in his Range Rover thirty minutes later. He spent a moment looking at the lock on the outdoor gate before he walked in. His cheeks glowed with the cold. His energy bounced against the deadness of my home.

"I'll bring a wrench over and fix that lock," he said. "It's loose." He put his arms around me and brought me in close to his chest.

"Oh, sweetheart," he said, as he squeezed me. "You are so cold."

My memory of Colin during this time is that he seemed to call or appear during my darkest moments, like an angel flying too close to the ground. I can't underestimate what his love contributed to my health—a lifeline at a time when most of my strength was gone, and I felt as if I was running on the last drops of adrenalin my body had to offer. He put on a kettle for a cup of tea and rubbed my shoulders as we waited for the water to boil. I was completely aware of the catatonic look of grief I wore during those weeks after David's death, and yet, Colin still came by, often without calling first, offering to help.

Given the trauma and complexity of my life at the time, I certainly could have chosen to shut off my heart, but instinctively, protectively, I knew I needed him. Since childhood, I'd only relied on myself for my care. The unsteady marriage to David had only solidified my belief that we can only depend on ourselves. And yet, with Colin, I was allowing the deepest defenses to fall. I let him take care of me.

He went to the coat closet and gathered my things—a scarf, a hat, my long black cashmere coat. As he tied the scarf around my neck, I felt weird. *I can tie my own scarf!* Why would I have such mixed emotions about finally, truly being cared for? I tried to let my shoulders drop and soften to Colin's kindness. He sensed my apprehension. "You okay?" he asked, holding onto my arm as he locked the door behind us.

## CHILDREN AND GRIEF

The American Academy of Pediatrics describes the differences between children's grief and adult's grief. Preschoolers may believe that death is reversible or that their loved one really isn't gone for good. Children between five and nine may understand death's finality, yet they may not accept that it can happen to them or their family.

Many therapists confided in me that it is best to let the child's grief be your guide. Sophie's emotions swung wildly during the first few months of David's absence, but she refused to talk about David's death with a third-party professional. Most therapists agree that it is not beneficial to have a child in counseling if he or she is resistant. Some children won't want to cope with the loss of their loved ones for years, or even decades. It is normal during the weeks following the death for some children to feel immediate grief or persist in the belief that the family member is still alive. However, long-term denial of the death or avoidance of grief can be emotionally unhealthy and can later lead to more severe problems.

Anger can be a natural reaction to a parent's death. It is not uncommon for the child to show anger toward surviving family members. The child may temporarily become more infantile, demanding food, attention, cuddling, and baby talk.

An extended period of depression may require assistance from a qualified mental health professional.

# Chapter Twenty-Two

The crematorium called again, asking when I would be ready to make a decision regarding David's remains. I called Margaret, a friend and attorney whom I knew could help me navigate this world without collapsing into emotion. When she answered, she didn't run down the laundry list of things she had to do. Instead she said, "I'll be right there."

Margaret had been the first to offer help in planning the reception after David's funeral. Her timing and generosity were not out of character. Margaret was a modern-day Mother Teresa: she spent her vacations building homes in poverty-stricken areas of Mexico, she volunteered her time for several nonprofits in town, and she still found time for her friends and family. We were both hard workers and had saved wisely. We'd invested in apartment buildings together after a few years of friendship. Margaret did the painstaking work of accounting for every dollar we made. She arrived at my doorstep in a St. John suit and sensible black pumps. She carried two newspapers she'd picked up from the snowdrift and held them away from her clothes.

"Hello, darling," she said, stepping inside. "Here are your papers. I've called the Bensons for the reception, I've coordinated with the girlfriends so that each person will bring a dish, and I've sent out the announcements."

"Margaret," I said, hugging her hard, "would you please quit your job and go run the war? We need someone like you."

She laughed, and on our way to the funeral home, we caught up on news of Sophie and her son Gavin. When we finally rounded the corner to the acres of graves, she said, "Weird, I've only ever come through here bicycling with the kids." She shook her head. "It takes on a brand-new meaning now."

We walked through the door of the funeral home, a massive place with too much marble and gold clashing with the somber tones of death. The carpeting, the couches, and the drapes all were in the same palette of tan. On the long granite countertop, four small candles burned with names in front of them. One said "David Krol." *David Krol*, I thought, *what's he doing here*?

I had to physically jerk my body to remind myself that David was dead. It was something I experienced over and over again, a stray confused thought that maybe he wasn't dead after all. Margaret looked at me, worried. She smiled, put her arm around me, and introduced us to the woman in the tan pantsuit behind the counter who spoke in low, measured tones. It occurred to me how tiresome it must be to show empathy all day long, every day.

She showed us into a small room adorned with plaques and memorial engravings full of samples of granite and marble. These are the decisions you face when someone dies. It is the ultimate Hallmark experience, summing up a person's life by choosing the right kind of casket or the best vase to hold their remains. David would have hated this place. He would have walked out the minute he saw the money-making room. "Something simple would be fine," I said.

"Most people prefer to have something longer lasting, something significant and tasteful," she said.

"Something simple will do." I noticed a beautiful, plain piece of unfinished pinewood pushed to the side of the choices. It was the type of wood David loved to shape and mold into projects. I'd seen him turn pine like that into a tree house, a chest, a fence at our first home.

"I'll take that," I said to the tan pantsuit woman.

"Are you quite sure?"

"Quite."

She pushed a folder of ten pages in front of Margaret. We sat at the long cherry wood desk. "We will need to read through each of these," she said. "Let me know if you need any help understanding any part of this."

Margaret gave me a sideways glance, pulled down her glasses, and began reading. To my surprise, the funeral director read the words out loud. "I, the widow of the deceased, David Krol," she said.

Margaret looked up at me to see how I reacted. I shrugged my shoulders. I didn't know how I felt. The terms felt so new and foreign. Widow. Deceased. I rolled the words around and around on my tongue, wondering why I was still in denial when I knew I was in denial. Deceased. That was it. I still did not believe David was dead. I hadn't seen his body. The medical examiner had transferred it straight here after determining he'd died from suicide. I hadn't seen a shred of evidence that he was dead. "I'd like to see my husband before you cremate him," I blurted out.

The woman looked up, concerned. "I don't think that's a very good idea," she said in sorrowful tones. "He's badly decomposed. He's been here a few days. I don't know how to say it, but there's an awful odor from the body."

"I don't care," I said, now convinced it was the right thing to do, to see evidence that might help me move from unbelieving and shock to believing and recovering.

The woman phoned someone and whispered, "Would you please come in here?" Soon, the morgue operator, or cremator, came in, still wearing green gloves. He explained to me something I already knew—if I were to go into that room, I would smell of death for days. I'd heard cops say it before after entering rooms where bodies had decomposed. The stink permeates your skin, your hair, your cells, and you can't wash it out.

"I can," he said, "take a picture for you, so that you can see your husband one last time."

I sat back down. Margaret told him, "I think that's a good idea."

A few minutes later, the morgue operator came back with three

Polaroid pictures and put them in front of me. They were close-ups of David's face. One from the front, another from the side, and a third of his left hand. His eyes were closed, his mouth slack-jawed, as if he had fallen asleep in front of the television. There were blue and purple marks on his face from frostbite, and deep dark purple bruising under his eyes and into his cheeks from the force of the bullet. Dried blood ran down from his head past his ear to his neck. There was a small hole an inch or so above his ear. He was painfully thin, like a cancer victim, no fat left on his face at all, just skin and bone, and his hair was as wild as it must have been that morning, when he left us all behind. Animals hadn't gnawed him. The force of the blast hadn't ripped his brains apart. I felt an overwhelming sense of relief looking at the photos. The officer who called me the night of his death was right: David did not look haunted at all. He was at peace, finally. I picked up the third photo and tears filled my eyes. On his finger was the gold ring I'd given him ten years earlier, on our wedding day.

## THE ESCAPE THEORY OF SUICIDE

Men account for four out of five suicides in the United States. Male suicide often follows job loss, business failure, relationship loss, or an embarrassing public disclosure.

Florida State University psychology professor Roy Baumeister analyzed suicide in terms of motivation to escape from aversive self-awareness. "The causal chain begins with events that fall severely short of standards and expectations. These failures are attributed internally, which makes self-awareness painful."

Baumeister points out that most people who kill themselves actually lived better-than-average lives. He argues that idealistic conditions actually heighten suicide risk because they often create unreasonable standards for happiness, "whether produced by past achievements, chronically favorable circumstances, or external demands." Baumeister notes that a "large body of evidence" supports this theory.

Baumeister emphasizes that the biggest risk factor for suicide isn't chronically low self-esteem per se, but rather a relatively recent demonization of the self in response to a negative turn of events. Feelings of worthlessness, shame, guilt, or inadequacy, or feeling exposed, humiliated, and rejected lead suicidal people to dislike themselves and to see themselves as unlikable and unacceptable.

Baumeister's escape theory applies well to male suicide. It depicts the individual struggling with some injury to self-esteem and shifting into a crisis mode in which the cognitive awareness of options narrows.

# Chapter Twenty-Three

As soon as David went missing, I played his favorite music in my home: Neil Young, Bob Dylan, Leonard Cohen, John Prine. David understood and felt the power of words more than most, and somehow, listening to the anthems of these men helped me feel again. It hit me hard one day when I was preparing for an onslaught of David's family to arrive. I'd put my iPod on shuffle, and the song "Forever Young" by Dylan came on. I stopped in my tracks, remembering the nights we played and replayed that album in the Utah desert. We'd hike all day, drink tequila, and eat from the garden at night, with Dylan in the background. Hearing it again, the sobbing took hold of me so violently I had to lie down on the bed. It lasted long enough to swell my eyes, clog my nose, and puff up my face again. David had always loved what I considered to be the highest musical form, artists who didn't pander to sentimentality or bow to commercialism. He'd chosen the music that moved him, and now, it moved me to a softer, more forgiving place.

The house filled up. David's sister Adele returned from Montreal with her estranged husband in tow and her two beautiful daughters, willowy and fresh-faced, reminding me of what Sophie would look like in another five to seven years. They brought wine and bags of Trader Joe's snacks: Cheetos, potato chips, crackers, pretzels—none of it appropriate for a meal. I laughed to myself, remembering how David had told me, "I am living proof a person can survive two years on junk food alone. I did it when I lived with Adele."

His mother arrived again from British Columbia, sullen and hardened, barely acknowledging me when she walked through the door. "We won't be staying long," she said, referring to her children and grandchildren. "We'll be getting a hotel tonight."

Of course. Of course she needed someone to blame for her son's death. I reached for her hands. "Alice, I loved David. I hope you know I tried."

She pulled away and immediately went to the hardwood cabinets where we displayed David's travel treasures. "If you don't mind," she said, "I'd like to take this with me." Alice held up an antique miniature bookcase David had said was a family heirloom.

"Of course," I said. "Take whatever you like." She gathered a few more of his things and left for the hotel.

David's nephew arrived with a friend and a trailer. I'd told him he could have the tools David used for carpentry and woodworking. There was tens of thousands of dollars worth of equipment in the garage—it would be of no use to me. Luke thanked me and then loaded the trailer until it overflowed with enough equipment to start his own woodworking business. David's family would need something to remember him by.

His sister Jill arrived with empty boxes and asked for David's books. I swallowed, hard. This was my fondest memory of David, his love of literature. We'd built the bookcases downstairs together because we'd filled up the library upstairs. We had loved some of the same authors: Bukowski, Carver, Gilbert, Hemingway, Kerouac. I wanted those books we'd both dog-eared, the ones we both loved. She was already filling the boxes when I resigned myself. He was gone. The books would not bring him back.

"Go ahead," I said.

Sophie was sitting in her bedroom the day before David's funeral, reading a book. I sat down next to her and asked, "Is there something of Daddy's you'd like to keep for yourself? Something to remind you of him?"

We walked together into David's room. She pulled out the third drawer, where he kept his boxers, and pulled the green pheasant shorts from the pile. "I think I'll keep these," she said smiling, "and I'll always remember that dance he did when he first wore them." That was it for Sophie. A pair of green boxer shorts, the ones that had made her dad laugh.

I tucked away a few of David's treasures for her: his family's signet ring, the compass he'd used on long canoe and camping trips, a pair of binoculars they'd both loved, his driver's license, and his cell phone. I packed those things, along with every photo I could find of David, and put them in the pine chest he'd built for Sophie when she was born. One day, I knew, she would treasure those things.

The day of David's funeral, in December 2006, Portland was hit by a freak ice and snow storm. We'd expected temperatures in the mid-sixties, but when I stepped outside to pick up the paper, there was a thin sheet of ice on the deck. My butt slammed against the deck and my elbow hit the ice, opening a small cut that bled quickly. I winced and then paused. The winds howled through the huge oak trees around our home, reminding me of David's habit of running straight into the wildest weather imaginable, his coat open, hair tangled and messy. This was his kind of day.

On Portland's black ice days, when the streets were impassable, David liked to chain up and drive around, like Mad Max, the Last Man on Earth. On many of the storm days, neighbors would see him slipping through the streets and ask him to pick up milk or eggs, or drop a sick family member at the hospital. He loved the drama of it all, him against the ice, his truck slipping this way and that. When the town was paralyzed, it was David who could move.

We'd decided on an outdoor amphitheater at Hoyt Arboretum for the funeral. He loved to picnic there, lying on his back on the tables and looking up at the soaring pitch of the timbered shelter. I'd ordered twelve large overhead heaters, just in case it was chilly. Now, as we got out of our cars, I realized temperatures had dropped into the twenties. A friend showed up with huge piles of big, fluffy blankets.

A musician friend of mine sat inside the amphitheater, playing soft acoustic guitar. Her fingers looked cold—when she saw me she smiled so warmly I blew her a silent kiss. Dozens of people dressed in long coats, scarves, and gloves filed in and huddled close together. We'd expected seventy-five people or so, but the chairs filled quickly and then the park benches, and by the time the funeral started, the entire amphitheater was filled with people who came to pay their last respects to our family.

The amphitheater looked out on hundreds of ferns and oak, pine, and cherry trees. Ice hung heavy on the branches, distorting the trees into fantastical creatures. The lawn appeared crystallized, frozen and still. I smiled to myself, knowing how much David would have loved this setting.

Sophie saw three of her friends sitting in the third row and asked, "Can I sit with my friends?"

David would have said yes. Her buddies put her in the middle of the pack, one on each side holding her hand.

David's friends were, by nature, great storytellers, and one by one, they came to the podium to share tales of his humor and his great penchant for haphazardly planned adventures. One friend, Matt Palmer, told a story of a river trip in which all of them nearly drowned because David insisted on taking a Category 5 route, one of the most difficult types of rivers to navigate.

"He just kept telling us we'd be okay," Matt said. "And we were. Until now."

Another told a story of one of David's fishing trips, when he'd promised to take care of the food and drink. "When we opened the cooler, there was beer, bacon, and bread. I'd never been so constipated, or so happy, in my entire life." The audience had tears in their eyes from laughing, not crying.

Colin had asked if he should come, and I'd said no—I thought it would be uncomfortable for everyone, especially David's family. But now, witnessing this outpouring of love for David, I wished Colin could be here, if only as a fly on the wall, to hear the stories of the man I'd fallen in love with. Colin only knew David as a person with a mental illness. He was so much bigger than that.

A friend of mine opened his Mac to start a slide show he'd put together for our family. He'd shown up days after David's death and offered to go through my carefully organized pictures, picking out ones that captured David's life. It was one of the most generous offerings in the days following his death. The musician played "Forever Young" as the images flashed before me.

There he was, smiling broadly, his oversized hands holding Sophie up to the sun at the beach—pride beaming from his face. I'd forgotten she was only two weeks old when we took her to the beach for her first stroll. The next photo was David feeding Sophie blended veggies in the highchair, him making a funny, wincing expression as she ate another spoonful.

There were several photos of him deep in a book in the corner. I'd remembered, when we first met, how I admired his ability to excuse himself at parties and family gatherings to read; toward the end of our marriage I'd resented the hell out of it.

Every indicator of David's illness, however subtle, had been there in the beginning for me to see—yet I'd embraced the exuberance and rejected the depression, never understanding why he could be so mean and irritable on the heels of so much charm and enthusiasm.

My mother handed me a Kleenex. She'd loved David always, knowing he was not the man in the pictures, but someone far more conflicted. She also understood why I stayed with him—my loyalty to family, our history.

## PRIVACY RIGHTS AND THE CAREGIVER'S RIGHT TO KNOW

The Federal Health Insurance Portability and Accountability Act, or HIPAA, often frustrates parents and caregivers of troubled adult children. The law restricts release of personal medical information for anyone eighteen or older. It is helpful for patients wishing to protect their confidentiality, but for caregivers or parents of people with a mental illness, HIPAA places numerous roadblocks to accessing information regarding the care of a mentally ill patient in need. For example, it prevents doctors from talking with family members in detail about a loved one's treatment plan.

The challenge for many families is to communicate with both their mentally ill loved one and their care team. Our family had very little information about David' diagnosis, his care plan, or his ongoing suicidal ideation. We would have benefitted from more information, more updates, and a clear assessment from his psychiatrists and social workers.

Other families encounter the problem of noncompliance—patients who refuse their medication because they believe the side effects are more harmful than the treatment. It is extremely common for patients with bipolar disorder and schizophrenia to become noncompliant because of the belief that medication dulls their senses. Parents and caregivers are often helpless against HIPAA in demanding medication compliance.

# Chapter Twenty-Four

"Deepak Chopra is here," my producer said, poking her head into my office. "Should I send him up?" Inessa's soft, beautiful face was scrubbed, and her makeup was applied so carefully I realized she must have prepared herself for Chopra's visit. If only I'd done the same.

It was my first day back at work, and I'd made it through the first hour with a lump the size of an avocado pit in my throat. My boss had hugged me warmly. He was not the suit-wearing, authoritarian type of boss I'd had in television newsrooms. Dale wore Birkenstocks, ate organic food for lunch, and stopped working on his computer when a particularly great piece of music came on. "You going to be okay?" he asked.

"I'm in the right place," I told him. "It's good to be back."

"We missed you," he said.

I kept my head down in the hallway, preferring not to have to look at the mournful expressions some people wore as I passed. Others offered sincere expressions of help: "If there's anything I can do . . ."

*Yes, there is something,* I fantasized. If you could pay the mortgage, or walk the dog, or figure out how Sophie will get home from school while I'm at work. *If you could tell me how to get her to sleep in her own bed again, or how to deal with the anger of David's family or, for that matter, my own rage bubbling up inside. Yes. There are so many things to be done.* David's creditors, many of them friends of our family, needed to be paid. And his debtors needed to pay his estate, but some of them refused, knowing a dead man can't testify against them in court. Instead of voicing any of this, I accepted the offers graciously. "Thanks so much," I repeated over and over again. "I'll let you know."

I slumped in my chair, already exhausted by the lethal combination of anxiety, fear, sadness, and guilt.

"Well," my producer said, "are you ready?"

"Oh, yes, right." Normally, I would have spent the night prior to the interview poring over highlighted sections of the author's most recent book. Instead, I'd held Sophie to my chest while her back heaved up and down in huge convulsions of grief and loneliness.

The door opened, and my producer said, "Sheila, meet Deepak Chopra."

I stood and forced myself to smile widely and shake his hand firmly. He was wearing a gold Indian-style jacket, not a traditional one, but a designer version that was perfectly tailored to his waist and hips. His hands were supple and strong, a combination that struck me odd as I asked myself, *Since when do spiritual leaders use such great hand cream?*

He didn't smile, but nodded calmly when I told him, "I'm humbled by your visit. Thanks for coming." I looked down to see fiery red Nike tennis shoes on his feet and black designer jeans on a frame that looked fit and firm.

"Love your shoes," I offered, and then I regretted it, confused by his interest in something so patently flashy.

"Thank you. Shall we begin?" He motioned toward the chair on the other side of the studio. He'd probably done twenty of these interviews already this week. Portland was the last stop on the West Coast book tours. No doubt he was exhausted and couldn't suffer small talk.

I nodded. He put on his headphones and placed both hands in his lap. His chest barely moved when he breathed. His eyes were so brown they were almost black—so calm he appeared bored. *Bored?! Could Deepak Chopra be bored by me?*

I sprang into professional mode, riding the sound levels on the board as he gave me a sound check, "One, two, three, four."

"Okay, Deepak, can I call you 'Deepak'?"

"Everybody does." He offered a hint of a smile.

I took a big breath, steadied myself, and began, "Deepak Chopra joins us this morning on *Speaking Freely*; his newest book is called *Life After Death: The Book of Answers*."

If I'd prepared myself the way I should have, the way I normally do, reading and rereading the publisher's notes, the author's bio, the prepared questions, I wouldn't have been so jolted by the words "Life After Death." Instead, the lump in my throat threatened to explode, and tears squeezed out the corners of my eyes. My voice halted, then broke, and I couldn't continue speaking.

I hit the space bar on my computer to stop the recorder.

Deepak leaned back in his chair.

"I'm so sorry," I said. "This is my first day back to work—my husband just died." The flesh in my nose swelled up, and my voice sounded weak. I could not continue with the interview until I got myself under control.

Deepak nodded. There was no change in his facial expression, none of the mournful, twisted expressions I'd seen on others' faces when I told them of David's death. Chopra was a spiritual leader revered by millions of people around the world, and he couldn't even offer sympathy?

I prodded him. "Suicide. He shot himself."

No change. His breathing pattern wasn't altered. He opened his mouth to speak, deliberately and carefully. His lips formed complete *o*'s and *e*'s.

"He is exactly where he needs to be, and so are you."

"Excuse me?" My blood pressure surged. I suppressed a rage building in me that had been buried for years, one in which my emotions, *my* emotions, had been ignored, sidelined, minimized by the people I cared most about. I loved Deepak Chopra; I'd read every one of his books, except for his latest. The least he could do was show compassion; Chopra *owned* the word compassion, for God's sake.

He folded his long fingers carefully on the desk and scooted forward in his chair. "What we're talking about is pertinent to the book. Would you like to continue?" he asked.

My cheeks flushed, and I felt my teeth grind together, a habit I'd never had before the last few months. "Yes, yes, of course," I said. "Let me just start over." I offered a weak smile. His lips turned up, slightly. He looked at the computer, so familiar with the process he probably could have run the recording equipment himself.

"Deepak Chopra is here with us today on *Speaking Freely*," I said, relieved that rage had cleared the stuffiness in my nose. "His newest book is called *Life After Death: The Book of Answers*." I sounded tight and hurried. I adjusted my tempo. "You've covered so many important spiritual topics in your previous books, but this must be the most pressing spiritual concern—what happens when we die?"

Chopra nodded. "I worked in the emergency room for many years, and I saw people in that final moment of death, filled with anxiety, fear, and trepidation. Now, contrast that with the experience I had watching my father die, in deep meditation, surrounded by the people he loved, in a state of peacefulness and grace. We can overcome our fear of dying and consider the fantastic possibilities that await us in the afterlife."

"But science tells us that death is final," I said.

"Correct, but the soul lives on, the bundle of consciousness that contains meaning and context and purpose and relationship. If you are in touch with that part of yourself, it is eternal and timeless; every experience is meaningful."

I caught myself—my mouth was slightly ajar. Chopra's cadence, his tone, his calming nature, resonated so deeply that my head suddenly felt completely clear. I was totally and completely open to his message.

Chopra continued, "There is abundant evidence that the world beyond is not separated from this world by an impassable wall," he said. "In fact, a single reality embraces all worlds, all times and places. At the end of our lives we cross over into the next phase of a limitless journey."

"So," I said, "the people who believe in heaven, meeting their relatives and all, do you believe their expectations will be met?"

Chopra chuckled. "Heaven, the afterlife, whatever, however you define it, it's all a reflection of your personal beliefs, expectations, and level of awareness. In the here and now, you can shape what happens after you die. By bringing the afterlife into the present moment, life after death opens up an immense new area of creativity. Ultimately there is no division between life and death—there is only one continuous creative project."

The rest of the questions came effortlessly, fluidly. I peppered him for a full thirty minutes with no notes or prompting. At the end, he calmly took his headphones off and said, "Thank you. You're very good at what you do."

I swallowed. The avocado pit was gone. I'd been tortured by my own thought process, my own guilt, my own belief that David's death proved nothing and meant nothing. But thirty minutes with Chopra had liberated me, at least temporarily. He'd at least offered a different way of reacting to the pain.

I looked Chopra in the eyes, and the boredom was gone, replaced by something so soft and beautiful my heart fluttered. "Thank you," I said. "This was so helpful to me."

Chopra rose, straightened his gold jacket, and extended his hand. "Good."

Inessa led him to the exit. He shook a few hands on the way out of the office. The last thing I saw were those red tennis shoes rounding the corner, swooshing off to his next interview. Nike, the goddess of victory. I smiled to myself, a radiance that must have seemed oddly timed to the rest of the world.

Dr. Bruce Perry is one of America's foremost experts on trauma. Perry has treated children faced with unimaginable horror: genocide survivors, witnesses to their own parents' murders, children raised in closets and cages. His work has revolutionized the methods used to ease the pain of traumatized children, allowing them to become healthy adults.

In his book *The Boy Who Was Raised as a Dog,* Perry says, "About 40 percent of American children will have at least one potentially traumatizing experience by age eighteen. This includes the death of a parent or sibling, ongoing physical abuse and or/neglect, sexual abuse, or the experience of a serious accident, natural disaster, or domestic violence."

In 1996, Perry founded the Child Trauma Academy, an interdisciplinary group of professionals committed to bringing treatments to traumatized children. Perry and his team are reporting phenomenal success with somatosensory activities such as yoga, meditation, deep breathing, singing, dancing, and drumming. The repetitive, rhythmic nature of these activities soothes a traumatized brain and sets the stage for healing.

Perry uses the neurosequential model of therapeutics (NMT), which includes making a developmental map of his patients' brains. Trauma healing, according to Perry, requires the patient to feel safe, and the activity must be developmentally matched to the individual. A nine-year-old girl whose father has just committed suicide is not a candidate for biofeedback therapy, but she will gravitate to the calm and repetitive nature of music. The rhythmic component of music allows the child's brain to decompress and begin to relax. After David's death, Sophie resisted traditional counseling and psychiatric intervention, but she turned her attention to music and songwriting, a creative outlet that allowed her to self-soothe in a way that is very similar to NMT.

There are few practices that engage our hearts and spirits

as successfully as listening to music. Perry's work as a clinician and researcher at the Child Trauma Academy has led many governmental agencies to consult him. He provided psychiatric care to traumatized children following the Columbine school shootings (1999), the September 11 terror attacks (2001), Hurricane Katrina in 2005, and the Sandy Hook Elementary School shootings in 2012.

# Chapter Twenty-Five

I waited for a sign, any sign that David's soul had moved on. After Chopra's visit, I read everything I could get my hands on about mindfulness and the afterlife. I thought the teachings might allow me to intercept any messages David might send.

It didn't happen. David didn't make as much as a cameo in my dreams. I didn't feel his presence behind me when I was scrubbing the kitchen counters the wrong way. I never got the sense that he was looking after us or intervening to keep us from harm. Once, I purposely ran a yellow light to see if his spirit might stop me. The light flashed red as I barreled through the intersection, untouched by angels.

One night, as I tucked Sophie into bed, I asked her, "Do you ever feel Daddy's presence, like he might be in your room?"

She looked at me, confused, her green eyes completely engaged in the question. "You mean, like a memory?"

"Yes, like that," I lied, wishing she'd felt or witnessed something miraculous, something that might make me believe David's spirit would be there to always watch over her.

"Sweetheart," I said tenderly, "how would you feel about visiting the Dougy Center?" I'd told Sophie about the center soon after David's death. It's an extraordinary program for grieving children.

Sophie lowered her chin, defiantly. “Seems like you want to go there more than I do, Mom.”

She was right. Sophie was coping much better than I was. The grief counselor had told me to be prepared for this. Kids often don’t want to process their loss until years, sometimes decades, later. But bedtime was always hardest for Sophie, the time of day when her defenses dropped to their low point and fatigue gave way to emotion. I put her to bed the same way every night, lying down beside her, with my arm around her waist, talking about the day’s events.

“So what was the high point of your day?” I asked, trying to find space for myself on her new full-size bed. Colin had helped move out her old mattress and box set after she complained she needed a grown-up room. We painted the room a shade of red that Sophie loved and drove three hours to Seattle to buy an Ikea bed with a ladder. Her desk and files and computer fit below, along with a hangout space for her and friends. The only weird part was when I awkwardly climbed the ladder at night to tuck her in.

“I dunno,” she said softly, her shoulders turned away from me. She hugged Bear tightly, his ears ragged and worn, the fur on his belly missing entirely.

“Are you doing okay?” Her tone worried me. The nightlight in her room illuminated the side of her face. The ceiling glowed with a warm white light. We’d stuck what seemed like a thousand fluorescent stars up there when we first moved in, Sophie handing me the tiny plastic shapes one by one and pointing at the place “in her sky” they should go. It was the one thing in her “little kid room” she didn’t want to let go of, the comfort of those stars, and her Bear.

“It’s not the same,” she said, curling in tighter to herself.

“I know.”

I breathed steady and deep, ready to listen, conscious of the importance of hearing, not judging or trying to make it better. As my therapist had said, “It’s as much as you may get from her for now. Take what you can get.”

I lifted her T-shirt to scratch her back, something she'd loved since she was a toddler. "Get the chicken bones," she'd usually say, "yeah, that's good, right there!" But this time, instead of oohs and aahs, she whimpered, and the whimpers turned into a sob.

"I miss him," she said. "I miss Daddy."

"I know, baby, I know," I whispered. "I'm sorry you are hurting."

"He never even said goodbye!" she said louder, her sobs turning into wailing, a sound that echoed up to the fluorescent stars and back again, ringing in my ears. I tried to remember a time I cried like that as a child, and couldn't. I had forced my sadness or isolation inside, sobbing silently into a pillow at night. Growing up, there was not much space for my emotion in a household as fragile as ours. I remembered developing the keen sense of gauging everyone else's moods to avoid causing more trouble. It was a coping mechanism I had carried through to my marriage, getting out of the way instead of confronting problems head on. My contributions to our family's failures were never far from my mind.

"Sweetheart, you have been through so much," I said.

She sat up in bed, suddenly struck by a thought that stopped the crying. The tears spotted her cheeks, and her nose needed to be wiped. I didn't move to get a tissue. I wanted desperately to hear her out, to not interrupt this moment. I sat up with her.

"I can't remember him, Mommy. I can't remember for sure what he looked like. I know what he looked like in the pictures and everything, but I'm worried I will forget him." The thought terrified her—her chest rose and fell quickly, and she squeezed Bear until I thought his worn head might pop from his body.

"Baby. You will always have Daddy in your heart. You will have the memories of him making you breakfast, and making you a fire, and reading to you. Remember how many books Daddy could read in a week?"

She nodded.

"Those memories are yours to keep forever. They won't ever go away."

She turned her chin down. "But what about Colin?"

I braced myself for something painful. "What about him?"

"I'm worried he will replace Daddy." The gravity of her insight hit me like a fist. My body recoiled, a sudden shock moving through my spine and neck, until I had to force myself to stay sitting up.

I spoke slowly. "Sophie, Colin is a good man."

She nodded.

"But, you have a daddy. David. You have his cheekbones, and his lips, and his long legs, and David will always be your dad, forever." I held her hand, sweaty and soft, in mine. "I don't want you to replace Daddy—ever. Colin wouldn't want that either. But your heart is big enough to love again, honey. You'll see. It's like you'll have a huge place for Daddy in your heart. And then, maybe you'll grow more room for Colin. Or not. You always get to decide who you want to love and how much. Nobody decides that for you. But when you do fall in love, and you will, you'll grow more room in your heart for your husband and your kids. It never stops—our capacity for love is limitless."

"Like infinity?" Sophie said.

"Just like that." I curled up next to her, lost in my thoughts. I had ignored the truth of David's illness so that Sophie could live with her father. Now, he was gone. I felt the burden of my illogical thinking every time I held Sophie.

"Hold my back, Mama," she whispered.

I spooned into her, breathing in her smell. Her hiccupping breathing pattern quieted after a while, into an even flow of air, in and out, in and out.

The most visible sign of David's death was the toll it had taken on me. After months of watching his mental health decline—months when I operated under maximum stress, doing everything at hyperspeed—my body felt poisoned and sluggish. David's death had started my own body's deterioration: for the first time, the skin on my arms and legs was so dry it itched at night, I had dark rings under my eyes, and my hair was thinning.

I ignored my condition until one day at work, in the middle of chatting on the air with my cohost, I couldn't find the word I needed. The topic was the stock market: "Negative territory, again," I said. "The . . ." My mouth was open, the word "Dow" was on the tip of my tongue, and uh, uh, uh, nothing. It was gone, *whoosh*.

My cohost looked at me, horrified, and then quickly filled in the blanks. "The stock market has left Sheila speechless," he quipped, before breaking for a commercial.

"What happened?" he asked, pulling the headphones from his ears.

I shook my head, dumbfounded. My career had been built on having the right word at the right time. I knew I needed help.

C. S. Lewis wrote about his wife's death from cancer in the book *A Grief Observed*: "Grief is like a winding valley where any bend may reveal a totally new landscape."

The acupuncturist squinted while she looked at my tongue, then *mmmed* and *aahed* while I described the mysterious symptom that had plagued me. She reached into a cupboard and pulled out more than two dozen sterilized needles. Expertly, with little more than a flick of her wrist, she placed needles in my wrists, near my elbows, in my earlobes, stomach, and legs, and all along the inside of my ankles. When she finished, she told me calmly, "Rest, relax. This is going to take a while."

*I don't have a while,* I thought, my mind racing like a tiger in a cage. *I'll be late for work.*

I'd been happy when she said she'd fit me in the schedule, even though I hadn't been in for regular visits in more than a year. Calming woodwind music played in the background. The sheets were pure white and clean smelling. But something still felt wrong. For one thing, it was too hot. The acupuncturist had politely cracked the window when I mentioned it.

I'd always loved acupuncture before. I'd used it on several occasions when big stories prevented me from sleeping or eating well. It restored my sense of balance, made my skin glow again.

This time, though, my hands were clenched tight, and my head banged with a headache that intensified every time I breathed in the incense. My tongue clacked against dry tissue in my mouth. I couldn't move to reach the water she'd set by the treatment bed for fear of breaking a needle.

That image of David standing at our kitchen sink, agitated and miserable, his tongue smacking dry, flooded over me. The smell of dental fillings overwhelmed me—it was the smell I associated with David whenever he took the antidepressants. Why hadn't his doctors listened to me? He'd had hepatitis after traveling in Africa. His liver was damaged. The drugs poisoned him, amped him up beyond control.

My heart palpitations increased, and my chest heaved up and down. The needles were suddenly beyond uncomfortable, stinging and probing in places they shouldn't have been. It felt like blood vessels were popping all over my body. I was in the middle of a full-blown panic attack.

Several of the needles came out as I flailed around, arms going this way and that. The stings felt like bee bites. I found the heavy bell the acupuncturist had told me to ring if I became uncomfortable. I swung it side to side so frantically I knocked over my glass of water.

The acupuncturist opened the door calmly, her voice still serenely balanced. "Yes?" she asked.

"You've got to get these out," I said. "I can't take it. I'm oversensitive, or something. Something's wrong with me."

She put her hands on the top of my head, like a blessing, warm, soft hands that made the thump in my head softer, more tolerable. "Do you want to tell me about it?"

"About what?" My eyes closed to everything except the ticking time bomb in my chest. It was a heart attack, I knew. I was having a heart attack. I was dying on an acupuncturist's table. *Please, please take the needles out*, I thought. *I can't take any more pain.*

"About your fear," she said, pressing her thumbs into the very spot on my forehead where the headache centered itself.

The slight crack in the window wasn't bringing in enough cold air. I needed to get up, to go, to get dressed and get to a hospital. I could feel every prick on my body where the needles stood, every opening screaming with pain. I started to talk and didn't recognize my own voice.

"I'm afraid I'm going to die," I said, my voice breaking. "I'm going to die and Sophie will be completely alone." The revelation cascaded through me, taking with it the sensation of a heart attack, the panic, and my intense need to flee. I started to sob, so loudly I worried the acupuncturist might call for help.

Instead, she smoothed my hair over and over again. "Yes, I know," she said calmly. "I know." She took a tissue out of the box and gently wiped my nose. "Breathe," she said. "Remember to breathe."

The spasms rippling through my chest reminded me of Sophie, who as a child could cry so hard she'd hiccup for half an hour after her tantrums. I would stroke her hair over and over until she fell fast asleep, but the erratic breathing would continue even into her dreams.

The smell of the room had changed. Now the scent enveloped and comforted me, the temperature had cooled just enough, and the needles no longer poked but instead felt anchored in just the right places. I imagined them reaching down to my central nervous system, to my circulatory system, to the organs themselves and stimulating all that had been broken and damaged.

My fingers unclenched. Blood flowed to my extremities.

Soon, I was in a state of complete relaxation, my body limp against the mattress, my eyes gazing at the ceiling tiles, my thoughts only on the magnificent gift I'd been given—breath, life, this moment.

The acupuncturist rose quietly and opened the door to let herself out. I didn't know how much time had passed, but it was the first moment of peace I'd had since David died. He had been in pain, too, a much more burdensome mental torture. He wanted relief. He wanted to sleep again. I understood.

My thoughts turned to Costa Rica, which we visited when Sophie was six years old. David and I had argued over whether it was safe to take Sophie into a cave we'd heard about from the rafting guides. They'd promised us a spectacular sight, the womb, they called it, with the clearest water and a rock face that sparkled like diamonds. I didn't want David to take Sophie; he'd argued that he could keep her safe by wading in with her on his back.

I followed reluctantly, pissed off that he always seemed to win those kinds of fights. I waded for several anxious minutes before finally rounding a corner to see him holding Sophie on her back, floating in the water, looking up at the rock wall the guides had promised us—the womb, glittering like a million stars at night. She was mesmerized.

I mouthed the word "Wow" to David, and he said apologetically, "I know."

The memory was so vivid I could see the blue of David's eyes, his big hands under Sophie's back, steady and strong.

## BABY BOOMERS AND SUICIDE

Suicide rates among middle-aged Americans rose sharply from 2001 to 2010, according to the Centers for Disease Control and Prevention. More people now die of suicide than in car accidents, according to the CDC's Morbidity and Mortality Report. In 2010, there were 33,687 deaths from motor vehicle crashes and 38,364 suicides. The surge in the suicide rate among middle-aged Americans is most troubling. From 1999 to 2010, the suicide rate among Americans ages thirty-five to sixty-four rose by about 30 percent. The most pronounced increases were seen among men in their fifties, a group in which suicide rates jumped by 50 percent. Historically, suicide rates rise during times of financial stress and economic setbacks. The increase coincides with the recession of 2008 and a decrease in financial standing for a lot of families. The CDC also cites widespread availability of opioid drugs like OxyContin (oxycodone), which can be deadly in large doses. From 2001 to 2010, there was a marked increase in intentional overdoses from prescription drugs, and of hangings.

# Chapter Twenty-Six

Jeff Brands knocked on my door in early February. His hands were stuck way down in his pockets, and every time he breathed, steam formed around his mouth.

"Come in, come in," I said. "Thank you for coming." He walked through my door and looked around the living room. His hair was mussed, and he ran his fingers through it before settling his gaze on the windows. I could spot lovers of modern architecture the minute they walked in. Their eyes always wandered up to the high ceilings that were finished in old growth wood to feel like the forest was above, below, and around you. The home's spare design was muted by the architect's soft spot for nature. The granite countertops were the same color as the forest outside. The lighting came from soft angles, above, to the side. The room was divided by furniture, not walls.

My sister, who had returned to help with the settling of David's affairs, sat at the kitchen table. She stood when she saw John. She came over and looked him directly in the eye. "Hello, I'm Diane. We spoke on the telephone."

The three of us sat at the table together, surrounded by some of the envelopes that Diane considered "pressing legal issues." John was a forensic accountant and had been referred to us by David's attorney.

"I'm the guy who can make sense of all the numbers," he said confidently. "I can tell you whether there's any money left in David's business and exactly how much he, or you, owes."

"I'm not confident the people who owe David money will pay." I showed him the yellow sheet David had scribbled for me in the hospital. "I called Dr. Tendale, the dentist. David claims Tendale owes him a hundred grand," I said. "Tendale claims David didn't finish the work on time, or up to spec, and he refuses to pay the bill." Another client, the owners of a local nightclub, made the same claim. They said that toward the end of David's illness, he made mistakes or got confused on the job, and his behavior and choices voided the contract.

John pursed his lips. Diane looked at him. "The bottom line is their creditor is dead," she said. "Who could testify against them in court?"

John's cheeks were still flushed from the cold. "Well, they may say that now, but if, when we take a look at David's books, we can determine he was owed money, they won't have a choice. The probate court will make them pay."

"I can't pay you for your time," I said, embarrassed. "I can barely make the mortgage on this house and keep Sophie in school."

John interrupted. "You won't have to pay. I'll do this on contingency. Your job is to take care of Sophie."

I bit my lip, overwhelmed with gratitude and humility. There had been so few times in my life when I needed other people's help. I'd always been so independent. These days, I needed humility more than pride. I touched John on the arm. "Thank you."

Diane nodded her head. "Sheila, he's right. It's probably best if you let us handle this until your stress level is down. I can stay another week and get John started. Then let him take it over. Get these piles out of your house. It's really bad for your energy level."

I reached over and hugged her, so grateful for her brains and her heart. John pulled a pen and a pair of reading glasses from his pocket and moved one seat over, closer to Diane. They hunkered down together, the Buddhist priest and the forensic accountant. What great friends to have when you are managing a crisis.

The next morning, with Sophie at school and Diane on a walk, I climbed the stairs to David's office. I tried to focus on the task, my task, the only task I'd been given. Clean the house. Get rid of David's chaos. I got four plastic bins from the basement and labeled them "Probate," "Recycle," "Keep for Family," and a huge question mark for the items that would need to be looked at before I could sort them away.

David's books had been removed from the bookshelves by his sisters, but there were still some remodeling magazines that could be recycled. I pulled them from the bookshelf and dust flew into my face. My eyes stung, my nose burned, and I threw open the drawers to David's desk to try to find some Kleenex.

I don't know why I hadn't seen it before, when David was sick in the hospital. Maybe I had seen it and it didn't mean anything to me at the time. A blue manila folder that said "Life Insurance Policy, prepared for David Krol."

I pulled the folder from the desk and opened the document. David had never carried life insurance before he met me. He'd told me it never occurred to him to get it. After Sophie was born, we'd agreed that he would take out a policy of some sort, something to make sure that, in the event of his death, she'd be taken care of.

I opened the policy and scanned it. There was a $500,000 death benefit.

If this policy were still in effect, we'd be able to stay in the house. I stifled something close to a gasp. I didn't want to get my hopes up. Somewhere, I remembered reading that insurance policies generally don't cover suicide. But I pulled out my cell phone and dialed our insurance agent. "Hello, Mark?" I said. "This is Sheila Hamilton."

"Hello, Sheila. How are you?" I imagined him working at his tiny northeast office—he'd always struck me as a man who should have been in the entertainment industry. I'd only been in his office a few times, but he always seemed to remember me.

"I don't know if you've heard, Mark." I paused. "David died."

"Oh, no. I'm so sorry to hear that. How did he die?"

I could hear him making notes, the routine information-taking that occurs after death, the number cruncher figuring out his next move.

I hesitated. "He committed suicide, Mark. They found his body in December."

Mark was typing into the computer, pulling up his data on David. He *mmmed*, then sighed. "Oh, that's awful. This is not good," he said.

"What is it?"

"David let his insurance policy lapse after just two months, Sheila. He took it out the day the three of you came into the office together, but he never paid the premiums. He hasn't had a policy in eight years."

He might as well have hit me in the stomach with a baseball bat. I leaned my forehead on the desk and muttered into the phone. "I shouldn't have bothered you."

Mark's voice dropped low and very quiet. "I'm so sorry. He was quite insistent when I called to remind him to pay or renew the policy that it wasn't something he thought he needed. Good luck, Sheila."

The luck I would receive would be in the form of legal advice, from Jeff Brands, real estate attorney Stu Parker, and divorce attorney Jody Stahancyk. All of these experts worked for pennies on the dollar to help me settle David's debts. David owed thousands of dollars in back taxes. The bank had already called due the $100,000 line of credit David used for his business, a loan that carried my name.

The clients who owed David money refused to pay, and his business was eventually declared insolvent. I was on the hook for all of David's personal debt. I eventually sold every piece of property in my name to settle David's debts, including our home, a lot at the beach, and the apartments Margaret (my former business partner) and I had managed together.

The indignities were great, especially knowing that some of David's subcontractors, his vendors, and other agencies would not be fully reimbursed. As late as 2010, the IRS was still sending payment notices for David's 2008 taxes—even though he'd been dead two years.

The pain of David's suicide never really diminished, but life's momentum is a powerful thing. We moved on.

## SUICIDE PREVALENCE

Actor Robin Williams took his life in August 2014, prompting a flurry of news stories and social media posts. But his death was one in 41,149 suicides in the United States that year, making suicide the nation's tenth leading cause of death and the second leading killer for people ages fifteen to thirty-four. In the months after Williams's funeral, stories about mental health faded from the headlines.

Imagine if the flu were claiming 41,149 people every year. The public health campaign would be immediate and extensive. Yet there is no systematic government-sponsored program to attempt to reduce suicide. Mental health services have been cut by federal, state, and county budgets, and the suicide research budget for the National Institute of Mental Health has been shrinking every year since 2011.

Only one organization has increased its research into suicide—the military. Suicide is now the second leading cause of death in the armed forces, with a suicide rate that tripled from 2004 to 2012.

The military and the U.S. government have now spent 230 million dollars to attempt to understand the skyrocketing nature of military suicide. Among those efforts is a study analyzing soldier suicides and tracking tens of thousands of troops to attempt to understand the suicidal mind. If we invest in suicide prevention, we can bring the rate of suicide down.

# Chapter Twenty-Seven

Sunday morning. A rain outside that reminded me of the "in like a lion" phrase. I'd just opened *The New York Times* and was on the editorial page, hoping for at least another hour in front of the fire. The phone rang.

I brightened at the sound of Colin's voice. "Hey, you, you want to get out?" he asked cheerily. I had tried to navigate the chaos of David's death on my own and involve him in the business affairs as little as possible. But the more I saw of him, the more I wanted him around. Sophie felt the same way, brightening whenever she heard our plans included Colin and his girls—we'd been to the beach together and spent many of our weekends strolling the city. I knew it was dangerous to get so close so early; everything I read warned against a relationship in the aftermath of death. But I'd been stripped raw by David's death, and for the first time in my life, I was asking for, and getting, the emotional support I needed from other people. The only antidote to David's death was choosing life, without apology or reservations. Colin's voracious appetite for living was inspiring.

He was not the type of father who let his kids hang around the house on the weekend. He saw them every other week, for five days at a time, and he did not want to waste a single moment.

"We're ready to roll—wanna join us?" His enthusiasm was so infectious; by now, it was a great source of comfort for me that Colin did not suffer huge mood swings. I looked at the still unopened sections of the *Times* and bit my lip, conflicted.

Sophie heard me on the phone and curled up beside me on the couch. "Is that Colin?" she asked. "Hi, Colin! Do you have the girls?" she yelled into the receiver.

"Hi, Sophs," he said. "Yeah, we're going swimming at the club. Wanna come?"

Sophie started bouncing up and down like Tigger. "Can we, can we, Mom?"

The legs of her pajama bottoms skimmed the middle of her shinbone. *I really should get her some new ones,* I thought. Her feet looked more like mine now, and she had slender, beautiful toenails with black and white polka dots she'd painted herself. How could I deny her? "Of course," I said into the phone, watching Sophie jump in the air and then dance around in circles like Rocky. "We'd love to join you."

"Great," Colin said. "We'll grab some dim sum after swimming."

I packed a bag for Sophie and myself, making a mental note to get Sophie a bigger bathing suit. Oddly, I still thought of her as being stuck at the size and the age when David died. In just three and a half months, so much had changed.

The pool was empty except for the lone lifeguard who yawned and looked bored. The windows looked out on a cold March day, but inside, the air temperature felt humid and comfortable. Colin jumped in with a cannonball that splashed the rest of the girls at the edge of the pool, and they shrieked with delight. Olivia stayed furthest from the edge, her six-year-old body so thin I sometimes worried about her resilience. She stood with her arms folded over her chest, protectively.

Charlotte and Sophie were nearly the same height, even though Sophie was a year older. They both wore bikinis, reminding me of little colts with legs too long and spirits that could not be reined in. Sophie dove in after Colin. Charlotte jumped in next.

Having a pool at home had given Sophie a rare advantage; swimming was now second nature to her. Colin's youngest, Olivia, still stood on the side, looking at the others. "Daddy, come get me," she yelled. "I will drown!"

Colin rolled his eyes and swam to the side. "You will not drown. Here, get on my back. I'll ride you around like a horse."

He managed to pull Charlotte behind him on an inflatable mattress while Olivia held tight to his back. Sophie bobbed up and down in the deep end. Every now and then, I would see her surface, taking in the scene of a dad playing with his daughters. Before I could figure out the emotion on her face, she'd submerge herself under the water. My stomach tightened in knots. I would never be able to replace the love of her own father. There would never be another man who would love her so fully.

"Do you want me to take one of the girls?" I asked as Colin rounded back toward me, pulling both girls on the mattress. I was still sitting by the side of the pool, my feet dangling in the water.

"No!" Olivia shouted. "I want my dad."

"Me, too," Charlotte said. "Daddy, it's my turn."

My cheeks flushed, and my skin got goose bumps. The newness of me, the fun of another adult around, had worn off. Now, I was just another person competing for their father's attention. I'd heard blending families was difficult. Somewhere, I'd read the divorce rate for second, blended marriages was around 75 percent! Colin shrugged his shoulders and looked at me apologetically.

"That's okay," I said. "If you decide you want to give your dad a break, you can always come with me." I sat on the edge of the pool, unsure of my next move.

Sophie swam over to Colin, anxious to play. "Colin, can you flip me from your shoulders?"

"Uh, I've got my hands full here, Soph," Colin said, his tone sharp and overwhelmed.

Sophie's face fell, and even though goggles protected her eyes, I knew there would be tears forming. I could stand rejection—I knew Sophie could not. My face must have tightened. My blood pressure rose suddenly, unexpectedly. I had waited to get in the water, but now I had a strange impulse to dive in, carry Sophie to safety, and never see Colin again. I could not afford to see her hurt or even dinged. Not yet, not now.

Colin sensed the impending disaster. "On second thought, let's do this. See the big clock on the wall?" He pointed to a round clock at the end of the pool. "I'm going to give each of you five minutes with me."

Olivia dissolved in protest. "No, Daddy, I don't want to let go."

"That's not fair at all!" Charlotte folded her arms and pouted on the side of the pool. "You are *my* dad!"

"It's the fair way, and it's the only way," Colin said. "We'll go from youngest to oldest, starting with Olivia. And wait patiently until it's your turn, okay?"

I wrapped a towel around my waist and sat on the sidelines to watch. It never occurred to me that Colin's penchant for order and fairness could work to his advantage in figuring out an emotion as complex as jealousy. I watched the clock—10:35. Olivia beamed at the other girls as her dad took her around the pool. Instead of spending their time swimming, Charlotte and Sophie sat with their arms folded, scrutinizing each tick of the clock.

At 10:40, they shouted, "Time's up!"

Charlotte jumped on Colin from the front and had him catapult her into the sky as many times as she could in her allotted time. Olivia clung to the edge and kicked her legs impatiently. Sophie's face took on a seriousness that worried me. This was very, very important to her. Colin looked weary; his shoulders slumped from the psychological and physical pressure of the outing. My chest hurt.

"It's 10:45," Sophie said. "My turn!"

Charlotte shouted, "It is not your turn yet. There are seven seconds left!"

Colin let Charlotte go gently. "I'm sorry, sweetheart. Your turn is over."

"This is not fair! You are *my* dad!" she said.

Sophie waded in tentatively, her shoulders slumped with anxiety. I stifled my own tears.

Sophie whispered something in Colin's ear. He nodded, and then he moved his hands underneath her back as she flipped over in the pool. She lay there with her face looking up at the pool ceiling, barely moving, but at peace, just as she had in Costa Rica, when David had found the cave with a million stars. She floated like that for the rest of her time with Colin, moving slowly, silently, the stillness of the water below her, her eyes shut tight beneath her goggles. Colin held both hands firmly beneath her back, gliding her through the water until the minute hand had made its five full rotations.

I brought my knees to my chest, to protect my heart. I hadn't prayed since David's death, angry with whomever and whatever entity there might be that allowed him to take his own life. At that moment, however, I needed a conversation with God, as one-way as it might be.

"Please, God," I said, "forgive me, this is awkward. Please let us do what is right for these little girls." I held my head to my knees and let the tears come, warmed by the strange humidity, heavy with a humility I would carry for a lifetime. David's death had changed the landscape of what I knew and how I believed. Death had preserved David at a certain age, in a certain time frame, and everything we'd been together had been shattered. There was nothing left except room for me to change.

## SUICIDE BEREAVEMENT

Suicide is self-inflicted and violates the fundamental norm of self-preservation. Consequently, suicide survivors may grieve differently than others grieving a natural death. Suicide survivors show higher levels of guilt, blame, and responsibility for the death than other mourners. They frequently feel that they may have directly caused the death through abandonment or mistreatment. Dr. Katherine Dunham, department co-chair of psychology at the State University of New York at Plattsburgh, noted that the spillover stigma from suicide attaches to the bereaved. These authors report that survivors of suicide tend to be viewed "as more psychologically disturbed, less likable, more in need of professional mental health services, and more likely to remain bereaved longer."

In Dunham's research, 76 percent of those bereaved by accidental death reported positive changes in social interactions, but only 27 percent of suicide survivors reported positive changes in social interactions. Withdrawal is a common reaction to suicide. It is difficult to explain the actions of the suicidal and therefore difficult to explain our reactions to our social networks. Survivors may pull away from their social groups out of shame, causing friends and even family members to pull away in frustration and confusion.

# Chapter Twenty-Eight

I heard the music of Frank Sinatra as I was coming up the steps, loaded down with two grocery bags full of ingredients for a chicken risotto dinner. I'd started cooking again—a healthy sign.

I paused to watch the two of them through the window—Colin, dressed in his work slacks, his jacket removed, shirt sleeves rolled up and tie unhitched, twirling Sophie around the living room floor. She'd changed into the white taffeta gown I bought her for Easter the year before, with shoes that looked oddly small on her feet. Every time he turned her, she watched him as carefully as she could, and then she'd whip her head around to catch his eye. Ha, he'd taught her how to spot! My arms felt weak from the surge of delight that moved through me. I opened the door, smiling.

"Who knew you two were so talented?" I asked.

"Mama!" Sophie said. "Watch, Colin's teaching me to dance!"

"Here, let me get those." Colin kissed me on the cheek before taking the bags.

Sophie turned her lip down, hands by her side, disappointed the dance had ended.

"No, no, don't stop. I'd love to watch you two," I said, flopping myself down on the couch and kicking off my heels.

Sophie put her arms back up in the stance of a ballroom dancer, and Colin rejoined her, twirling her to the tune of "Fly Me to the Moon." Colin had mentioned he'd taken ballroom dancing in college;

now he counted out the steps for Sophie carefully, "One, two, three." He moved around the room as if he were Fred Astaire and she were Ginger, saying, "One, two, three."

Sophie smiled at me over her shoulder, struggling to keep up with Colin's fluid steps. "Let's do the lift," she said, "the lift!"

Colin put his hands on her hips and swooped her high to the air, an angel flying above his head. Sophie's cheeks flushed pink, her body nearly skimming the ceiling, Colin holding her expertly as he sashayed around the floor. Sophie's eyes danced, too. Then she touched his head as if to say, "I'm dizzy."

In one way, I was worried that Sophie had bonded with Colin so quickly. I wanted her to protect her heart, to hold her most emotional self at bay. This was my old pattern repeating itself, looking for safety in defense. Sophie did just the opposite, relying on Colin's consistency and his goodness to help her heal. She read with him, called him on the telephone, and jumped into his arms when he arrived home. Over time, she learned how to navigate the jealousy she felt when Colin's girls arrived for their biweekly visits.

Blending families is an unnatural act, but we were determined to make it work. I'd never met a man who doled out so much affection to his children or was fairer or more capable of juggling the demands of domesticity than Colin. Sophie learned valuable lessons in sharing, patience, and kindness because of her stepsisters' refusal to treat her differently than they treated one another. We never romanticized the difficulty of bringing two families together, and the challenges, though many, always led to personal breakthroughs. I'd been through much tougher, and far less valuable, experiences.

In the same way that mental illness forces us to make decisions about how we will react, blending families presents an opportunity—do we choose to withhold or to expand our love? Can we be more generous, more present, and more available? I challenged myself to say yes.

Things were changing at the radio station as well. My cohost and I were promoted to the morning show, and I settled into an early morning routine others consider grueling—I saw it as a necessary part of working the most coveted time slots on the radio. The alarm sounded at 3:30 a.m. I showered and tiptoed out the door at 4:15.

From 4:15 until 5:30 a.m., I researched the morning's news—local, national, and international; I downloaded sound clips from CNN and MSNBC; and wrote eight newscasts and found as many "kickers," or the types of stories that add a little levity to the show. I edited two interviews, one that would air in a newscast and another that would air on our website. I prepped for the interviews with the artists who would be calling in later, posted pictures and stories to the website, tweeted and blogged, and checked up on the constant chatter of email from our listeners.

After the live show, I settled back into my editing, a chance to breathe, slow down, and enjoy the conversations with authors, artists, and musicians. On this day, the interview was with Chris Martin, the lead singer of Coldplay and the husband of actress Gwyneth Paltrow. The digital recording of his interview was displayed on my computer screen in what is called wave form—sound waves that look a little like the up and down lines of a seismograph. Seeing the wave form made it easy to edit the interview. It also gave distinct clues to people's personalities: those who are animated have waves that show up as wild and erratic as a heart attack reading. Depressed or dour interviewees often show up as a long, flat line, with very little emotion on the high or low end of their voices. Children's waves are thinner and weaker. Trained speakers often have thick sound waves that look like the jagged ups and downs of the Dow.

David never would allow me to record his voice. I often wondered if he suspected the sound waves might reveal something he didn't want to see.

Chris Martin's voice was in my headphones. I was totally engaged in what he was saying about the making of his most recent album. The white light in the studio flashed, a sign that the phone was ringing.

I took off the headphones and picked up the receiver. "Hello, Sheila, dear, I do hope I haven't disturbed you." It was Alice, calling from a new number. "I've moved closer to Nini. I just thought it would be better to be closer to family after Lew's and David's deaths. I thought you might want the number."

"Yes, yes, of course," I said, turning away from the computer. "How are you?"

"I'm better. I'm getting stronger. The asthma attacks have subsided for now." That's right—I reminded myself of his family's propensity to suffer from asthma. Even David had started to have breathing problems later in his life. I made a mental note to myself to watch Sophie for any early signs of the disorder.

She paused. "I thought you might need some support during this week."

I nodded. "Yes, David's birthday. It's a tough day, but they all are, really. I thought, somehow, that time would make it easier, but in fact, it's just the opposite. When the shock wore off, I had a new round of grief to deal with."

"Quite right," she said. "How is our lovely Sophie?"

I hesitated before I spoke. Sophie was great, incredible really, for what she'd been through. She'd started going to a new school; she was happy at home and healthy. "She's fine, Alice, thanks for asking. She's reading a ton of books, playing tennis again. It's been a good summer for her."

Alice drew in a breath. "Does she speak of David?"

I considered my words carefully. "She is in a different place right now, Alice. When David first died, Sophie grieved long and hard. I would lie with her at night while she cried so hard I thought she might break. But after a few months, she stopped talking about him. She stopped wanting to hear my funny stories about him. We're in a different phase now. I'm sure it will change." I waited to breathe. The truth was so hard, but I was through with secrets—it was the secrets in my marriage that had destroyed us. I hoped Alice would accept my candidness in kind.

"Hmm," she said. "Well, I suppose we all grieve differently, don't we. Especially children. They just need more time."

"Yes," I said. "Sophie still refuses to see a psychologist."

"Well, I certainly understand that," she interrupted. "I still think those people did David more harm than good."

"I was just going to say that I hope one day she will be willing to talk to someone other than me about what she's gone through. I expect she'll need to process it all at some point."

"Or, perhaps not," Alice said. "As I said, we all grieve differently."

For a split second, I was back in Diedra's cabin with Alice, her face drawn by the realization that David was gone for good, knowing the experts we'd hoped could help him couldn't save him any more than we could. The memory sent a strange sensation through my body, the same way a flu bug feels when it first announces itself in your stomach. His family had denied the gravity of his illness, denied me the truth when I first met them. I considered asking her why, and then I stopped myself. I knew the reasons: they were the same reasons that had prevented me from telling my family the truth about my crumbling marriage. We were both ashamed.

For a moment I fell silent, forgiving myself, David, his family. We were wounded, all of us. David had escaped his pain in the way he thought best.

"I do hope to see Sophie again," she said. "Perhaps next summer?"

"I'm sure she'd like that," I said.

I weighed the obligation of keeping David's memory alive for Sophie—the stories, the pictures, the reminders I put on her calendar to write her relatives and thank them for the cards they sent on her birthday. She would one day want to know more exactly what went wrong, why her father decided to leave her so abruptly. Even if she avoided the pain of David's memory now, Sophie would want to know the whole story; she always did. I would write it down, knowing my memory would be clouded, my objectivity hampered, the sharp, instinctive tools of a reporter deadened by overwhelming emotion and personal involvement in my own story.

The fact that David hadn't left a note, denying us any written record of his final moments, or any insight into his decision, troubled me. Because of his illness, so much of his purpose in the world went unclaimed. He wouldn't live to see his greatest achievement, Sophie, learn French, or win a tennis match, or ski a black diamond run. David's story was so unfinished.

I once heard a pastor speak about suicide, about how those who take their own lives force us all to examine our untapped promise, our purpose, the reasons we put our dreams on hold. I'd been thinking about it so much, examining how I had loved, how deeply, what my part was in David's life and his death. My own purpose had come under searing self-scrutiny. Even if I could never forget him or move on from him in the way other people described, I was claiming the promise David left behind.

I put my headphones back on. Chris Martin was talking about living a life he, too, never imagined, one with infinite possibility. "If your wife had slept with Brad Pitt, you'd be shaking your head too." I threw back my head and laughed out loud.

Grief is like an unwelcome stranger, an abductor who comes just at the moment you least expect and puts a black sack over your head, whisking you away to a dark, unknown place. Just when I thought I could cope with the idea of David's absence, I would wake up confused and traumatized all over again. His birthday, Easter, Christmas, and the anniversary of his disappearance all seemed to tear at the scab that had formed over the emotional wound.

Two years had passed since David's death, and I could not shake the feeling that there was something more I needed to do to fully understand David's decision.

I had overwhelming feelings of despair at the most unexpected times: Watching Sophie kick the soccer ball reminded me of the dozens of nights she and David spent kicking the ball across the hardwood floor in our kitchen. When Sophie sang the lead in the school play, I was reminded of how David would prod Sophie to sing louder at our campfire gatherings. Sophie skied the way he did, cracked jokes with the same rhythm, shared his nose and his cheekbones and thick, thick hair—how could he have left her? Were there reasons that made sense at least to him? Was there a logic, however twisted? Or was it just the disease, the darkness, something no one, not even David, could understand?

I petitioned the doctors for his medical records, desperate for any answer. When the documents were ready, I drove to the hospital and parked in the same parking space I had used to visit David. It was the first time I'd been back to the hospital since his lockdown.

The skateboarders I'd seen on so many nights during David's hospitalization were there again, along with the familiar clackety-clack of their skateboards against the cement. It immediately took me back to the lonely nights I'd entered and exited the hospital, awash in emotion and anxiety.

One of the young guys dressed in baggy pants and a T-shirt looked up at me and grinned. I smiled back. Had I seen this particular teenager before? I could not recall seeing any of the skateboarders' faces before today. Except for the vivid sound of the sport, I'd remembered the skaters only as dark sketches at the recesses of my memory. I wondered how much else I'd missed during David's illness.

In the lobby, clerks stared at their computer screens while families waited in the reception area for word of their loved ones. A young woman paced back and forth while talking on her cell phone. She wore a business suit, her face haggard from the day. People come to hospitals on their bad days, not their good ones. The panic, the anxiety, the smell of pharmacology and mental illness flooded my senses again. Dizzy, I leaned up against the reception desk. "I'm here to pick up my husband's medical records."

A clerk arrived with a massive file, three hundred or so pages. On the top of the stack: a discharge summary dated October 24.

*Final Diagnoses: Bipolar disorder, mixed state.*
*Suicidal ideation, resolved.*
*Partner relational problems.*
*Complicated bereavement.*
*Severe Secondary to financial problems, separation from spouse and daughter, death of father.*

A note from his psychiatrist read, "David was discharged this morning. I wrote a thirty-day supply of medications for him. He was very pleased with how well he was doing and he acknowledged that while his brain wasn't all the way back it was most of the way back and he felt comfortable with leaving. His friend has written a letter regarding her concern that the firearm, which he had shot twice in the woods, was still lost. David has assured everyone that he does not know where it is.

"David does not feel that we need to call her and feels that the issue is resolved. He is not planning to go look for it and he thinks that it is just simply lost in the woods."

The discharge note continued, "David's mother had set plans that either she, or his sister, Adele, would be with David constantly and felt comfortable that he would be okay. He was no longer expressing a plan to kill himself."

My chest lifted with a breath of air that I couldn't let out. It was caught at the back of my throat, trapped with the anger and frustration I'd felt two years prior, when I tried so desperately to make sure the staff behind the glass windows realized the man they were treating needed their attention.

That David would lie about his planned suicide did not shock me. He'd lied to me plenty about everything from life insurance to his intimate relationships. But how could trained psychiatrists, the last line of defense, the people most expert at detecting the deceit and vagaries of bipolar, also be defrauded? And if it's as easy as David made it sound in those exit interviews, what hope is there of ever preventing suicide? What separates those who can be saved from those who, like David, simply can't believe in a future beyond their illness?

I sat in the hospital lobby reading through the documents for two hours. I called Ted Oster, the social worker who had been so helpful to me during David's hospitalization. "Sheila," he said warmly, "how are you?"

"I know it must be odd to talk to me after all this time," I said, "but I just can't *shake* this question, this question of why. I think I was shielded by shock and grief for the first year, Ted. But I really need to know. How could David have done this to Sophie?"

Ted grew quiet. "He could have used more time, undoubtedly. Unfortunately, there is no funding for transitioning patients. We do as much as we can."

The weight of the hospital documents felt heavy on my lap. Ted drew in a breath and continued, "But David, David was unreachable, Sheila. The staff talked about it at length—his affect, his holding the staff at arm's length, his refusal to tell the truth about his gun. We were all very concerned. We, too, take this loss very personally."

I thanked Ted for all he'd tried to do and hung up the phone. An unfamiliar noise escaped my mouth, the kind of guttural sound that comes from unresolved loss. Whether he knew it or not, Ted had given me an essential piece to the puzzle I'd tried to put together for two years, one I would never completely solve.

*David had been unreachable*: to me, to his family, and in the end, to his doctors. A series of memories flashed vividly through my mind: him pulling away at the coffee shop when I'd first moved in to appreciate his smell, his distant and clouded affect the day of our wedding, his excuses as to why we shouldn't make love during my pregnancy. He was not mine from the beginning, and certainly not at the end, when he grew weary of the added isolation of mental illness. Everything I'd done to try to reach David was useless against his mistaken belief that we are alone in this world.

If mental illness caused David's isolation, I was powerless against it. But if it was the opposite, if isolation actually helps create mental illness, we might all avoid that fate—by allowing true intimacy in our lives, by telling the truth, by embracing our own authentic selves.

I would later read about a research project that highlighted the importance of intimacy and relationships in helping the mentally ill recover. Jay Neugeboren's brother, Robert, had been in the New York mental health system for nearly forty years and had been given nearly every antipsychotic medication known to humankind. Jay began interviewing hundreds of former mental patients who had been institutionalized, often for periods of ten or more years, and who had recovered into full lives: doctors, lawyers, teachers, custodians, social workers. He was fascinated with the question—what had made the difference?

Some pointed to new medications, some to old. Some said they had found God. No matter what else they named, they all said that a key element was a relationship with a human being. Most of the time, this human being was a professional, a social worker or nurse, who said, in effect, "I believe in your ability to recover, and I am going to stay with you until you do." The author points out that his brother had recently recovered from his mental illness, without a recurrence for more than six years, the longest stretch in his adult life.

Of all the research I've read about breakthroughs in mental illness, this message resonates most loudly. We need one another to lead healthy lives, and when faced with the prospect of illness, be it mental or physical, we need to believe others can help us through to the other side. We need to believe that it is no different to ask for help with a mental illness than it would be for a cancer patient to ask for chemotherapy. We need to have faith in our own ability to endure, and when hope wanes, as it will with the illogical ups and downs of brain diseases, we should find our way back to our hearts.

I filed the papers back into the manila folder and walked to my car. My phone buzzed with a text message: "Hi Luv, Can't wait to see U and the girls tonight. Your man, C."

Two weeks later, Colin and Sophie charged headstrong into another huge set of Kauai waves with their boogie boards. Sophie's back was crisscrossed with tan lines; her legs were long and strong from all the outdoor exercise. When had she grown so tall?

Another big wave came, and Colin heaved Sophie forward on the board so that she could get the longest ride possible. She rode the slipstream, shouting, "Whoo-hoo! Mom, watch! This is so cool!"

A jagged outcropping of black rock framed one side of the beach. It was beautiful—more beautiful than any postcard. Colin caught the next wave, riding up alongside her as if they'd planned the whole show. I smiled and waved, wondering whether to trust the bubble of joy I'd suppressed all week. It was, he was, this was, all too good to be true.

The warm sand underneath my thighs was real. The air, its moist, reassuring humidity, reminded me to drink it all in, the beauty, the water, the incredible fruits and vegetables.

But this joy? Could I trust it? Would I ever get over the feeling that another huge wave would come along and wipe out everything I loved?

Sophie ran from the water, dripping, her skin glowing and her long hair bleached an even lighter shade of blonde from the sun. "Mom," she said, trying to catch her breath, "you've got to come try it."

"I am having so much fun watching you do it, Soph," I said. "I want to get some more video before we have to go to dinner."

Sophie leaned down, put her two arms on my shoulders, and said, "Thanks for bringing me, Mommy. This is the most amazing vacation I've ever had."

I caught my own breath and smiled back. "I'm so glad, sweetheart. It wouldn't be the same without you."

Sophie rejoined Colin in the water, the two of them jumping up in the air every time another wave came, making their way farther and farther out, to the big waves that make the best rides. The drift was strong, and Colin kept his hand on Sophie's board or her hand to keep her close. Then he positioned her toward the beach and pushed her fast so she could ride the crest of another magnificent wave. Sophie screamed all the way in. "Whoo-hoo! I'm flying!"

She waved at me from the ocean, her long arms reminding me again of David. It left me wishing he could see Sophie again, so happy, so beautiful.

*David—if only. What if I'd . . . ? Why?* I would never answer those questions. No matter how hard I tried to enjoy at least one day without his memory, or the guilt of his death, or the profound absence made by his loss, I hadn't succeeded. His remarkable genetic influence on Sophie was even more profound as she aged. Her looks, her sense of humor, even her stubbornness, were David's. I missed him terribly. His memory, and my current state of hopefulness, were too raw a combination. The tears came up from nowhere, surprising me when they squeezed out the sides of my eyes.

I looked up to see Sophie and Colin climbing up the black rocks. They jutted out like a spit along the beach, a perfect place for jumping into the ocean. Colin climbed behind Sophie, careful to make sure she had every handhold and foothold before she took the next step upward.

My heartbeat quickened. "Colin," I yelled, wiping my face with a sandy hand. "She's afraid of heights!"

He couldn't hear me. The wind had come up, and the waves were too loud. I sprinted to the rock, awkwardly running in the sand and the slope, desperate to get to them before they jumped. "Colin, don't," I shouted. "Sophie is afraid of heights!"

They were at the top of the outcropping now, an immense cluster of rocks that stood maybe ten feet above the water. Sophie would be terrified.

She stood on the rock, holding Colin's hand. Her shoulders were back squarely, and her stance was like a warrior's. She yelled back to me, "I really want to do this, Mom. Let me go!" Her goggles were on her eyes, her chin jutting out defiantly, and suddenly, she looked another year older to me, not just physically, but emotionally—more confident, on the verge of something important.

Colin shrugged his shoulders, apologetically, and shouted, "It is really safe, honey."

"Okay," I said. "Please hold her hand."

The two of them walked gingerly to the edge of the rocks and then started a countdown together: "One, two, three!" They swung their arms back and forth, then *whoosh*, they leapt into the air, the blue Pacific sky behind them, hands and arms outstretched to the setting sun, a god and goddess, their trim bodies disappearing like long spears into the surf. I ran to the edge of the water, my hands to my lips.

After what seemed like several seconds, their heads finally bobbed back to the surface, smiling and laughing together. I exhaled and jumped into the air. "That was beautiful!" I said, running into the surf to join them, the unexpected chill of the water splashing up against my legs and chest and finally across my forehead, soaking my hair, soaking me with their joy, our joy, until I was finally baptized into a new beginning.

# Epilogue

One of the reasons I wrote *All the Things We Never Knew* was to more clearly understand the genetic risk of bipolar illness and suicide. For too long, I'd missed it entirely in David. I need to be vigilant about my daughter and her inherited risk of having the illness.

In this book, I've painted a picture—one that illuminates many of the signs and much of the foreshadowing of serious mental illness. I hope that my choice to share this personal journey might help families and friends be aware of those signs and might encourage those at risk to seek treatment before depression or substance abuse takes away that option.

Many people view suicide as preventable and avoidable, and some hold that because I was married to David, a measure of the inevitable blame was mine to bear. But too few realize the toll mental illness has on a marriage, in anger, resentment, sexual infidelity, hopelessness, and verbal abuse. David's doctors believe he suffered from the illness from the onset of puberty, but because of his intellect, he was able to compensate for his illness until the profound stressors of life became too much to bear. College is also a particularly risky time for the onset of depressive illness—the use of alcohol and drugs, and radically altered sleep patterns, can precipitate psychotic episodes.

Because Portland, Oregon, is a relatively small city and many people are aware of the circumstances of David's death, I am stopped every now and then by someone who whispers, "My mother committed suicide," or "My ex committed suicide." In our culture, we're much less likely to whisper about the death of a loved one from cancer or heart failure, yet the stigma attached to suicide forces us into the shadows with our grief and our questions—most notably, "WHY?"

Some days, I am content with Chopra's view that David's death was part of his inevitable journey. Other times, I am struck with the emptiness of it all, how permanent an end he chose to his temporary suffering. It was not the answer.

The role of antidepressants in David's suicidal state is a topic large enough for a book of its own. It was just three days after David started on antidepressants (Lexapro) that he had his first suicidal thought. I was concerned that because of his poor liver function, the drugs made him more toxic. Antidepressants, if prescribed alone, rather than with mood stabilizers such as lithium or anticonvulsants, can precipitate the type of mania David experienced for the first time on the drug. His initial diagnosis was bipolar disorder type II, mixed state, with suicidal ideation. David had admitted in his initial interview that he had had recurrent depression but had never experienced a full-blown manic episode until three months before his death. In my opinion, David should never have been placed on Lexapro.

The medical summary I received details the psychiatrist's first attempts at a Self-Administered Battery and Personality Assessment. David was unable to complete the task. The doctor finally learned that he believed he'd been "frozen" for several months, unable to bill his work and confused about why his brain was becoming so muddied. David related several periods in his past in which he'd had a brief inability to work, but never as bad as that particular situation.

He admitted to being hypersexual, and told the psychiatrist, "I think I have lost my mind. I'm a completely different person now than I was. Every day I'm getting more different. I have trouble tolerating this moment, any moment. Everything seems so unreal to me. I don't want this to be real." David told the doctor he believed his life was done, even though he was still alive. He said, "The life I had before was a good life, a zillion times better than this one, due to my own actions. I let it go. It is completely my fault."

There is one fact that is particularly potent that I believe should be shared with every loved one of someone who is hospitalized with bipolar disorder: people with manic depression are most likely to kill themselves following their release from a psychiatric hospital.

The transition out of hopelessness, lethargy, and despair is commonly mixed with rapidly swinging mood states. When patients are released, a resurgence of vitality makes it possible for them to act out previously frozen suicidal thoughts and desires. According to Dr. Kay Redfield Jamison, one of the leading experts in the field, psychiatrists are often baffled by the suicides of those patients who appear calmer and in "better spirits" than those who do not. The period during and immediately after a patient's first hospitalization is, at best, a gamble. The family members of the mentally ill should be aware of this and be trained to deal with the dangerous period of uncertainty following their loved one's psychiatric hospitalization.

Of all the authors who brought me closer to understanding David's illness, I'd like to offer a special thanks to one who never treated him: Dr. Jamison. Her ongoing battle with manic-depressive illness, and the numerous books she's written on the topic, had a profound effect on me.

Jamison, too, has attempted suicide, and her vivid writing about the terror of battling a mood disorder allowed me to frame David's decision in the context of his illness, not as a selfish act or a defiant one. Jamison keeps the last line of a poem on her desk that draws her in when things go dark and she is exhausted by the futile attempts to pull meaning from life. It is from Douglas Dunn's "Disenchantments," and I have copied the line to help me through my darkest hours.

*"Look to the living, love them, and hold on."*

## RESOURCE ORGANIZATIONS

*American Association for Marriage and Family Therapy (AAMFT)*
The professional association for the field of marriage and family therapy that represents the professional interests of more than 50,000 marriage and family therapists in the United States, Canada, and abroad. Founded in 1942, AAMFT aims to increase understanding, research, and education in the field of marriage and family therapy. The organization conducts a national exam for marriage and family therapists used for licensure in most states. www.aamft.org.

*American Psychiatric Association*
Founded in 1844, the American Psychiatric Association is the world's largest psychiatric organization. It represents over 36,000 psychiatric physicians from the United States and around the world. Members specialize in the diagnosis and treatment of mental and emotional illnesses and substance use disorders. www.psych.org.

*American Psychological Association (APA)*
A scientific and professional organization that represents psychology in the United States. With nearly 130,000 members, it is the largest association of psychologists worldwide. Founded in 1892, it aims to advance psychology as a science and profession and as a means of promoting human welfare by promoting research, establishing and maintaining standards, and diffusing knowledge. In 1992, APA established the Disaster Response Network (DRN) to work collaboratively with the American Red Cross and other relief organizations to provide licensed psychologists onsite to aid disaster victims and relief workers. More than 2,000 psychologists have received required disaster response training and are DRN members. www.apa.org.

*Center for Mental Health Services (CMHS)*
A component of the Substance Abuse and Mental Health Services Administration (SAMHSA), Public Health Service (PHS), and Department of Health and Human Services (DHHS), CMHS is charged

with leading the national system that delivers mental health services and administers programs and funding for assisting people with mental illness with treatment, employment, housing, and transportation. CMHS was established under the 1992 *ADAMHA Reorganization Act*. The Emergency Mental Health and Traumatic Stress Services Branch (defined below) is housed within CMHS. http://samhsa.gov/about-us/who-we-are/offices-centers/cmhs.

***Children's Advocacy Centers***
Established by the Office of Juvenile Justice and Delinquency Prevention within the U.S. Department of Justice to assist communities in improving their response to child abuse, the centers provide information, consultation, training, and technical assistance; help to establish child-focused programs; and support coordination among agencies responding to child abuse. www.ojjdp.gov.

***Department of Health and Human Services (DHHS)***
The U.S. government's principal agency for protecting the health of all Americans and providing essential human services, especially for those who are least able to help themselves. The department's 300 programs cover a wide spectrum of activities and purposes, from medical and social science research, disease prevention, and food and drug safety to health insurance for elderly, disabled, and low-income Americans and maternal and infant health. In the Federal Response Plan (FRP), DHHS is the lead agency responsible for carrying out Emergency Support Function number 8 (health and medical care) and plays a supporting role in mass care and information and planning. www.hhs.gov.

***Department of Veterans Affairs (VA)***
The VA is the U.S. government agency charged with providing benefits and services to veterans and their dependents. Its health care system provides a broad spectrum of medical, surgical, and rehabilitative care and also houses the National Center for Post-Traumatic Stress Disorder, Readjustment Counseling Service, and the Emer-

gency Mental Strategic Health Care Group. In the Federal Response Plan, the VA plays a supporting role for four emergency functions: public works, mass care, resource support, and health and medical services. www.va.gov/about_va/history.

*Emergency Mental Health and Traumatic Stress Services Branch*
A branch of the Center for Mental Health Services that is responsible for meeting the mental health needs of disaster survivors and responders, the EMHTSSB works in collaboration with FEMA to implement the Crisis Counseling Assistance and Training Program when a state has applied for a Citizen Corps Program (CCP) grant after a federally declared disaster. The grants may be for immediate services, which support services for sixty days past the declaration date, or for regular services, which support services for nine to fifteen months past the declaration date. www.fema.gov/additional-assistance#0.

*International Critical Incident Stress Foundation*
A nonprofit foundation dedicated to preventing and mitigating disabling stress through the provision of education, training, and support services for all emergency services professions, including continuing education and training in emergency mental health services for psychologists, psychiatrists, social workers, and licensed professional counselors, and consultation in the establishment of crisis and disaster response programs for varied organizations and communities worldwide. www.icisf.org.

*National Association of Social Workers (NASW)*
A membership organization that promotes, develops, and protects the practice of social work and social workers, NASW also seeks to enhance the effective functioning and well-being of individuals, families, and communities through its work and its advocacy. www.naswdc.org.

*National Center for Post-Traumatic Stress Disorder (NCPTSD)*
A seven-site consortium created by public law and housed within

the Department of Veterans Affairs. The mission of the NCPTSD is to advance the clinical care and social welfare of America's veterans through research, education, and training in the science, diagnosis, and treatment of PTSD and stress-related disorders. As a leading authority on PTSD, NCPTSD serves and collaborates with many different agencies and constituencies, including veterans and their families, government policymakers, scientists and researchers, doctors and psychiatrists, journalists, and the lay public. www.ptsd.va.gov.

*National Institute of Mental Health (NIMH)*
A part of the U.S. government's National Institutes of Health, PHS, and DHHS, the NIMH is responsible for research on mental health and mental disorders, including research on the mental health consequences of and interventions after disasters and acts of mass violence. www.nimh.nih.gov.

*National Organization for Victim Assistance (NOVA)*
NOVA is a private, nonprofit organization of victim and witness assistance programs and practitioners, criminal justice agencies and professionals, mental health professionals, researchers, former victims and survivors, and others committed to the recognition and implementation of victim rights and services. Its mission is to promote the rights of and services for victims of crime and crisis. www.try-nova.org.

*Office for Victims of Crime (OVC)*
A federal agency established by the 1984 *Victims of Crime Act* to oversee diverse programs that benefit victims of crime. OVC provides substantial funding to state victim assistance and compensation programs, the lifeline services that help victims to heal. The agency supports training designed to educate criminal justice and allied professionals regarding the rights and needs of crime victims. OVC is one of five bureaus and four offices with grant-making authority within the Office of Justice Programs, at the U.S. Department of Justice. www.ojp.usdoj.gov/ovc.

*Public Health Service (PHS)*

A major division of the Department of Health and Human Services, PHS is the principal health agency of the U.S. government. PHS is responsible for promoting and ensuring the nation's health through research into the causes, treatment, and prevention of disease. www.os.dhhs.gov/phs/phs.html.

*Substance Abuse and Mental Health Services Administration (SAMHSA)*

The leading mental health services agency of the Department of Health and Human Services includes the Center for Mental Health Services (CMHS) and the Emergency Mental Health and Stress Services Branch within CMHS. Through these divisions, SAMHSA provides assistance with assessing mental health needs and training disaster workers in mental health. SAMHSA also assists in arranging training for mental health outreach workers, assesses the content of applications for federal crisis counseling grant funds, and addresses worker stress issues and needs through a variety of mechanisms. www.samhsa.gov.

# Notes

## INTRODUCTION

*According to a 2004 report . . . 90 percent of the people who die by suicide*

Nock MK, Borges G, Bromet EJ, Cha CB, Kessler RC, Lee S. Suicide and Suicidal Behavior. *Epidemiologic Reviews*. 2008; 30(1):133-154. doi:10.1093/epirev/mxn002.

*Dr. Bruce Perry,* M.D., Ph.D., is an American psychiatrist, currently the senior fellow at the Child Trauma Academy in Houston, Texas.

Cavanagh JT, Carson AJ, Sharpe M, et al. Psychological autopsy studies of suicide: a systematic review. *Psychological Medicine*. 2003; 33:395–405.

See also: https://www.afsp.org/understanding-suicide/frequently-asked-questions.

*Neurosequential model of therapeutics*

Bruce D. Perry and Erin P. Hambrick. "Going Beyond the Medical Model." *Reclaiming Children and Youth* 17, no. 3 (Fall 2008) (www.reclaiming.com), pp. 38–43. Accessed via the Child Trauma Academy. http://childtrauma.org/wp-content/uploads/2013/08/NMT_Article_08.pdf.

Caplis, Catherine F. "Feasibility and Perceived Efficacy of the Neurosequential Model of Therapeutics." Antioch University, Psy.D. dissertation, 2014, pp. 2–6.

***Collaborative problem-solving method developed by Dr. Ross Greene***

Greene, R. W. "Collaborative Problem Solving." In R. Murrihy, A. Kidman, and T. Ollendick, eds., *A Clinician's Handbook of Assessing and Treating Conduct Problems in Youth*. New York: Springer Publishing, 2010, pp. 193–220.

***The Flawless Foundation***

"The Flawless Foundation takes a stand for children living with brain-based, behavioral challenges by promoting educated awareness about neurodevelopment, providing evidence-based, holistic treatment programs and by advancing environmental prevention focused research." http://flawlessfoundation.org/mission-and-vision. Accessed March 17, 2015.

*Dr. Elisabeth Kübler-Ross* was a Swiss-American psychiatrist, a pioneer in near-death studies, and the author of the groundbreaking book *On Death and Dying*. See ekrfoundation.org. Elisabeth Kubler-Ross. "Bio." A&E Television Networks, 2015. Accessed March 28, 2015.

## STIGMA

***Nearly one in five American adults (18.5 percent), or 43.8 million adults, had a mental illness in 2013***

Substance Abuse and Mental Health Services Administration. *Results from the 2013 National Survey on Drug Use and Health*. Mental Health Findings, NSDUH Series H-49, HHS Publication No. (SMA) 14-4887. Rockville, MD: Substance Abuse and Mental Health Services Administration, 2014.

***The profound reluctance to be a mental health patient***

Thornicroft, Graham, et al. "Stigma: Ignorance, Prejudice or Discrimination?" *British Journal of Psychiatry* (March 2007): pp. 115–190.

"Stigma 'Key Deterrent' in Accessing Mental Health Care." *Science Daily*, February 25, 2015. www.sciencedaily.com/releases/2014/02/140225193406.htm. Original study by Sarah Clement et al. "What Is the Impact of Mental Health–Related Stigma on Help-Seeking? A Systematic Review of Quantitative and Qualitative Studies." *Psychological Medicine* (2014).

Wahl, Otto F. "Mental Health Consumers' Experience of Stigma." *Schizophrenia Bulletin* 25 (1999): 467–478.

## EARLY TREATMENT

***The National Institute of Mental Health reports that "unlike most disabling physical diseases . . ."***

National Institute of Mental Health. "Mental Illness Exacts Heavy Toll, Beginning in Youth." Press release, June 6, 2005. http://www.nimh.nih.gov/news/science-news/2005/mental-illness-exacts-heavy-toll-beginning-in-youth.shtml. Accessed March 2015.

***Early Assessment and Support Alliance (EASA)***

"About EASA." Early Assessment and Support Alliance. www.easacommunity.org/home/ec1/smartlist_61/smartlist_61/. Accessed March 17, 2015.

McGorry, Patrick D., and Henry J. Jackson. *The Recognition and Management of Early Psychosis: A Preventive Approach*. Cambridge: Cambridge University Press, 1999, pp. 3–7.

***The current system of mental health care . . . is broken***

Tamara Sale, director, EASA Center for Excellence at Portland State University Regional Research Institute. Quoted in Robert Wood Johnson Foundation, "Oregon's Approach to Early Intervention and Prevention of Psychosis." Case study, Early Detection and Intervention for the Prevention of Psychosis Program, March 2013. www.rwjf.org/content/dam/farm/reports/reports/2013/rwjf405619.

All other quotes by Sale and/or the Robert Wood Johnson Foundation come from the case study cited above.

Tamara Sale interview with Sheila Hamilton, KINK radio https://soundcloud.com/kink-fm/extraordinary-hope-for-people-suffering-from-psychosisearly-intervention-works.

## SIGNS AND SYMPTOMS

***One in five Americans***

Mayo Clinic. "Mental Illness—Risk Factors." mayoclinic.org/diseases-conditions/mental-illness/basics/risk-factors/con-20033813. Accessed March 13, 2015.

Mental Health America. "Mental Illness and the Family: Recognizing Warning Signs and How to Cope." mentalhealthamerica.net/recognizing-warning-signs. Accessed March 19, 2015.

## HYPERSEXUALITY

***57 percent of people with bipolar disorder***

National Alliance on Mental Illness, "Opening the Door on Hypersexuality." Excerpt from the spring 2009 issue of *BP* magazine. www2.nami.org/Template.cfm?Section=Cleansweep&template=/ContentManagement/ContentDisplay.cfm&ContentID=77393. Accessed April 2, 2015.

Schneider, Jennifer P. "Rebuilding the Marriage During Recovery from Compulsive Sexual Behavior." *Family Relations* (National Council on Family Relations) 38, no. 3 (July 1989): pp. 288–294.

*Dr. Barbara Geller*, M.D., is professor emerita of psychiatry at Washington University in St. Louis.

***43 percent of children***

Balanced Mind Parent Network. "Hypersexuality in Children with Bipolar Disorder." November 29, 2001, updated January 6, 2010. www.thebalancedmind.org/learn/library/hypersexuality-in-children-with-bipolar-disorder. Accessed March 17, 2015.

Geller, Barbara, et al. "Phenomenology of Prepubertal and Early Adolescent Bipolar Disorder: Examples of Elated Mood, Grandiose Behaviors, Decreased Need for Sleep, Racing Thoughts and Hypersexuality." Abstract. *Journal of Child and Adolescent Psychopharmacology* 12, no. 1 (2002): pp. 3–9.

Fristad, M. A., E. B. Weller, and R. A. Weller. "The Mania Rating Scale: Can It Be Used in Children? A Preliminary Report." *Journal of the American Academy of Child and Adolescent Psychiatry* 31 (1992): pp. 252–257.

***Jamison reported that women with bipolar disorder***

NAMI. "Opening the Door on Hypersexuality."

## MENTAL ILLNESS AND DRUG USE

***Nearly one-third of people with mental illness***

National Alliance on Mental Illness. "Dual Diagnosis: Substance Abuse and Mental Illness." Reviewed by Ken Duckworth, M.D., and Jacob L. Freedman, M.D., January 2013.

www2.nami.org/Content/NavigationMenu/Inform_Yourself/About_Mental_Illness/By_Illness/Dual_Diagnosis_Substance_Abuse_and_Mental_Illness.htm.

Kessler, Ronald C., et al. "Lifetime Co-occurrence of DSM-III-R Alcohol Abuse and Dependence with Other Psychiatric Disorders in the National Comorbidity Survey. *Archives of General Psychiatry* 54 (1997):pp. 313–321.

Regier, D. A. "Co-morbidity of Mental Disorders with Alcohol and Other Drug Abuse Results from the Epidemiologic Catchment Area (ECA) Study." *Journal of the American Medical Association* 264 (1990): 2511–2518.

Sheehan, M. F. "Dual Diagnosis." *Psychiatry Quarterly* 64, no. 2 (Summer 1993): 107–134. http://link.springer.com/article/10.1007%2FBF01065865. Accessed April 2, 2015.

***NAMI reports: "Abuse of drugs and alcohol . . ."***
NAMI. "Dual Diagnosis."

## ANOSOGNOSIA

***Frontal lobes organize information***
National Alliance on Mental Illness. "Anosognosia." www2.nami.org/Content/NavigationMenu/Mental_Illnesses/Schizophrenia9/Anosognosia_Fact_Sheet.htm. Accessed March 17, 2015.

Treatment Advocacy Center. "Anosognosia." www.treatmentadvocacycenter.org/problem/anosognosia. Accessed April 2, 2015.

Amador, Xavier F., and D. H. Strauss. "Poor Insight in Schizophrenia." *Psychiatric Quarterly* 64 (1994): pp. 305–318.

Amador, Xavier. F., et al. "Awareness of Illness in Schizophrenia and Schizoaffective and Mood Disorders." *Archives of General Psychiatry* 51 (1994): pp. 826–836.

Arango, Celso, and Xavier Amador. "Lessons Learned About Poor Insight." *Schizophrenia Bulletin* (2010). December 16, 2010 online. http://schizophreniabulletin.oxfordjournals.org/content/early/2010/12/15/schbul.sbq143.full.

***In Oregon, intervention is allowed***

Treatment Advocacy Center. "State Standards Charts for Assisted Treatment: Civil Commitment Criteria and Initiation Procedures by State." www.treatmentadvocacycenter.org/storage/documents/State_Standards_Charts_for_Assisted_Treatment_-_Civil_Commitment_Criteria_and_Initiation_Procedures.pdf, p. 9.

Treatment Advocacy Center. "Involuntary Treatment Civil Commitment Standards," p. 2. Accessed March 21, 2015.

Copeland, D. A., and M. V. Heilemann. "Getting 'to the Point': The Experience of Mothers Getting Assistance for Their Adult Children Who Are Violent and Mentally Ill." *Nursing Research* 57, no. 3 (2008): pp. 136–143.

Treatment Advocacy Center. "Oregon: Getting Your Loved One Help." www.treatmentadvocacycenter.org/index.php?option=com_content&view=article&id=233&Itemid=168. Accessed March 17, 2015.

## CARE FOR CAREGIVERS

***In 1979, families frustrated with the lack of services***

National Alliance on Mental Illness. "Supporting Recovery." www.nami.org/Find-Support/A-Family-Member-or-Caregiver/Supporting-Recovery. Accessed March 21, 2015.

National Alliance on Mental Illness. "Teens: CIT for Youth." www2.nami.org/template.cfm?section=CIT_for_Youth. Accessed March 21, 2015.

Markey, Dana, et al. *Responding to Youth with Mental Health Needs: A CIT for Youth Implementation Manual.* National Alliance on Mental Illness. July 2011. www2.nami.org/Content/NavigationMenu/Find_Support/Child_and_Teen_Support/CIT_for_Youth/CITYouthWorkbook_Web.pdf.

Steadman, H., et al. (2001). "Comparing Outcomes of Major Models of Police Responses to Mental Health Emergencies." *Psychiatric Services* 51: pp. 645–649.

## CAREGIVER DENIAL

***Depression is a painfully slow, crashing death***

Lovelace, David. *Scattershot: My Bipolar Family*. New York: Dutton, 2008, p. 107.

## GUILT

***Nearly all relatives . . . feel guilty***

Woolis, Rebecca. *When Someone You Love Has a Mental Illness*. New York: Penguin, 1992, pp. 58–70.

## MENTAL ILLNESS, THEN AND NOW

Shorter, Edward. *A History of Psychiatry: From the Era of the Asylum to the Age of Prozac*. New York: John Wiley and Sons, 1997, p. iii.

See also: Shorter, quoted in Frances, Allen. "Is This the Worst Time Ever to Have a Severe Mental Illness?" Excerpted August 20, 2014. http://historypsychiatry.com/2014/08/20/is-this-the-worst-time-ever-to-have-a-severe-mental-illness.

***More than 50 percent***

"Survey of Inmates in State and Federal Correctional Facilities." *Mental Health, United States, 2010*. Prepared by RTI International. Rockville, MD: U.S. Department of Health and Human Services/SAMHSA, 2010, pp. 123–124.

"Survey of Inmates in State and Federal Correctional Facilities" (2004) and "Survey of Inmates in Local Jails" (2002), Bureau of Justice Statistics (BJS), Washington, DC. Unpublished data delivered upon special request by Lauren E. Glaze, BJS Statistician, and verified by Tracy L. Snell, BJS Statistician, March 2, 2009.

James, D. J., & Glaze, L. E. *Mental Health Problems of Prison and Jail Inmates* (NCJ-213600). Washington, DC: U.S. Department of Justice, Office of Justice Programs, Bureau of Justice Statistics, 2006. Retrieved from http://bjs.ojp. usdoj.gov/content/pub/pdf/mhppji.p.

## HEALING THE MIND

***A large percentage of survivors***

Author interview with Brian Goff.

*Dialectical behavioral therapy*

Linehan, M. M., et al. "Cognitive-Behavioral Treatment of Chronically Parasuicidal Borderline Patients." *Archives of General Psychiatry* 48, no. 12 (December 1991): pp. 1060–1064.

*Cognitive behavioral therapy*

Slee, N., et al. "Cognitive-Behavioral Intervention for Self Harm: Randomized Controlled Trial." *British Journal of Psychiatry* 192, no. 3 (March 2008): pp. 202–211.

E. Evans, et al. "The Prevalence of Suicidal Phenomena in Adolescents: A Systematic Review of Population-Based Studies." *Suicide and Life-Threatening Behavior* 35, no. 3 (June 2005): pp. 239–250.

Brandon A. Gaudiano, James D. Herbert, and Steven C. Hayes. "Is It the Symptom or the Relation to It? Investigating Potential Mediators of Change in Acceptance and Commitment Therapy for Psychosis." *Behavioral Therapy* 41, no. 4 (December 2010): pp. 543–554. www.ncbi.nlm.nih.gov/pmc/articles/PMC3673289/.

*"Western medicine moves the locus of control"*

Interview with Sheila Hamilton, June 20, 2014.

## MINDFULNESS

*Two controlled clinical trials*

Ma, S. Helen, and John Teasdale. "Mindfulness-Based Cognitive Therapy for Depression: Exploration of Differential Relapse Prevention Effects." *Journal of Consulting and Clinical Psychology* 72, no. 1 (2004): pp. 31–40.

Teasdale, John D., et al. "Prevention of Relapse/Recurrence in Major Depression by Mindfulness-Based Cognitive Therapy." *Journal of Consulting and Clinical Psychology* 68, no. 4 (August 2000): pp. 615–623.

Frank, E., et al. "Three-Year Outcomes for Maintenance Therapies in Recurrent Depression." *Archives of General Psychiatry* 47, no. 12 (December 1990): pp. 1093–1099.

Frank, E., et al. "Efficacy of Interpersonal Therapy as a Maintenance Treatment of Recurrent Depression." *Archives of General Psychiatry* 48, no. 12 (December 1991): pp. 1053–1059.

## SUICIDE AND PSYCHOTROPIC DRUGS

***In a study of thirty-eight bipolar patients treated with an antidepressant . . .***

***Researchers find that "there are significant risks"***

El-Mallakh, R. S., and A. Karippot. "Use of Antidepressants to Treat Depression in Bipolar Disorder." *Psychiatric Services* 53, no. 2 (May 2002): 580–584.

***Use of antidepressants may "destabilize the illness . . ."***

Koukopoulos, A., et al. "Duration and Stability of the Rapid-Cycling Course." *Journal of Affective Disorders* 73, nos. 1–2 (January 2003): 75–85.

***Forty percent of patients***

El-Mallakh, R. S., and A. Karippot. "Antidepressant-Associated Chronic Irritable Dysphoria (ACID) in Bipolar Disorder," *Journal of Affective Disorders* 84, nos. 2–3 (February 2005): 267–272.

***Antidepressants can induce a "chronic, dysphoric, irritable state"***

Schneck, C., et al. "The Prospective Course of Rapid-Cycling Bipolar Disorder." *American Journal of Psychiatry* 165, no. 3 (March 2008): 370–377.

## INVOLUNTARY HOSPITALIZATION

***When a loved one needs immediate psychiatric intervention or help***

Amador, Xavier. *I Am Not Sick, I Don't Need Help!* Peconic, NY: Vida Press, 2001, p. 56.

## NEW BREAKTHROUGHS IN THE UNDERSTANDING OF PSYCHOSIS

Keller, William R., et al. "A Review of Anti-Inflammatory Agents for Symptoms of Schizophrenia." *Journal of Psychopharmacology* 27, no. 4 (2013): pp. 337–342.

Ibid., pp. 2–5.

***Dr. Tyrone Cannon says markers of proinflammatory cytokines***

"Development of Psychosis: Gray Matter Loss and the Inflamed Brain." *Science Daily*, January 13, 2015, www.sciencedaily.com/releases/2015/01/150113090458.htm, citing Cannon, Tyrone D., et al. "Progressive Reduction in Cortical Thickness as Psychosis Develops: A Multisite Longitudinal Neuroimaging Study of Youth at Elevated Clinical Risk." *Biological Psychiatry* 77, no. 2 (January 2015), pp. 147–157.

Dantzer, R., and K. W. Kelley. "Twenty Years of Research on Cytokine-Induced Sickness Behavior." *Brain, Behavior and Immunity* 21, no. 2 (February 2007): pp. 153–160.

Dantzer, R., and K. W. Kelley. "Stress and Immunity: An Integrated View of Relationships Between the Brain and the Immune System. *Life Sciences* 44, no. 26 (1989): pp. 1995–2008.

Dantzer, R. "Cytokine-Induced Sickness Behavior: Where Do We Stand?" *Brain, Behavior, and Immunity* 15, no. 1 (March 2001): pp. 7–24.

***The research suggests that activation of microglia . . . is involved in tissue loss.***

Hart, B. L. "Biological Basis of the Behavior of Sick Animals." *Neuroscience Biobehavior Review* 12, no. 2 (Summer 1988): pp. 123–127.

***The authors of a 2010 review of the literature***

Smieskova, R., et al. "Neuroimaging Predictors of Transition to Psychosis: A Systematic Review and Meta-Analysis." *Neuroscience Biobehavior Review* 34, no. 8 (July 2010): pp. 2–12.

Benros, Michael E., William W. Eaton, and Preben B. Mortensen. "The Epidemiologic Evidence Linking Autoimmune Diseases and Psychosis." *Biological Psychiatry* 75, no. 4 (February 2014): pp. 300–306.

***A study reported in March 2015***

Dantzer, R. "Cytokine-Induced Sickness Behavior: Where Do We Stand?" Brain, Behavior, and Immununity 15, no. 1 (March 2001): pp. 7–24.

***Scientists hope to develop anti-inflammatory drugs***

"Anti-Inflammatory Treatment of Schizophrenia." Clinical Trials: A Service of the U.S. National Institutes of Health. www.clinicaltrials.gov/ct2/show/NCT01514682.

Nitta, Masahiro, et al. "Adjunctive Use of Nonsteroidal Anti-Inflammatory Drugs for Schizophrenia: A Meta-Analytic Investigation of Randomized Controlled Trials." *Schizophrenia Bulletin* (2013): sbt070.

## CHAPTER SEVENTEEN

***Suicide is the third leading cause***
***Author interview with Ross Szabo, Director of Youth Outreach for the National Mental Health Awareness Campaign.***

Kay Redfield Jamison, *An Unquiet Mind*, Random House (2005) p. 66–68.

***One study, reported in*** The **New York Times**
Cooper, Brian. "Nature, Nurture and Mental Disorder: Old Concepts in the New Millennium." *British Journal of Psychiatry* 178, no. 40 (April 2001): s91–s101. DOI:10.1192/bjp.178.40.s91.

***The 1995 National College Health Risk Behavior Survey***
Douglas, Kathy A., et al. "Results from the 1995 National College Health Risk Behavior Study." *Journal of American College Health* 46, no. 2 (September 1997): pp. 55–67.

## EARLY INTERVENTION AND PREVENTION

*Chris Bouneff, Executive Director, NAMI Oregon*

***Robert Wood Johnson Foundation.*** "EDIPPP Intervention Reduces Conversion to Full-Blown Psychosis Among At-Risk Young People, Says RWJF-Funded Study." July 28, 2014. www.rwjf.org/en/about-rwjf/newsroom/newsroom-content/2014/07/edippp-intervention-reduces-conversion-to-full-blown-psychosis-a.html. Accessed March 17, 2015.

## "MAGIC BULLETS": PSYCHIATRIC DRUGS

***850 adults and 250 children every day***
Whitaker, Robert. *Anatomy of an Epidemic: Magic Bullets, Psychiatry Drugs, and the Astonishing Rise of Mental Illness in America.* New York: Crown, 2010, p. 1.

***Carlat writes***
Carlat, Daniel. *Unhinged: The Trouble with Psychiatry—A Doctor's Revelations About a Profession in Crisis*. New York: Simon and Schuster, 2010, pp. 10–12.

*Diagnostic and Statistical Manual of Mental Disorders, Fifth Edition* (DSM-5). Arlington, VA: American Psychiatric Association, 2013.

Wilson, M. "DSM-III and the Transformation of American Psychiatry." *American Journal of Psychiatry* 150, no. 3 (March 1993): 399-410.

Kapur, S., A. G. Phillips, and T. R. Insel TR. "Why Has It Taken So Long for Biological Psychiatry to Develop Clinical Tests and What to Do About It?" *Molecular Psychiatry* 17, no. 12 (December 2012): pp. 1174-1179.

## THE CONTINUUM OF MENTAL HEALTH

***"Thanks to early detection"***

Insel, Thomas. "Toward a New Understanding of Mental Illness." TEDx Caltech, January 2013. www.ted.com/talks/thomas_insel_toward_a_new_understanding_of_mental_illness?language=en.

Insel, Thomas R. "Translating Scientific Opportunity into Public Health Impact: A Strategic Plan for Research on Mental Illness." *Archives of General psychiatry* 66, no. 2 (February 2009): 128–133.

Insel, Thomas R., and Remi Quirion. "Psychiatry as a Clinical Neuroscience Discipline." National Institute of Mental Health: My Blog. www.nimh.nih.gov/about/director/bio/publications/psychiatry-as-a-clinical-neuroscience-discipline.shtml. Accessed March 19, 2015.

## AFTER SUICIDE

***40,600 people completed suicide***

Smolin, Ann, and John Guinan. *Healing After the Suicide of a Loved One*. New York: Simon and Schuster, 1993, p. 115.

## CHILDREN AND GRIEF

***The American Academy of Pediatrics describes***

Mishara, Brian L. *Impact of Suicide*. New York: Spring, 1995.

Bailey, S. E., M. J. Kral, and K. Dunham. "Survivors of Suicide Do Grieve Differently: Empirical Support for a Common Sense Proposition." *Suicide and Life-Threatening Behavior* 29, no. 3 (Autumn 1999): pp. 256–271. www.ncbi.nlm.nih.gov/pubmed/10531638. See also: http://johnjordanphd.com, especially under Publications.

## THE ESCAPE THEORY OF SUICIDE

***Florida State University psychology professor Roy Baumeister analyzed suicide in terms of motivation to escape***

Baumeister, Roy F. "Suicide as Escape from Self." *Psychological Review* 97, no. 1 (1990): 90–113.

## HEALING FROM TRAUMA

***About 40 percent of American children***

Perry, Bruce, M.D., Ph.D., and Maia Szalavitz. *The Boy Who Was Raised as a Dog and Other Stories from a Child Psychiatrist's Notebook*. New York: Perseus, 2006, p. 1.

Franey, Kris, Robert Geffner, and Robert Falconer, eds. *The Cost of Child Maltreatment: Who Pays? We All Do*. San Diego, CA: Family Violence and Sexual Assault Institute, 2001, pp. 15–37.

See also R. F. Anda, et al "The Enduring Effects of Abuse and Related Adverse Experiences in Childhood: A Convergence of Evidence from Neurobiology and Epidemiology." *European Archives of Psychiatry and Clinical Neuroscience* 256, no. 3 (April 2006), pp. 174–186.

## BABY BOOMERS AND SUICIDE

***The surge in the suicide rate among middle-aged Americans***

Sullivan, Erin M., et al. "Suicide Among Adults Aged 35–64 Years—United States, 1999–2010." *Morbidity and Mortality Weekly Report,* May 3, 2013. Centers for Disease Control and Prevention. www.cdc.gov/mmwr/preview/mmwrhtml/mm6217a1.htm. Accessed March 20, 2015.

## SUICIDE PREVALENCE

***One in 41,149 suicides in the United States that year, making suicide the nation's tenth leading cause of death***

Xu, Jiaquan, et al. "Mortality in the United States, 2012." NCHS Data Brief no. 168 (October 2014). Centers for Disease Control and Prevention.

***Suicide is now the second leading cause of death in the armed forces***

Corr, William P. "Suicides and Suicide Attempts Among Active Component Members of the U.S. Armed Forces, 2010–2012: Methods of Self-Harm Vary by Major Geographic Region of Assignment." *Medical Surveillance Monthly Report* 21, no. 10 (October 2014), p. 2. A publication of the Armed Forces Health Surveillance Center. www.afhsc.mil/documents/pubs/msmrs/2014/v21_n10.pdf.

See also "Defense Department to Do More to Assist Warfighters with Mental Illness." Health.mil: The Official Website of the Military Health System and the Defense Health Agency (March 20, 2015). www.health.mil/News/Articles/2015/03/20/Defense-Department-to-do-More-to-Assist-Warfighters-with-Mental-Illness.

## SUICIDE BEREAVEMENT

***Dr. Katherine Dunham***

Bailey, S. E., M. J. Kral, and K. Dunham. "Survivors of Suicide Do Grieve Differently: Empirical Support for a Common Sense Proposition." *Suicide and Life-Threatening Behavior* 29, no. 3 (Autumn 1999): pp. 256–271. www.ncbi.nlm.nih.gov/pubmed/10531638.

# Acknowledgments

Portland is a writer's town, and before David died, my favorite evenings were spent at a Pinewood table in Joanna Rose's home. The writers I met there continue to inspire me with the depth of their talent and the generosity of their hearts. Scott Sparling offered so many tender comments and suggestions about this book, I cried over the notes he wrote in the margins. Laura Stanfill helped me edit a second draft while her new baby, Trixie, slept in her arms. Stevan Allred gobsmacked me with every new poem and short story. Suzy Vitello, at another table across town, offered poignant advice on loss and love, even as she came to terms with her own magnificent loss.

I began this book in the year after David's death. The manuscript might have stayed on the top shelf of my desk if not for the tenacity of my agent, Sandra Bishop, who never, ever, ever gives up. My brilliant editor at Seal Press, Laura Mazer, prompted me to go back over the manuscript with a reporter's eye to reveal the signs and symptoms I'd missed and share my research on mental illness. For that idea, and a thousand others that make this book more relevant and accessible, thank you.

And to David's family: Thank you for your support. We have changed names to protect your privacy, but your family's legacy is still very much alive in Zasha, aka the amazing Soph.

# About the Author

Five-time Emmy-winner Sheila Hamilton is the news director and morning show co-host at KINK-FM in Portland. Hamilton's storytelling resume runs through film, commercial television, radio, and print. She began her career as an Associate Producer for public broadcasting and then anchored and reported commercial television news for KTVX in Salt Lake City, Utah and KATU in Portland, Oregon.

Hamilton was recently voted Oregon's Best Radio Personality. She also writes cover stories for *About Face Magazine* and is a frequent speaker and emcee for her favorite causes—mindful mental health and empowerment for girls. She serves on the board of Girls Inc., an organization empowering girls to be strong, smart, and bold and The Flawless Foundation, a mental health advocacy organization. Find her online at SheilaHamilton.com.

author photo © Deneb Catalan

## SELECTED TITLES FROM SEAL PRESS

*Shades of Blue: Writers on Depression, Suicide, and Feeling Blue,* edited by Amy Ferris. $16.00, 978-1-58005-595-6. This anthology collects stories from well-known writers about depression, sadness, and attempted suicide, offering empathy to those who have been affected by these issues.

*Riding Fury Home: A Memoir,* by Chana Wilson. $17.00, 978-1-58005-432-4. A shattering, exquisitely written account of one family's struggle against homophobia and mental illness in a changing world—and a powerful story of healing, forgiveness, and redemption.

*Under This Beautiful Dome: A Senator, A Journalist, and the Politics of Gay Love in America,* by Terry Mutchler. $17.00, 978-1-58005-609-0. The true story of a journalist's secret five-year relationship with a member of the Illinois Senate reveals the devastation caused when gay and lesbian couples are denied acceptance and equal rights.

*We Hope You Like This Song: An Overly Honest Story about Friendship, Death, and Mix Tapes,* by Bree Housley. $16.00, 978-1-58005-431-7. Bree Housley's sweet, quirky, and hilarious tribute to her lifelong friend, and her chronicle of how she honored her after her premature death.

*Dancing at the Shame Prom: Sharing the Stories That Kept Us Small,* edited by Amy Ferris and Hollye Dexter. $16.00, 978-1-58005-416-4. A collection of funny, sad, poignant, miraculous, life-changing, and jaw-dropping secrets for readers to gawk at, empathize with, and laugh about—in the hopes that they will be inspired to share their secret burdens as well.

*Gorge: My Journey Up Kilimanjaro at 300 Pounds,* by Kara Richardson Whitely. $17.00, 978-1-58005-559-8. In this inspiring and unforgettable memoir, Kara Richardson Whitely recounts her journey to the top of the world while struggling with food addiction and fat prejudice.

Find Seal Press Online
www.sealpress.com
www.facebook.com/sealpress
Twitter: @SealPress